I0813015

Postcard History Series

Woodmont on the Sound

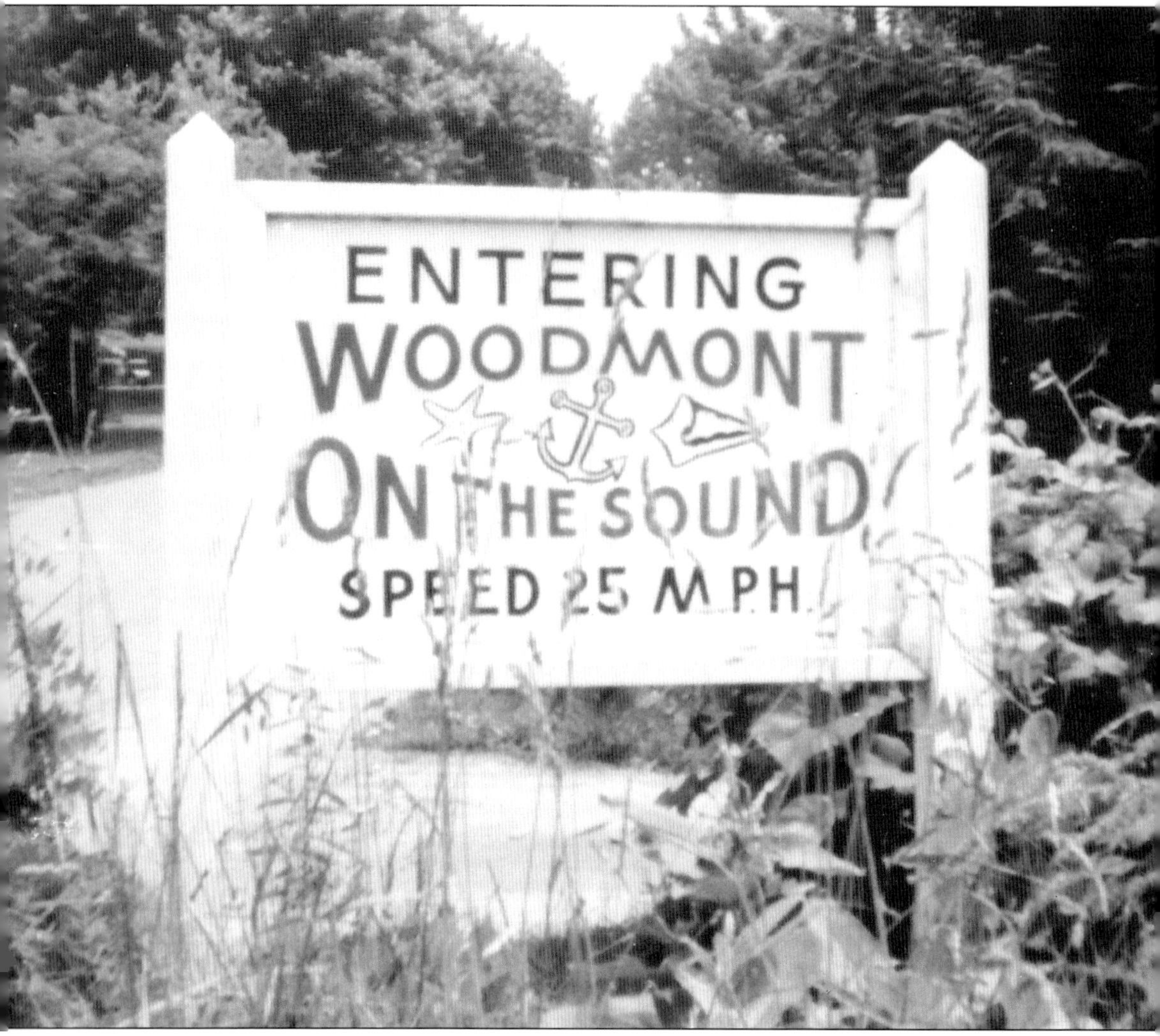

ENTERING WOODMONT ON THE SOUND. Please drive slowly. As early as 1907, the governing board of Woodmont voted "that large signs, bearing the name 'Borough of Woodmont' be erected at each end of the Borough, where the trolley line crosses our boundary and also at the entrance to the Borough near the Union Chapel and at the Oyster River Bridge." That tradition continues today, with signs welcoming visitors to Woodmont at those locations.

On the front cover: **MERWIN'S POINT.** With a view of the Merwin's Point flagpole to the west, this *c.* 1909 postcard shows two young girls playing on the beach. A boy, perhaps their brother, has his fishing gear on the rocks, and their mother sits on the sand reading on the right. (Courtesy of the author's collection.)

On the back cover: **ANCHOR BEACH.** Bathers enjoy Anchor Beach in Woodmont, with Signal Rock in the distance. This postcard was mailed to "the Misses Griswold in Meriden," at 5:00 p.m. on August 5, 1930. The inscription on the back reads, "Just had a nice dip. F.G. and I are staying here for a few days at the 'Anderson Towers.' It's quite a nice place. Love to both, Katharine." (Courtesy of the author's collection.)

POSTCARD HISTORY SERIES

Woodmont on the Sound

Katherine Krauss Murphy

ARCADIA
PUBLISHING

ISBN 978-0-7385-4968-2

Published by Arcadia Publishing
Charleston, South Carolina

Printed in the United States of America

Library of Congress Catalog Card Number: 2006935850

For all general information contact Arcadia Publishing at:
Telephone 843-853-2070
Fax 843-853-0044
E-mail sales@arcadiapublishing.com
For customer service and orders:
Toll-Free 1-888-313-2665

Visit us on the Internet at www.arcadiapublishing.com

To Mike, who loves Woodmont more than anyone I know;
and to Heidi, Jill, and Sarah—Woodmont gave them their roots;
their wings they found on their own.

Contents

Acknowledgments

Many people who share a love of Woodmont contributed to *Woodmont on the Sound*. Special thanks to Nancy Holt, professional photographer and owner of Photography by Joseph in Woodmont, who has the most amazing collection of historical photographs of Woodmont anywhere, and generously shared her images for this book.

Thanks to individuals who loaned their photographs and postcards: Joseph Cullen; Jerome Fiorentino, former burgess of Woodmont; Nancy Dunbar; Phyllis Medvedow, burgess of Woodmont; Hilda Beckas Mursko; Joseph Mursko; George Peacock; Kristina Sancher; Michael Schreiber; Richard Schwartz; Lowell Beach Sykes; Mary Treat; and Marlette Weiglein. Thanks to those who provided access and information: Richard Austin, warden of Woodmont; Glenn Behrle; Edward Bonessi Jr., burgess of Woodmont; Timothy Chaucer; Patricia Markle Levy; Richard Pepe; Roy Schlachter; and John Volk.

Thanks also to those organizations that are dedicated to preserving our local history: the Antiquarian and Landmarks Society in Hartford, the Milford Historical Society, the New Haven Museum and Historical Society, and the Shore Line Trolley Museum.

Thanks to those who gave me the technical expertise I lacked: designers Tracy Cole and Laurie Fried, and photographer Robert Lisak.

Thanks to Mary Donnelly, and her parents John and Catherine before her, who made it possible for me and my family to live in Woodmont in the first place. And to Michael Krauss, who taught me most of what I know about Woodmont. And to the late Alex Uspenski, who first made me realize what a wonderful corner of the world I had stumbled upon, when he said, in his beautifully accented English, "Voodmont is the most vonderful place in the vorld!"

INTRODUCTION

Like most of early Connecticut, Woodmont was mainly farmland and woods. Although Native Americans had enjoyed the coast for centuries, local farmers had little use for the shorefront property, which was rocky, inhospitable, and useless for farming. Indeed, farming in Woodmont was short-lived.

The attraction to saltwater has lured people to the shore for centuries. In the 1870s, three gentlemen from Waterbury "discovered" Woodmont.

"In 1870, Woodmont was nothing but a strip of unused meadow land in the town of Milford, and its beginning as a shore resort was simply a matter of chance," according to a 1906 issue of the *Saturday Chronicle*, a society newspaper published in New Haven between 1903 and 1916. The *Chronicle* article, called "Beginnings of Woodmont," claimed that the first beach cottage in Woodmont was built near Oyster River in the summer of 1874 by Dr. Joseph Anderson, the pastor of the First Congregational Church in Waterbury.

The Reverend Anderson had heard about Woodmont from another Waterbury resident named Mr. Ayres, who had stumbled upon it in 1872 while he and his wife were taking a horse-and-buggy riding trip through the state. They liked it so much they purchased one of two vacant houses there, on a hill, with a view of the water. When Anderson mentioned to Ayres that he was thinking of building a cottage on one of the Thimble Islands in Branford, Ayres suggested he consider what is now Woodmont and took him there.

The Reverend Anderson purchased about three-and-a-half acres of property from Edward Beach Clark, a descendant of one of the earliest settlers of the area, and built a waterfront cottage in the summer of 1874. Although Ayres died shortly after, Anderson and Ayres were the Woodmont pioneers. But it was Ayres who gave the name Woodmont to the area, meaning the wooded mount set back from the shore.

The second beach cottage was built later that year by Charles Perkins, also of Waterbury, at Merwin's Point, the opposite end of Woodmont. After those first two cottages, the growth was constant over the next 10 years. By 1906 there were about 150 cottages between the Anderson and Perkins cottages—a distance of about a mile and a half. Just 32 years after Ayres and Anderson first came to Woodmont, the summer population had grown to about 2,000.

In that short time, the land that had sustained American Indians and farmers for centuries had found a new use—tourism. Woodmont on the Sound was born.

What put Woodmont on the map, literally and figuratively, were the trolleys that extended from New Haven through Woodmont in the 1890s. The trolleys made the area accessible from the nearby cities and ushered in a real estate boom along the shore, which had been largely undeveloped meadows and swampy marshland, beyond the few family-owned farms.

The local farmers, or "planters" as they were called then, began to sell off their land. Farmland and woods were subdivided into dozens of small lots, and summer cottages began to spring up around the beginning of the 20th century. At the same time, several large wooden hotels with wraparound, multifloor porches opened. During its heyday, between 1895 and 1940, Woodmont had several large hotels, numerous smaller inns, cottages, stores, and restaurants, all catering to the annual flood of summer residents.

The primary relaxation activities were bathing, fishing, sailing, and sitting out on the porches to keep cool. With offshore breezes, the average temperature in Woodmont in the summer was probably a good five degrees cooler than inland. The hotels supported leisure activities such as dancing hops, whists (whist was a card game widely played in the 18th and 19th centuries—a forerunner of bridge), and musical concerts, theatrical presentations, croquet, and tennis and golf tournaments. Summer was a time for rest, relaxation, and socializing.

According to a clipping from an unidentified newspaper in August 1935, few went bathing in the Victorian era, in fact, "nothing much in the way of excitement happened in those days at a summer hotel except when one of the ladies tripped over a croquet wicket in the dark or the hired man came back from the village with the smell of ginger beer on his breath."

While Woodmont boasted about a mile and a half of shoreline, the two most popular beaches over the years were Anchor Beach and Crescent Beach. All the Woodmont beaches were populated with large shale rock formations, on which moss and barnacles grew below the high tide line, and which were responsible for many cuts and scrapes by waders, bathers, and fishermen. These rocks, however, have always been favorite fishing spots for those who did not have boats.

Although Woodmont was predominantly a summer community, a community it was. It was soon home to small businesses, houses of worship, a school, and a country club. A commercial center developed on Cherry Street, with a pharmacy, market, hardware store, department store, and post office.

Peddlers were a common sight in Woodmont from the beginning of the 20th century right through the 1950s. There were milkmen from local dairies, fruit and vegetable wagons, and the fish man who tooted a long trumpetlike horn. Local farmer John Quirk delivered eggs, and Mr. Bryan delivered coal and removed snow from the borough sidewalks with a horse-drawn plow. During the summer he delivered blocks of ice for the iceboxes.

In 1901, residents formed the Woodmont Association, a community improvement organization. Two years later the association was granted a charter by the Connecticut legislature, and Woodmont became an official borough within the town of Milford on June 18, 1903.

The "summer people" (the cottage dwellers who came to the shore for the weekends, for a week or two, or for the entire summer) came from all over, with large numbers coming from New Haven, New York, and inland Connecticut towns such as Meriden, Middletown, Ansonia, Derby, Bristol, and Waterbury. After Labor Day, most things shut down and most families moved back to the city.

Just as the introduction of the trolley helped establish Woodmont as a summer resort, the demise of the trolley signaled the end of that era. The last trolley to Woodmont ran on November 20, 1937. World War II was really the beginning of the end of Woodmont as a summer resort. A severe postwar housing shortage led many families to winterize their cottages for year-round use. The hotels, in some cases, became apartments, and others burned down or were simply torn down so new homes and businesses could be built.

The 1950s were a transitional period, but by the 1960s, Woodmont's life as a seaside resort was over.

Today there are about 762 households in Woodmont and 1,750 people, many of them second-, third-, and fourth-generation Woodmonters. Even in the 21st century, Woodmont continues to attract those who love the shore, the salt water, and the look and feel of days gone by. As Roy Schlachter, who spent his boyhood summers in Woodmont and continues to make the periodic pilgrimage back 60 years later, once said, "Hail, Woodmont, oh hail! May your majestic waters, rocky shores and sandy beaches continue to comfort and delight all those who partake of your pleasures."

One

The Early Years

The first inhabitants of Woodmont were Paugusset Indians who had a small village near the river now known as Oyster River. For hundreds of years, they hunted, planted, and fished in the woods, fields, rivers, and the sound. Game was plentiful in the woods, as were fish, clams, crabs, oysters, and lobsters in the sound. They planted maize, beans, squash, pumpkins, artichokes, and tobacco. Nuts, berries, and wild beach plums were abundant along the shore. But then America was "discovered," and the world would never be the same.

In 1639, the town of Milford had been founded by a group of settlers led by Peter Prudden who traded goods to the Paugussets in exchange for the land near the Wepawaug River. The settlers were mostly planters who lived peacefully with the Paugussets and renegotiated with them several times for more plots of land for farming over the next two decades.

Twenty years later, in 1659, the land from Indian River to Oyster River—including modern-day Woodmont—was purchased by Alexander Bryan and Robert Treat from Ansantawae, the sachem of the Paugusset Indians. For this piece of land, the settlers offered 26 pounds of goods, protection for Chief Ansantawae and his family, and the right to fish in their old waters.

For the next 200 years, this parcel of land was simply known as Burwell's farm. Two farms occupied the land, Burwell's farm east of Indian River, and Merwin's farm west of Oyster River. Gradually dirt roads replaced the old American Indian trails, including Burwell's farm road, which came to be called the "Road to New Haven," and later New Haven Avenue. The land was suitable for farming, but the road was nearly impassable at high tide. In 1662, Great Bridge (or Indian Bridge) was built over the Indian River, and the Oyster River Bridge was built in 1753.

Woodmont was home to several well-known farms over the years—Merwin, Burwell, Bryan, Beach, and Treat farms. The Robert Treat Farm still exists today, but farming was not to be Woodmont's future.

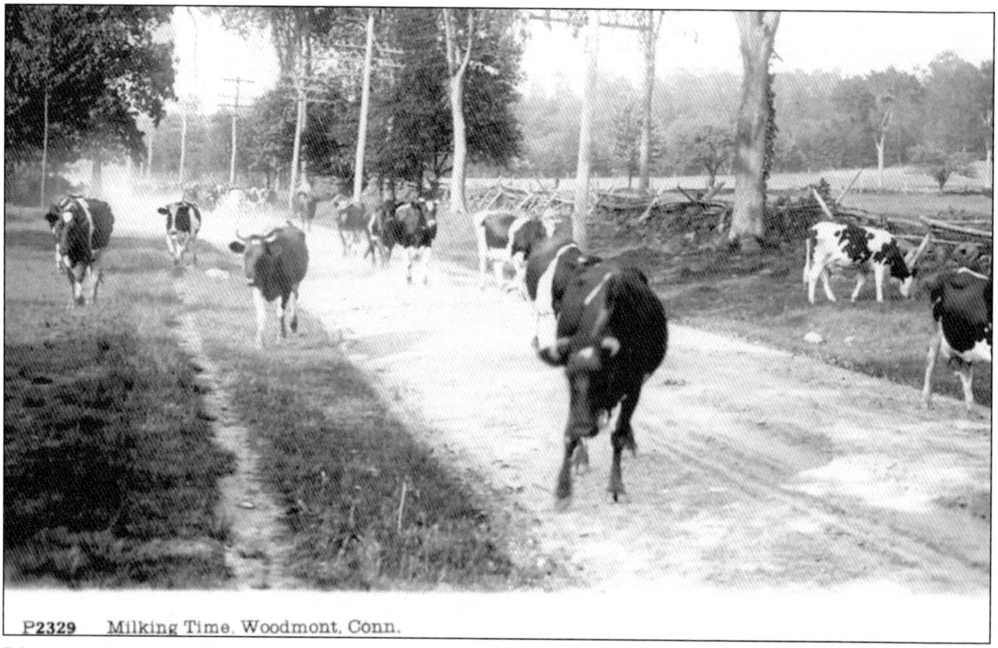

MILKING TIME IN WOODMONT. In its earliest days, Woodmont, like most of early Milford, was farmland. The farmers, like the Native Americans before them, enjoyed wild fruit and berries along the shore and game, which was plentiful in the woods. This postcard is postmarked 1914.

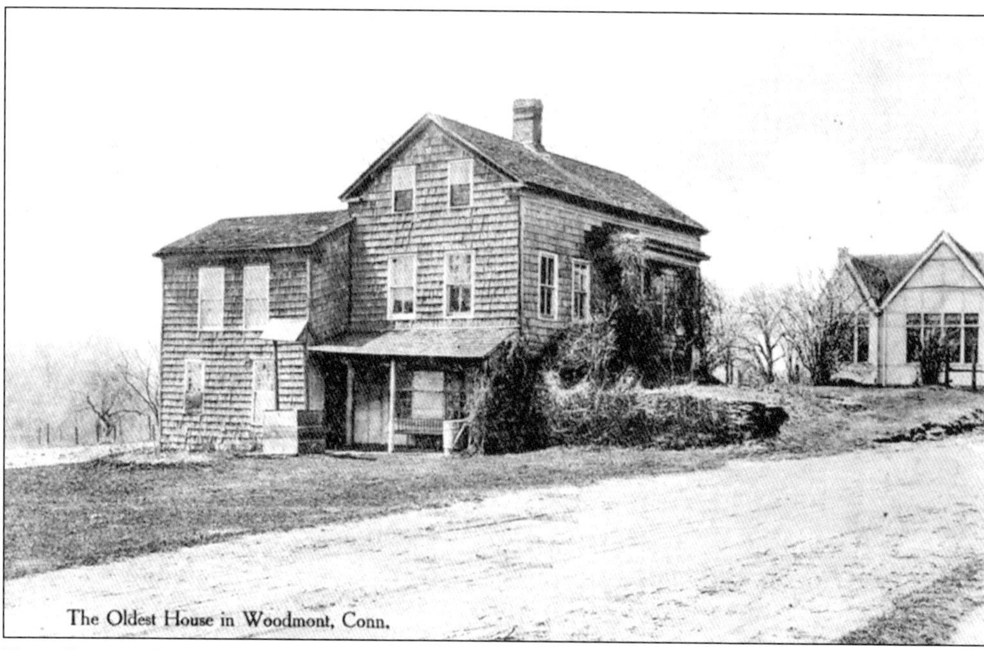

THE BRYAN HOUSE. Part of what is now Woodmont was first known as Bryan's Farm. The Bryan House at 71 Chapel Street (the corner of Chapel Street and Merwin Avenue) is Woodmont's oldest house, built around 1790. This postcard is postmarked 1921.

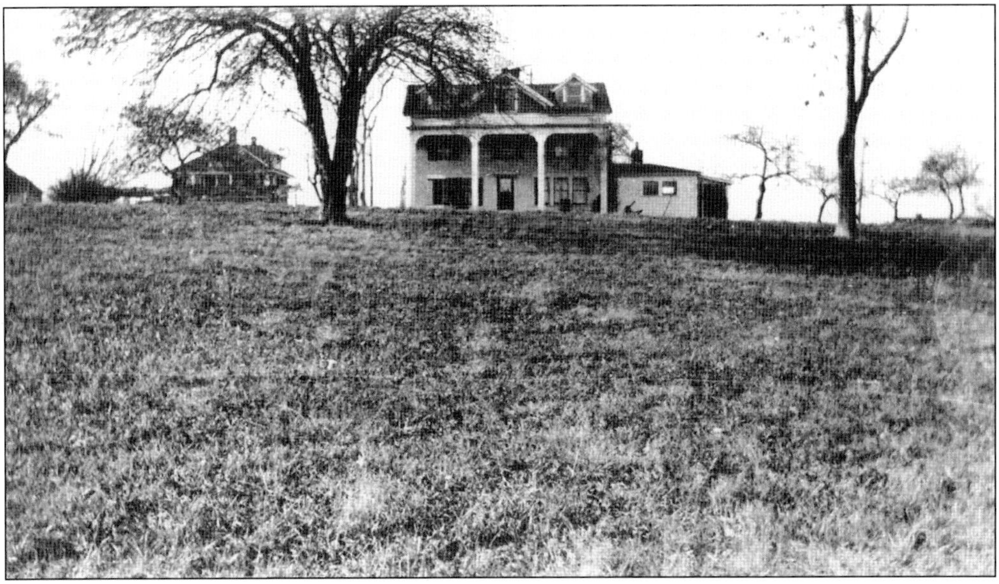

An Early Woodmont Farmhouse. This farmhouse, identified as Quirk's, was located on the Road to New Haven. Before 1900, between that road and the shore, about a half-mile away, there was nothing but fields and woods. (Courtesy of Photography by Joseph.)

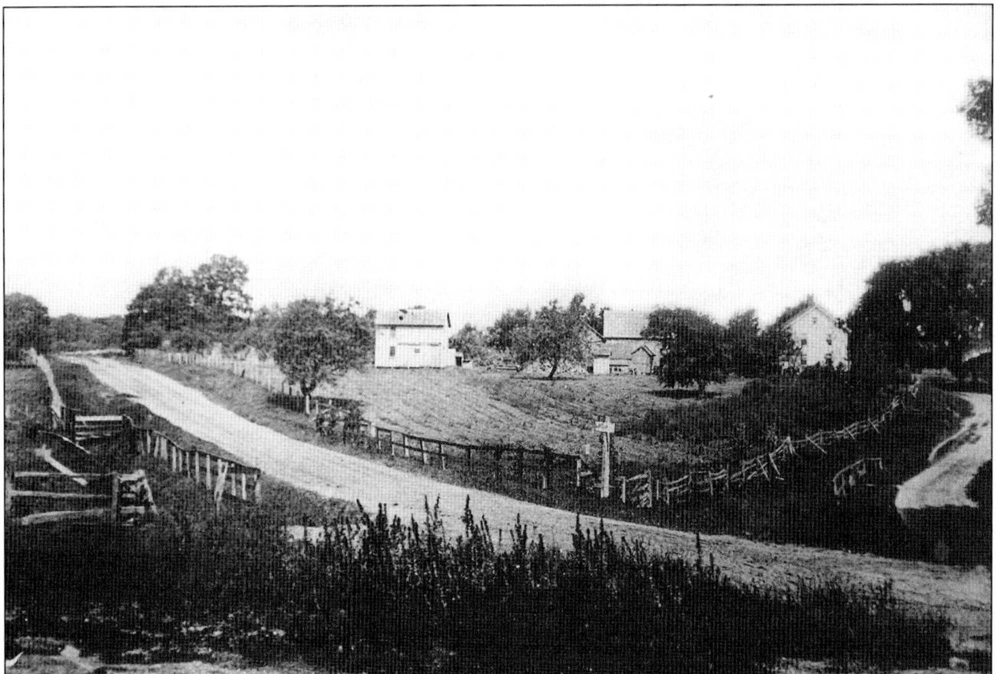

Farms and More Farms. The Lock's Farm was located off Merwin Avenue in the vicinity of the current Five Corners. An early railroad station was built beyond this farm; hence the current name Depot Road. (Courtesy of Photography by Joseph.)

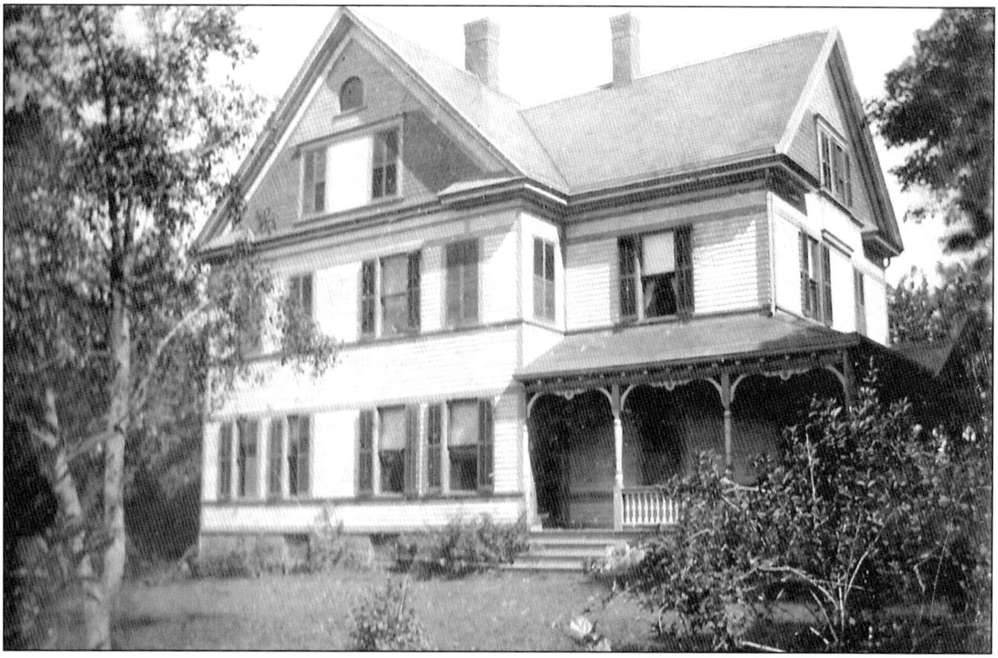

Maple Shade Farm. This house on Maple Avenue (now Merwin Avenue) was built by Theodore Beach, son of John Beach who started the Beach farm around 1818. The 15-acre farm had grown to 150 acres by the 1940s, raising seed corn, onion seed, and potatoes in the early days, as well as garden produce, a herd of cows, and chickens. (Courtesy of Lowell Beach Sykes.)

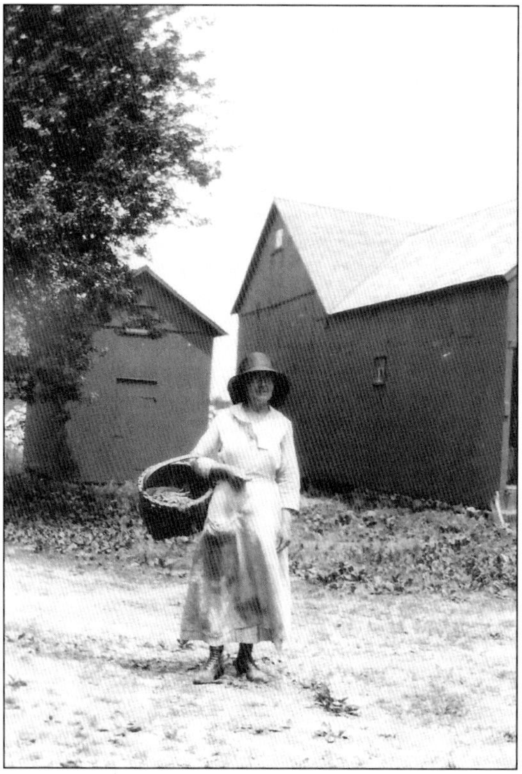

Coming from the Garden. Eda Rhodes Beach, wife of Frank J. Beach who is the grandson of John and son of Theodore, is in front of the feed barn and the cow barn. After World War II, Ralph Beach, a seventh-generation Beach farmer, sold 30 acres, which became Milford Lawns, the first housing development in the area. The farmhouse was torn down in 1970 to make way for the Ocean Crest condominiums, to the left of the modern St. Agnes Roman Catholic Church. (Courtesy of Lowell Beach Sykes.)

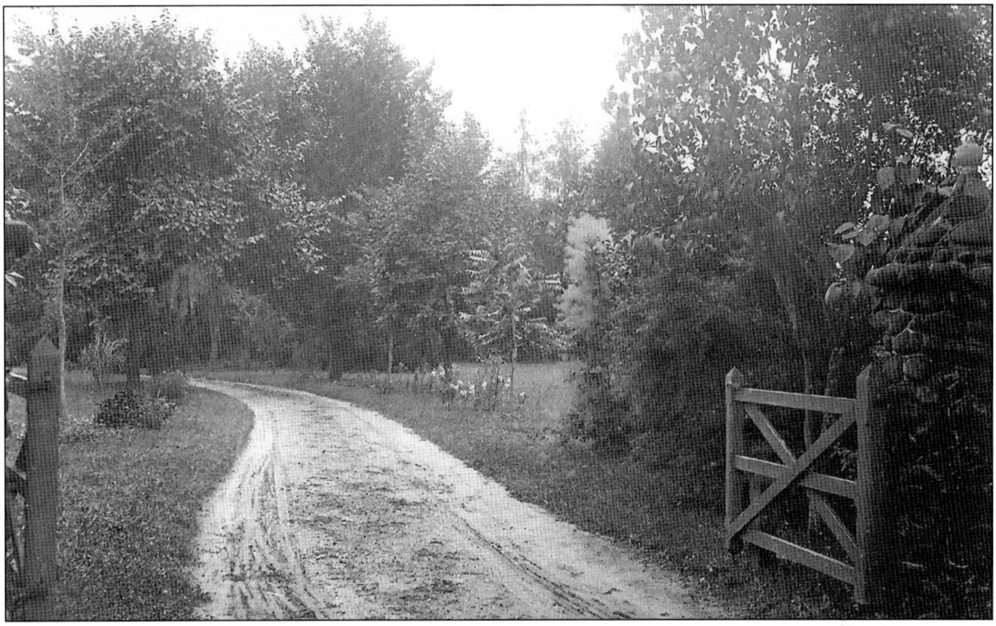

THE ANDERSON GATES. In 1873, the Reverend Dr. Joseph Anderson bought three and a half acres of land adjacent to Oyster River from Edward B. Clarke. This photograph, taken around 1900, is of the New Haven Avenue entrance to his property, and the dirt road shows buggy tracks, which led to his barn. The two stone pillars, which once held wooden gates, still exist today. There were no cottages there at this time—the land was owned by Milford farmers.

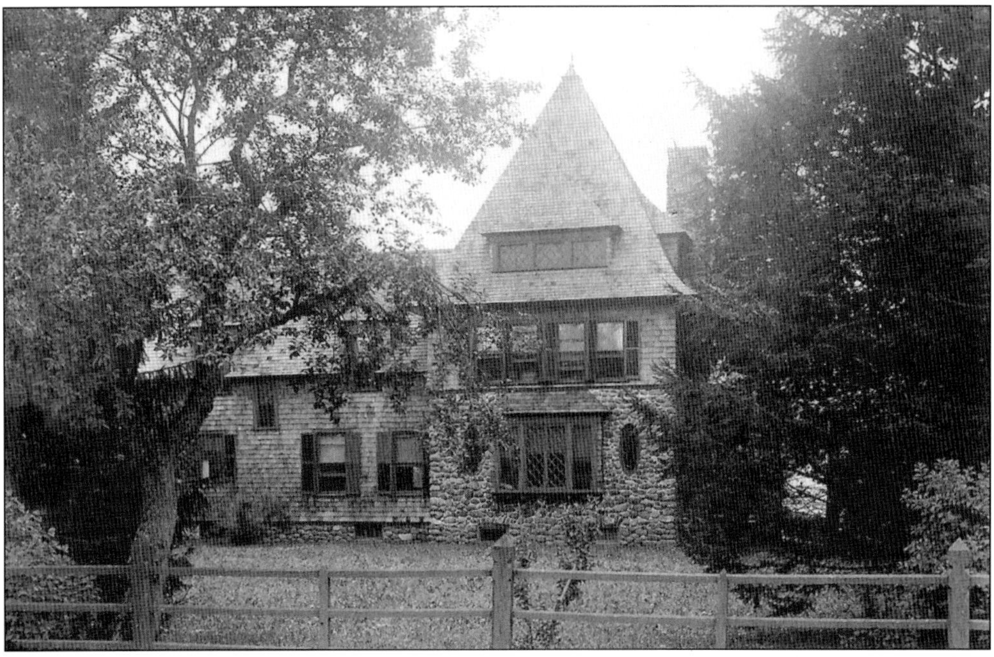

ANDERSON TOWERS. Dr. Anderson liked Woodmont so much that around the beginning of the 20th century, he built a year-round house on his property near the cottage. Anderson Towers, as it was called, is a massive Victorian house of fieldstone and wooden shingles. Anderson spent more than 40 years in Woodmont before he died there on August 18, 1916.

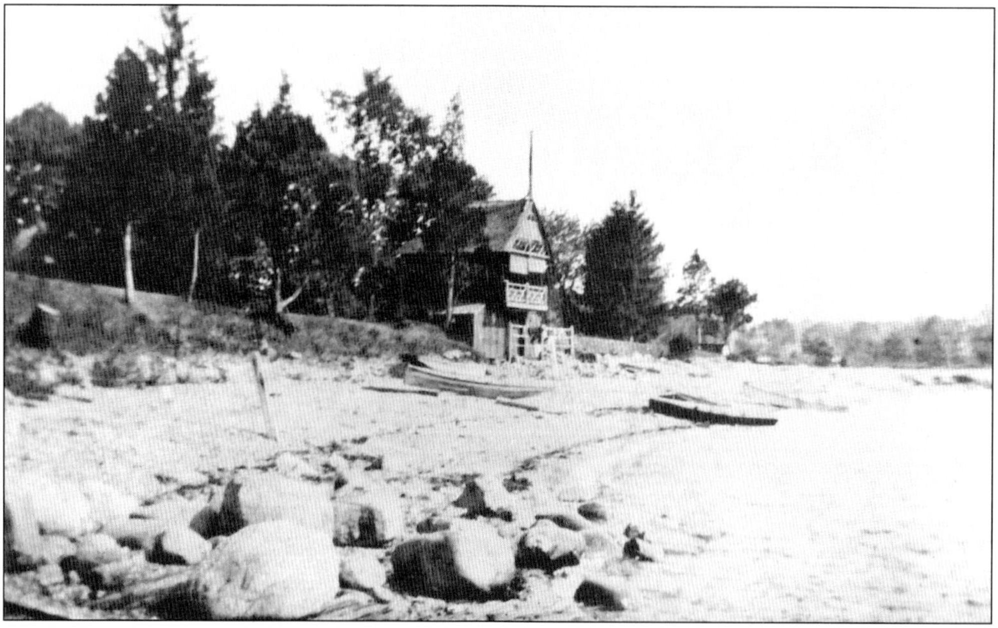

Site of the First Woodmont Cottage. The first Woodmont beach cottage was built by the Reverend Joseph Anderson of Waterbury in 1874 near Oyster River, at what is now called the Anderson Avenue Beach. Dr. Anderson's two-story cottage and barn, eclipsed by trees in the far right of this 1917 postcard, still exist along the beachfront on Rosemary Court. (Courtesy of Photography by Joseph.)

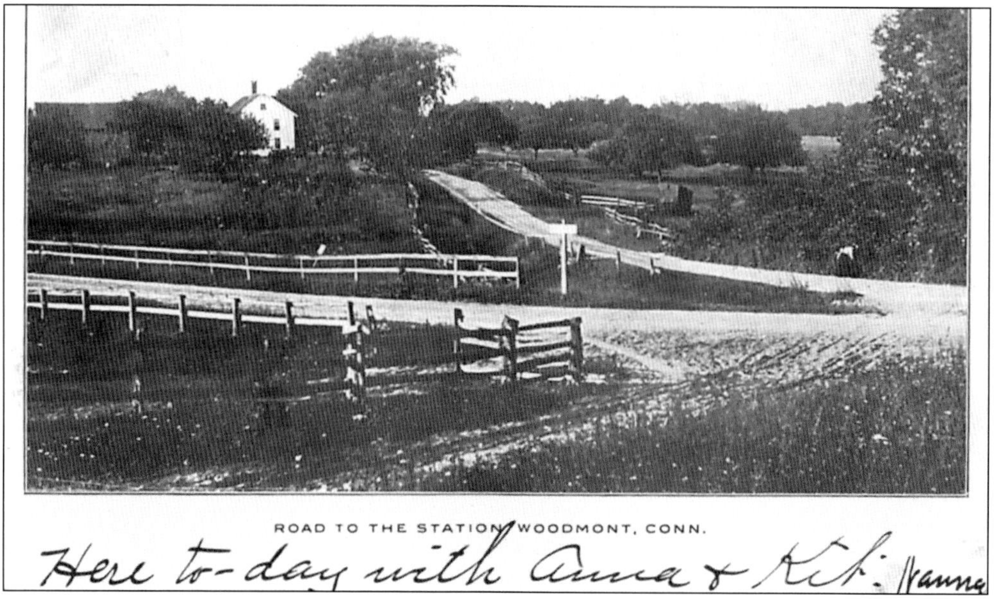

Road to the Station. Dr. Anderson first heard of Woodmont from another Waterbury resident named Ayres. Ayres's son, Russell W. Ayres, a Waterbury lawyer, believed Woodmont could be profitably developed, and he was instrumental in getting a railroad station developed there. For many years, Woodmont was served by its own mail line railroad station on Depot Road, off the current Five Corners intersection, with regular stops on the New York, New Haven and Hartford Railroad. This postcard is postmarked 1907. (Courtesy of George Peacock.)

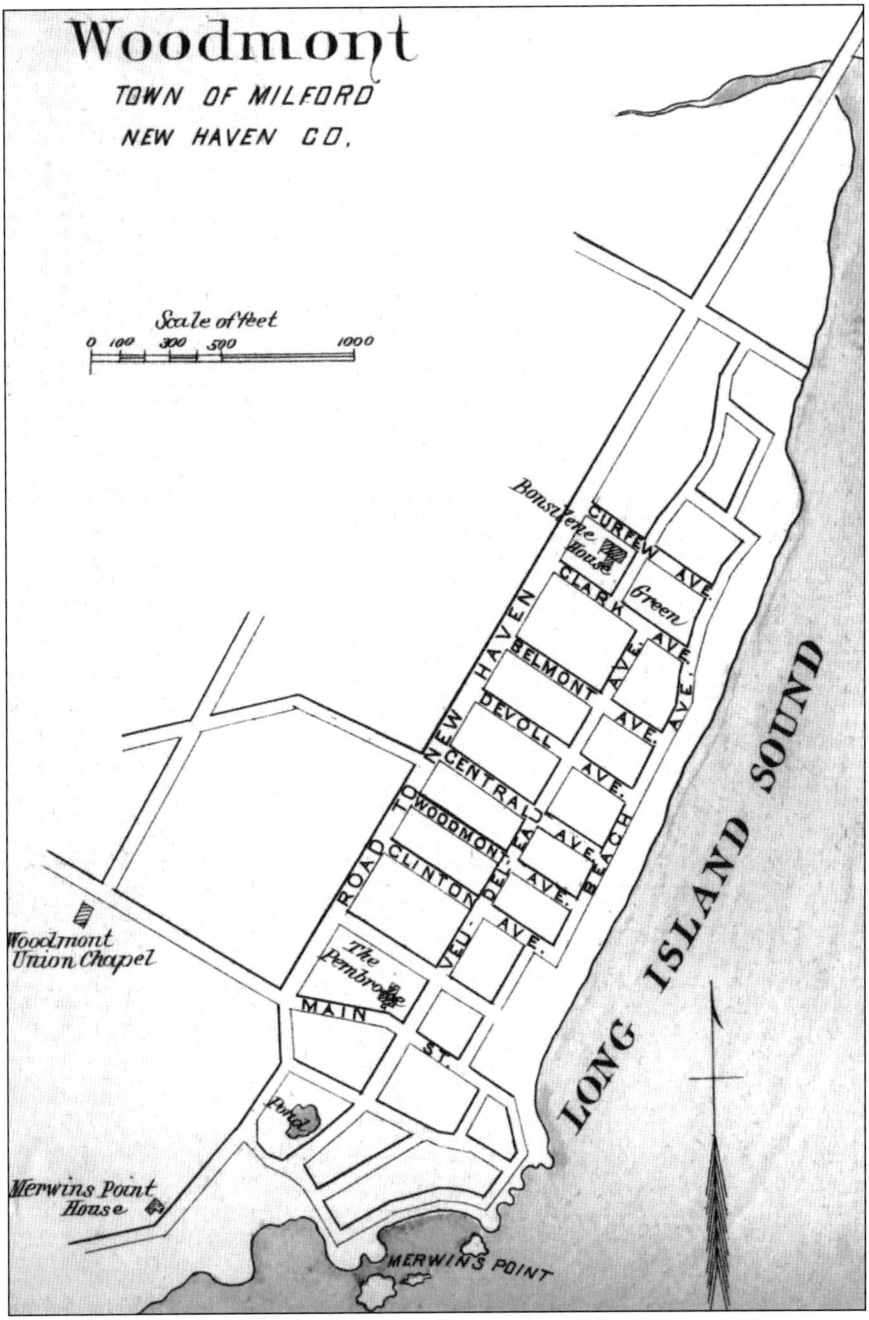

A Woodmont Map, 1893. Woodmont started out with haphazard, unnamed dirt paths between the cottages, but by 1893, had become organized with three long main avenues parallel to the shore—Beach Avenue, Vue de L'eau Avenue (later Hawley Avenue), and the Road to New Haven (later New Haven Avenue)—and less than a dozen cross streets, many of them unnamed. This map shows the chapel and the three earliest hotels—the Pembroke, the Bonsilene, and the Merwin's Point House. The map also identifies a pond that no longer exists, right where the Sanford House hotel was later built. The Sanford House had drainage problems for years. Its owners might not have known of the existence of the pond, which by then had been filled in.

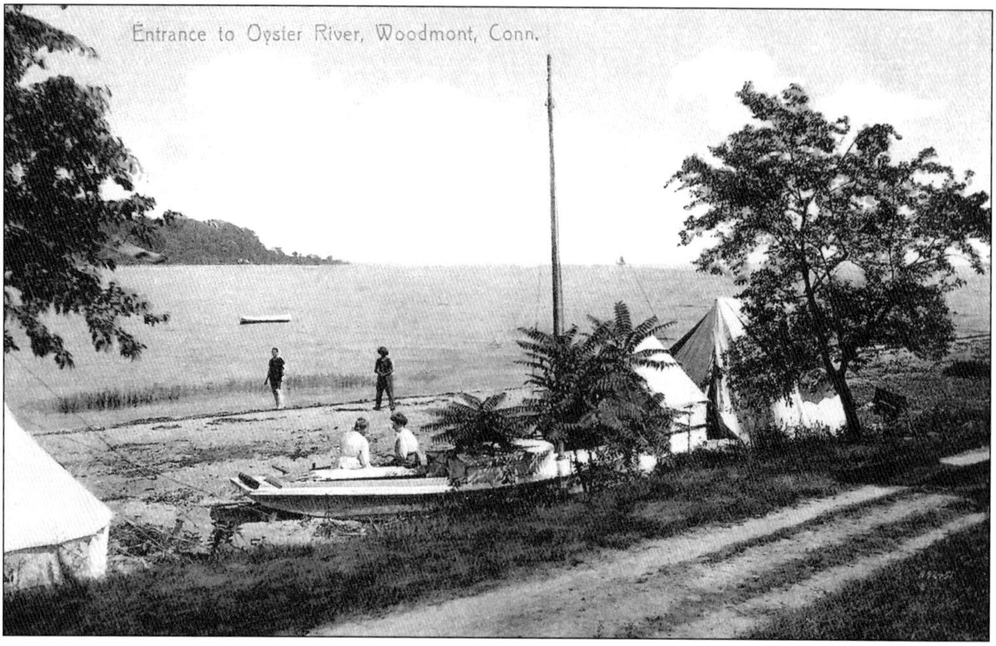

Camping at Oyster River. The Reverend Anderson's property abutted Oyster River Bay, a popular spot for oystering, clamming, and camping. (Courtesy of George Peacock.)

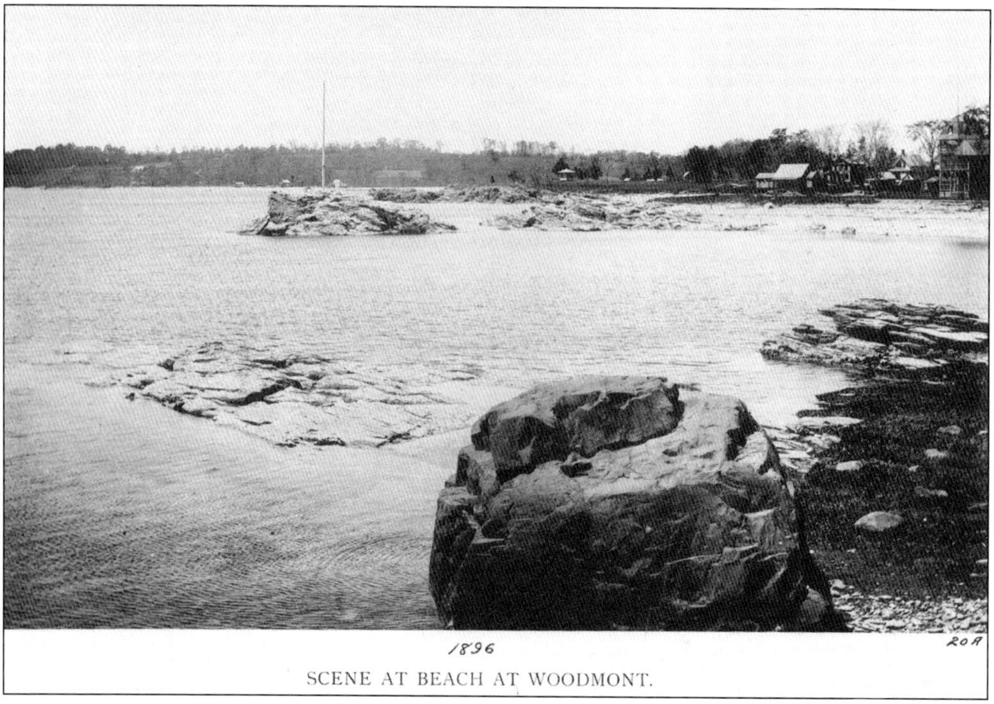

Woodmont's Second Cottage. Shortly after the Anderson cottage was built, Charles and Angeline Perkins of Waterbury constructed Woodmont's second cottage. They bought the property at the point from John Merwin in December 1874. In this photograph, dated 1896, there is no house at the tip of the point and just a handful of cottages in view, one of which must have belonged to Perkins. (Courtesy of New Haven Museum and Historical Society.)

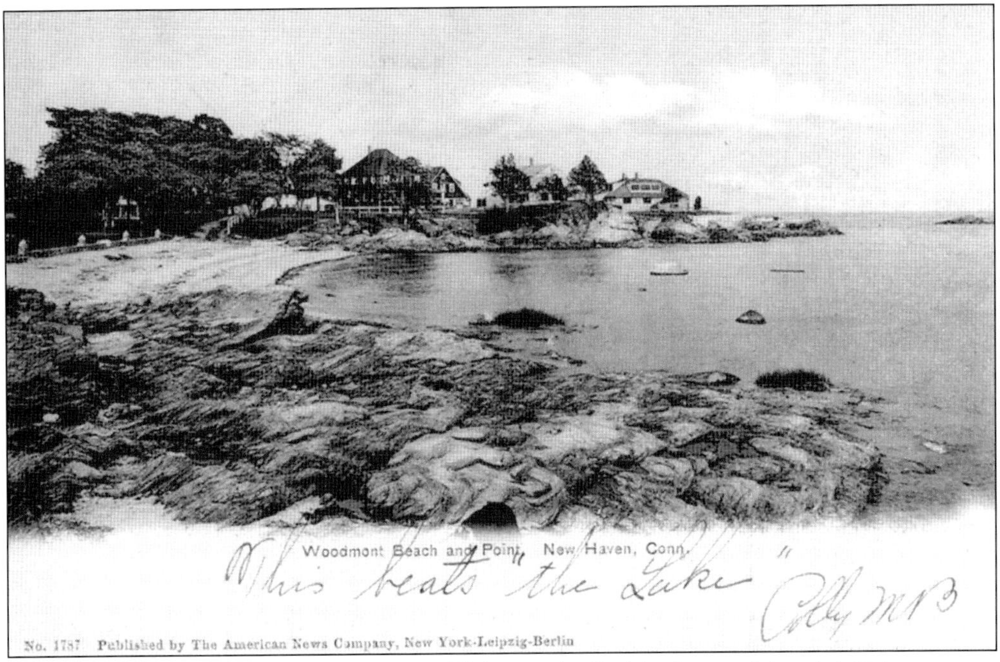

MERWIN'S POINT, LOOKING EAST. In addition to the Perkins house, Merwin's Point grew to include a half dozen prominent homes, as well as Woodmont's first guesthouse or hotel—the Mark Merwin House. The message on the postcard, postmarked in 1906, is "This beats the lake!"

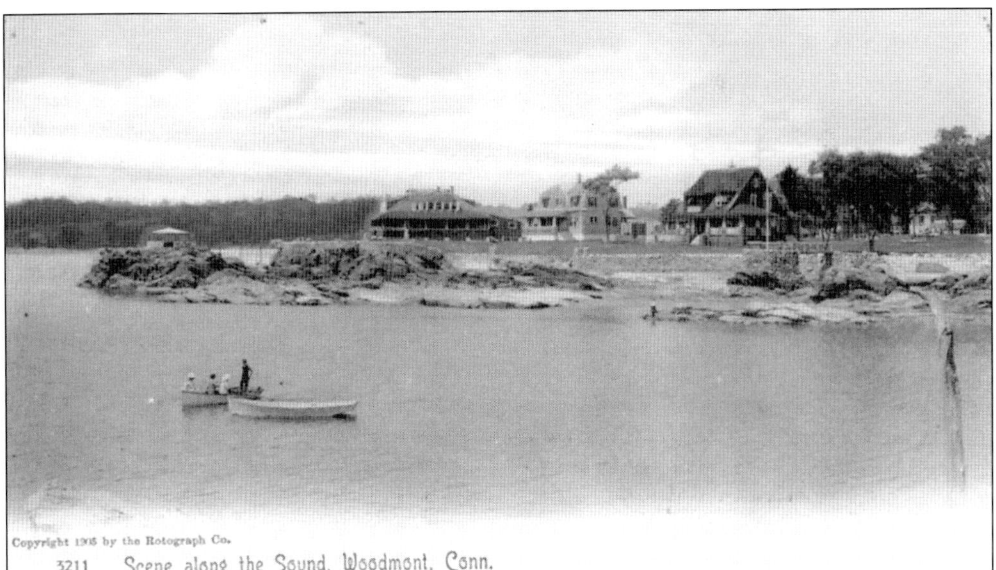

MERWIN'S POINT, LOOKING WEST. Historically Merwin's Point has been known throughout the state for excellent fishing. According to the *Saturday Chronicle* of September 1, 1906, "Thirty or forty years ago, Merwin's Point, which is now included in Woodmont, was well known all over the state as a place for a day's fishing."

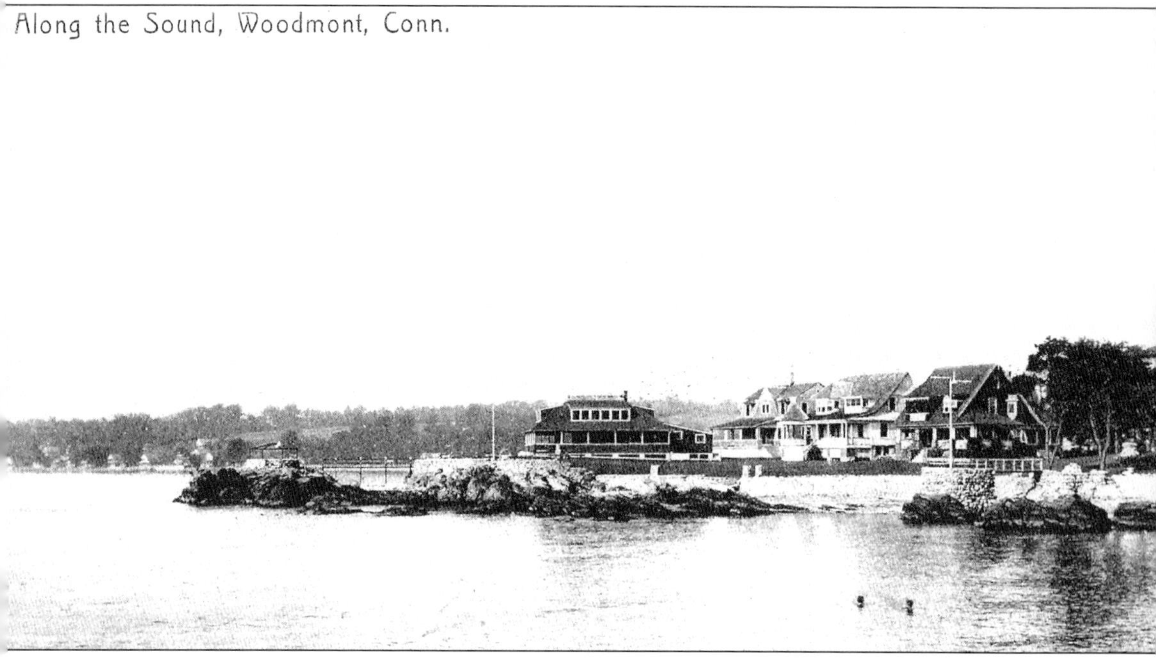

A Panorama of Merwin's Point. "Near Merwin's Point is a large house owned by W. W. Walker of Hartford. It is built on a rocky knoll directly on the water, the summer house a short distance to the front, being over the water at high tide. There is a good deal of entertaining at the Point, and Mr. Walker and members of his family do considerable themselves. Mr. Walker

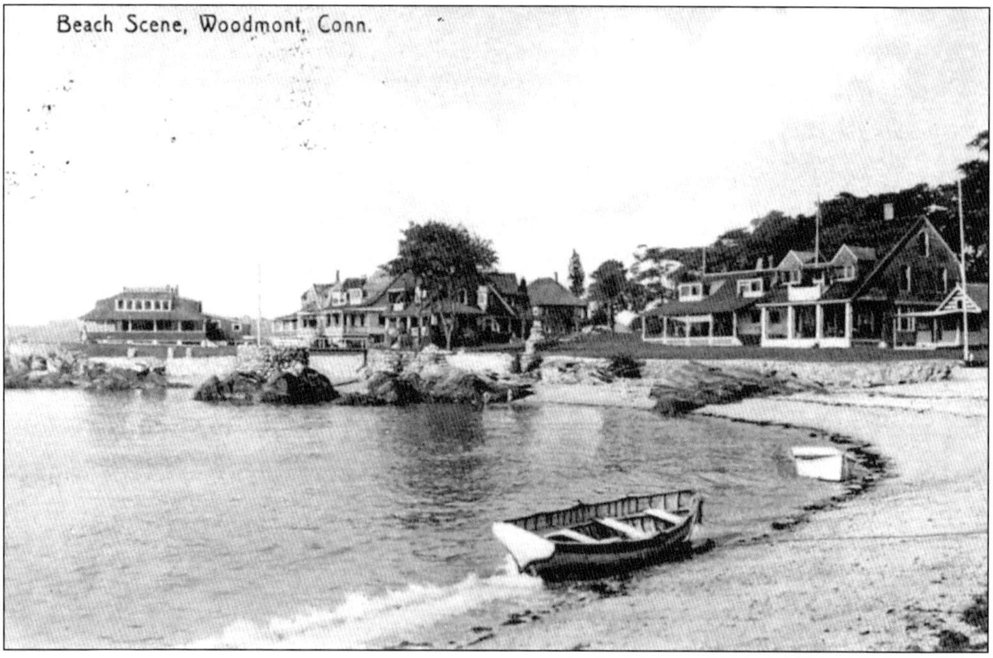

Merwin's Point and Anchor Beach. More postcards exist of Merwin's Point than any other scene in Woodmont. In the late 18th century, the largest amounts of land were owned by John W. Merwin and the Usher brothers, who sold it for building lots, which in 1906 were worth about $35 a front foot. This postcard is postmarked 1907.

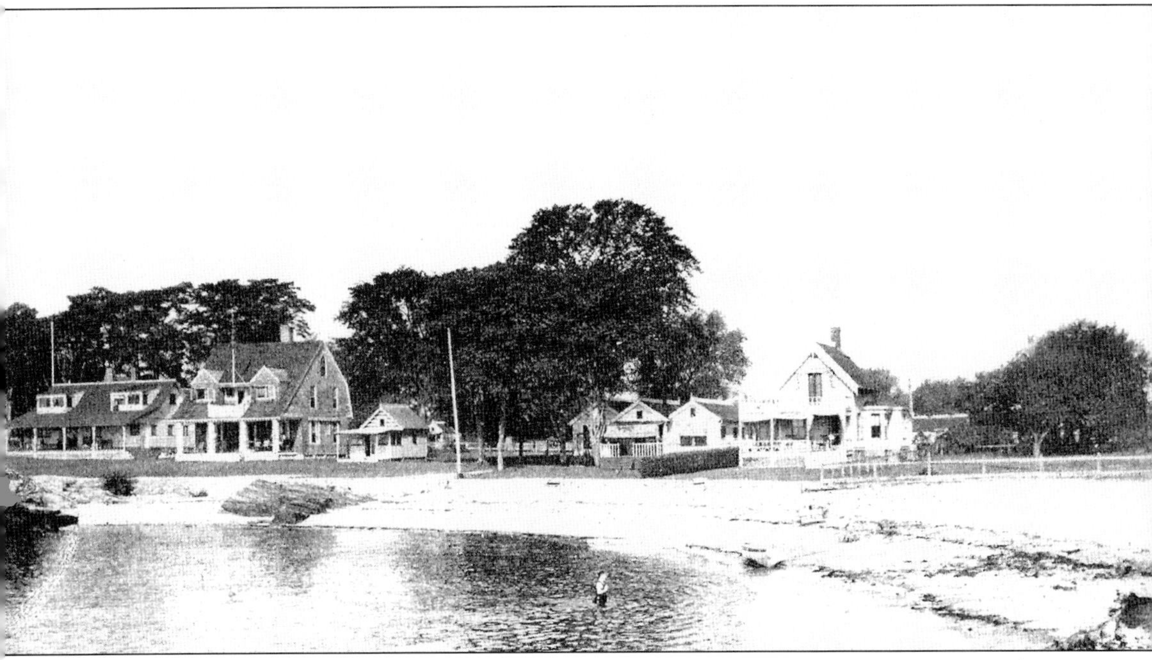

has always been a prominent member of the Woodmont Golf Club, and in past years, has put up several cups. This season also there will be several tournaments arranged," reads the *Saturday Chronicle* of July 21, 1906. The Merwin's Point homes were among the most prestigious in Woodmont.

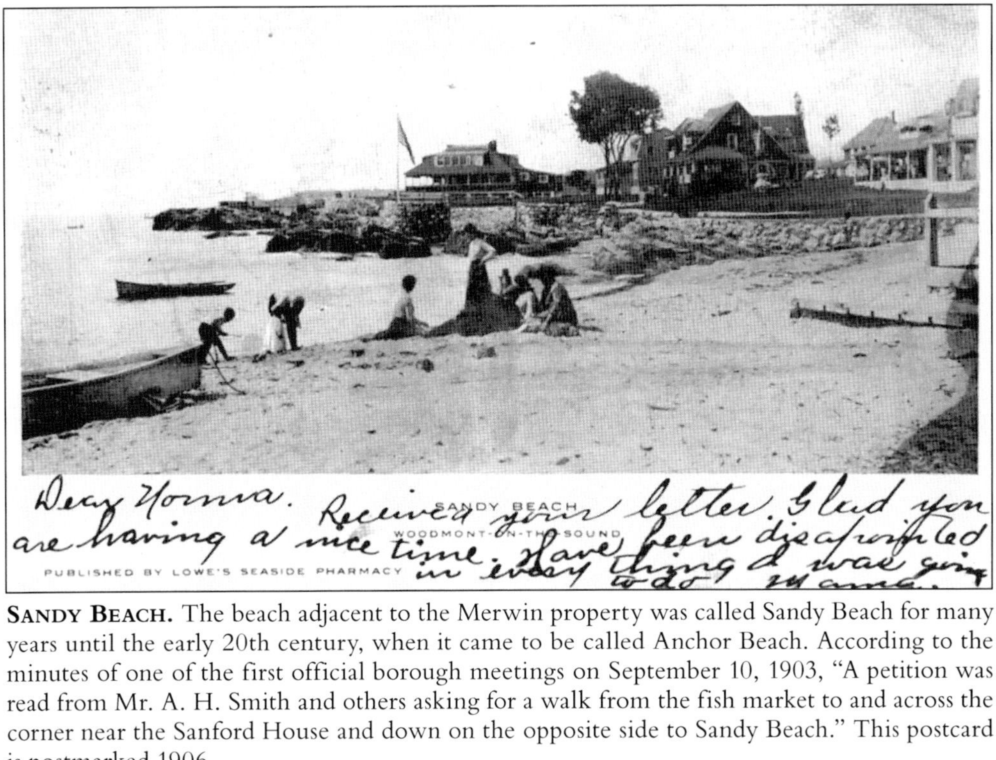

SANDY BEACH. The beach adjacent to the Merwin property was called Sandy Beach for many years until the early 20th century, when it came to be called Anchor Beach. According to the minutes of one of the first official borough meetings on September 10, 1903, "A petition was read from Mr. A. H. Smith and others asking for a walk from the fish market to and across the corner near the Sanford House and down on the opposite side to Sandy Beach." This postcard is postmarked 1906.

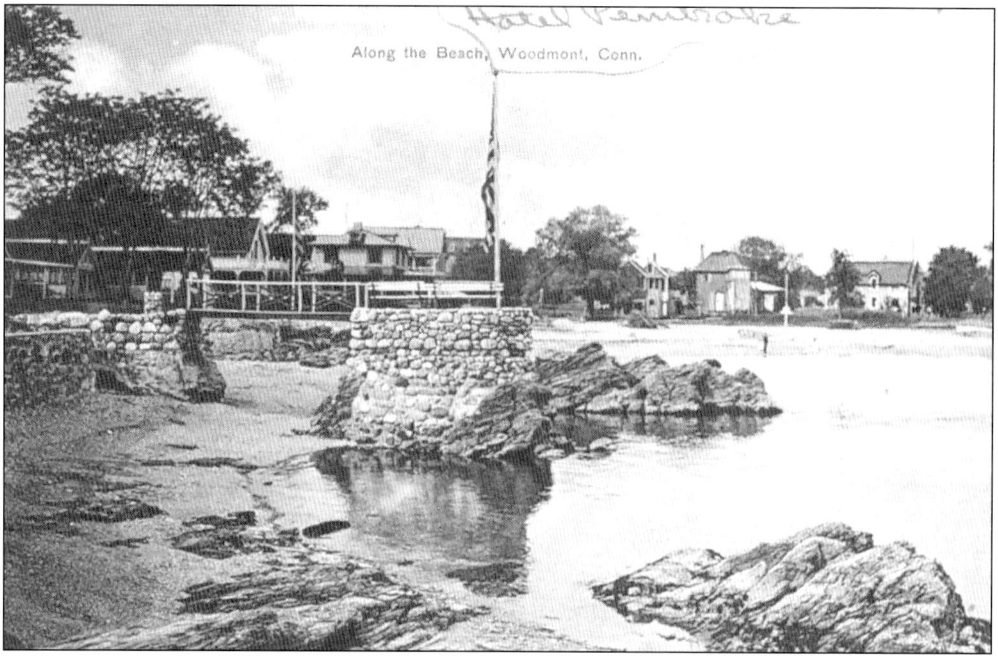

MERWIN'S POINT FLAGPOLE, LOOKING EAST. The view from Merwin's Point, looking toward Anchor beach, shows the large outcropping of rocks along the coast of Woodmont. The soil contained a tremendous number of stones, so when fields were cleared and houses constructed, the fieldstones were used for stone walls, foundations, fireplaces, gateposts, and flagpole bases. This postcard is postmarked 1912.

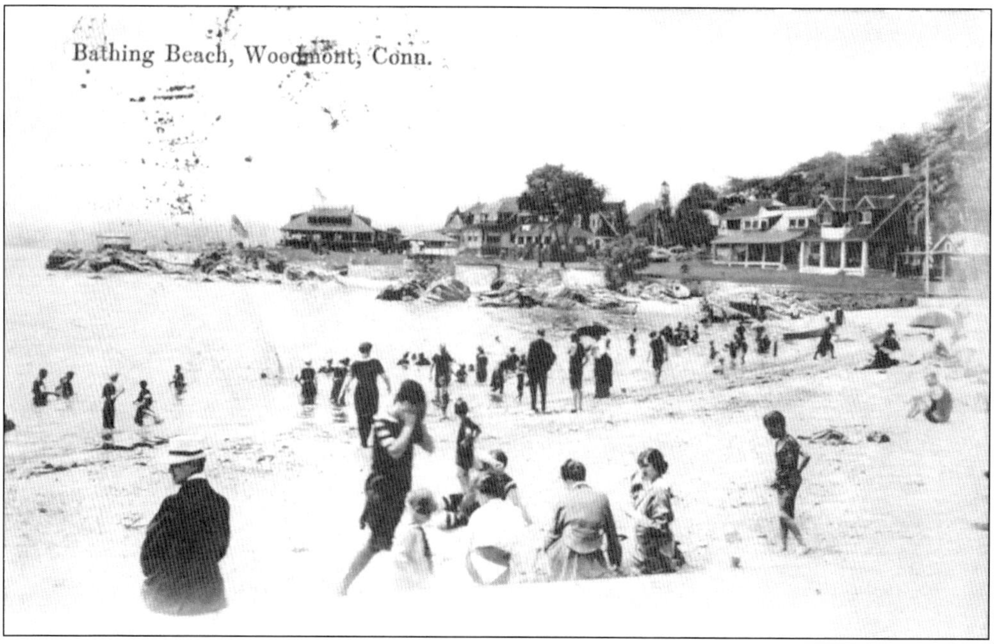

LOOKING WEST, TOWARD MERWIN'S POINT. Seen here is a view of a busy Anchor Beach in August looking toward Merwin's Point. This postcard is postmarked 1916.

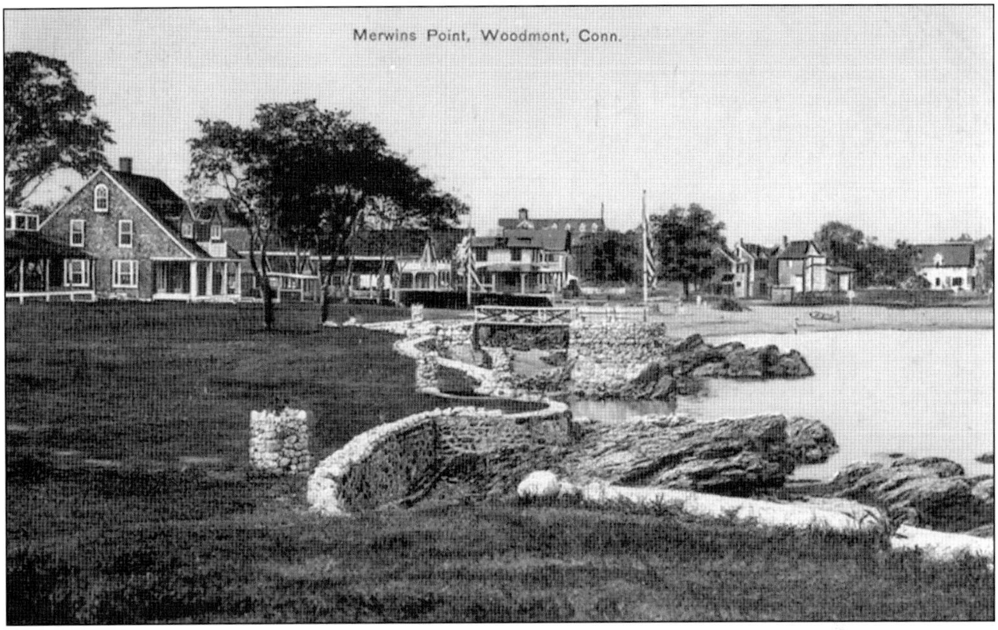

MERWIN'S POINT, WOODMONT, CONNECTICUT. This photograph was taken from Merwin's Point, looking east toward Anchor Beach. In the center of the *c.* 1905 postcard, the roofline and cupola of the Pembroke Hotel can be clearly seen in the distance, even though it is almost three blocks from Anchor Beach. Along these yards, the fieldstones formed retaining walls to protect the lawns and houses from the water at high tide and during storms.

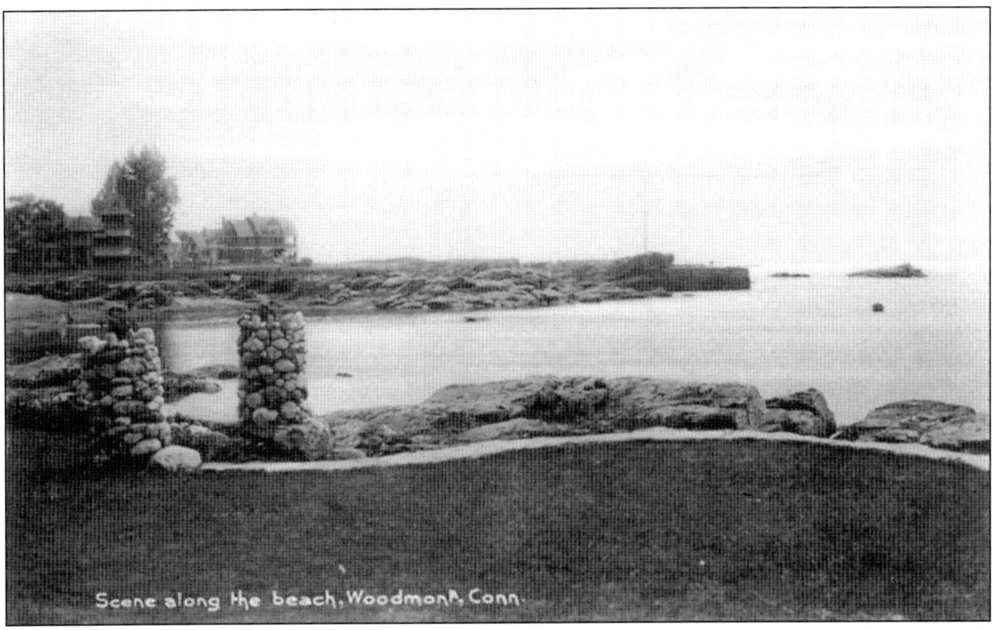

STONE PILLARS AT MERWIN'S POINT. This *c.* 1905 postcard shows the lawn at the Merwin's Point houses. Many of the cottages on the point used the fieldstones so abundant in the area for landscaping, stone pillars, and grottos.

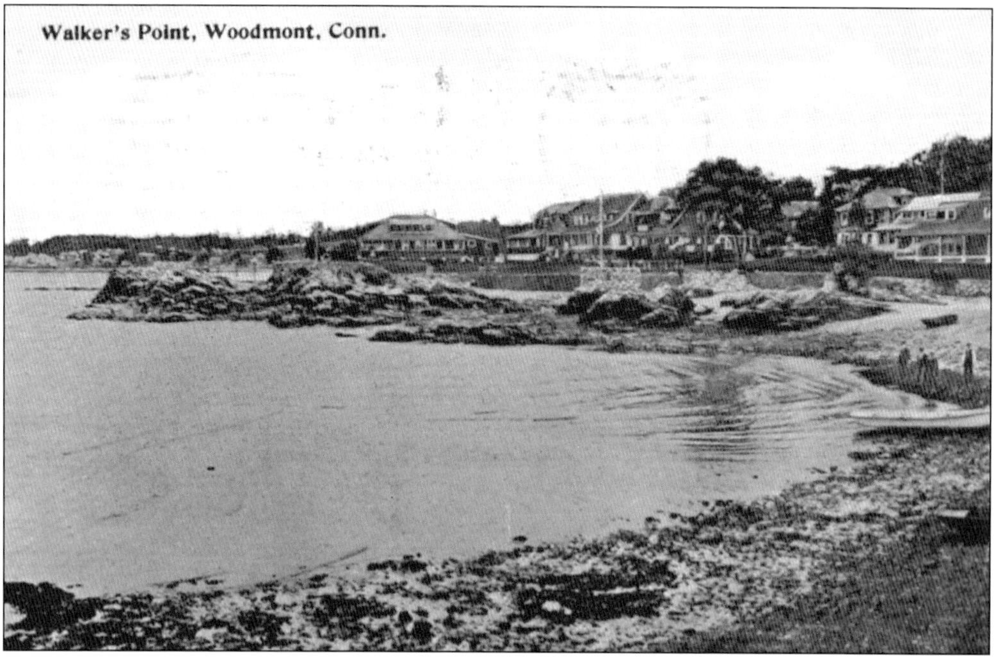

Walker's Point. Around 1899, the Merwin's Point property was sold to Werton W. Walker, and for a time it was called Walker's Point. In the 1920s, it was briefly called Sweezy's Point after owners Jerome and Mary Sweezy. Despite the various attempts to rename the point after current owners, today the area is still called Merwin's Point. This postcard is postmarked 1912.

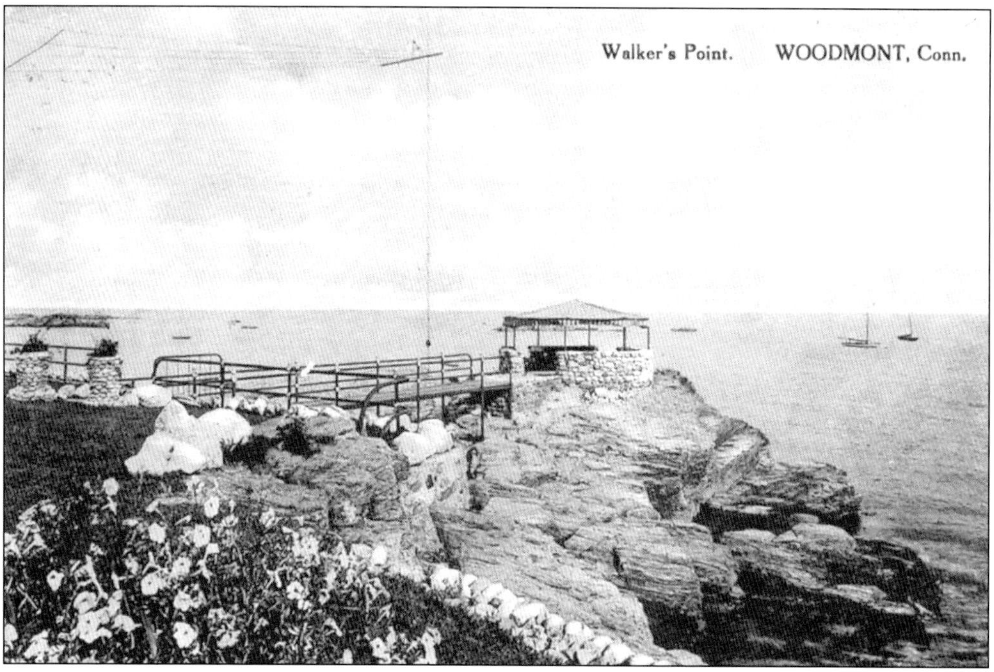

Walker's Point Gazebo. Addressed to Master Raymond Sceery, the message on this 1905 postcard reads, "There are lots of little boys down here playing in the water every day. From Aunt Mae."

Two

THE TROLLEYS ARRIVE

The Gay Nineties marked the beginning of Woodmont as a popular summer vacation area. A horse-drawn streetcar—the New Haven and West Haven Horse Railroad—had connected the centers of New Haven and West Haven since 1867. Shortly after that, it was extended to the West Haven shore where the Savin Rock amusement park attracted crowds every summer. But that was the end of the line.

In 1893, however, the West Shore Railway was created to extend the car line west from Savin Rock to Milford. The owners of the electric street railway hoped that if they laid trolley tracks along the shore, they would attract more picnickers and bathers in the hot summer months. The trolley owners were correct in their theory. Woodmont was the beneficiary of one of the region's first electrified trolleys. Where the horse-drawn railway traveled at a top speed of six miles per hour, the electric railway could go three times that speed.

The West Shore Railway ended about a mile west of Oyster River. Beyond that point, tracks were built by Connecticut Railway and Lighting (CR&L), which extended the trolley service from the western border of Woodmont to the center of Milford in 1898, and soon continued it into Devon and the western beaches of Milford. Woodmont was strategically located between Bridgeport and New Haven, and both cities were connected by the trolleys that ran right through Woodmont.

Before the trolley's arrival, most of the Woodmont coast consisted of a few family-owned farms, thick woods, and some swampy marshland of little use, but after the trolley made the area easily accessible, real estate developers turned it into profitable land. Hotels and summer cottages, large and small, began to spring up.

The trolleys, or electric street railways, started a real estate boom, and the summer resort business became Woodmont's newest industry.

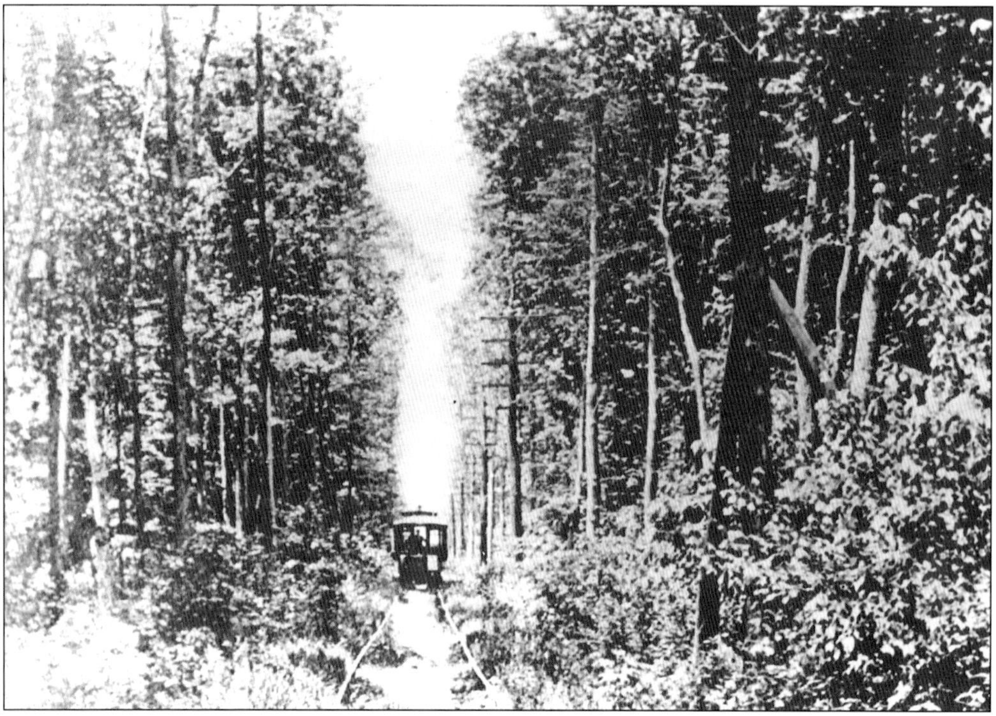

AN EARLY TROLLEY. This trolley is heading east from Woodmont toward Anderson Avenue and the marshes near Oyster River (the West Haven-Woodmont border). Electric trolleys, which usually went no faster than 20 miles per hour on city streets, could go as fast as 35 to 40 miles per hour in the woods or fields. (Courtesy of Photography by Joseph.)

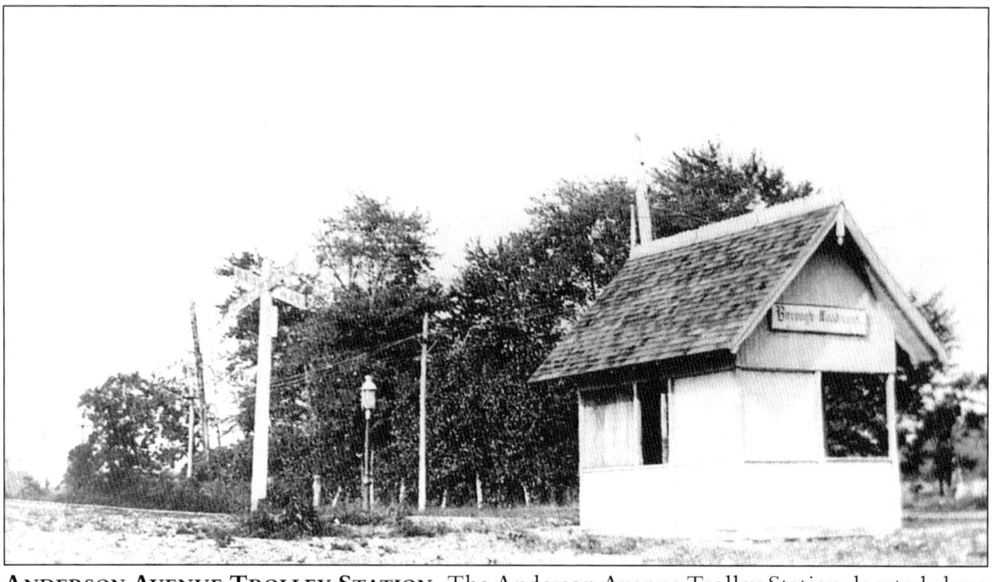

ANDERSON AVENUE TROLLEY STATION. The Anderson Avenue Trolley Station, located along the marshes by Anderson Avenue on the eastern end of Woodmont, was the first trolley station entering Woodmont from New Haven. The trolleys made Woodmont accessible when they were extended from New Haven through Woodmont in the 1890s. (Courtesy of Photography by Joseph.)

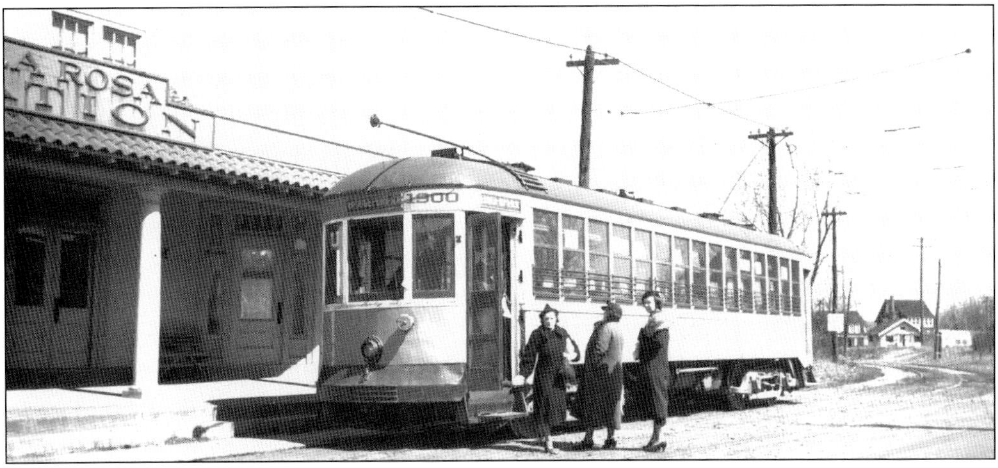

THE VILLA ROSA TROLLEY STOP. In this photograph, taken on March 22, 1937, car No. 1900 has just discharged three women dressed for a cold spring day. Sylvester Z. Poli had built this new trolley station across from his mansion in 1927. But within 10 years of opening the new trolley stop, the trolleys were gone. In 1949, a Poli nephew, Thomas Poli Nolan, became enamored with the then-retired trolley station and transformed it into Tom's Villa Rosa Restaurant. Over the past 50 years, the building continued to house different restaurants. It became the Beach House in 2004. (Photograph by Charles Duncan; courtesy of Shore Line Trolley Museum Library Collection.)

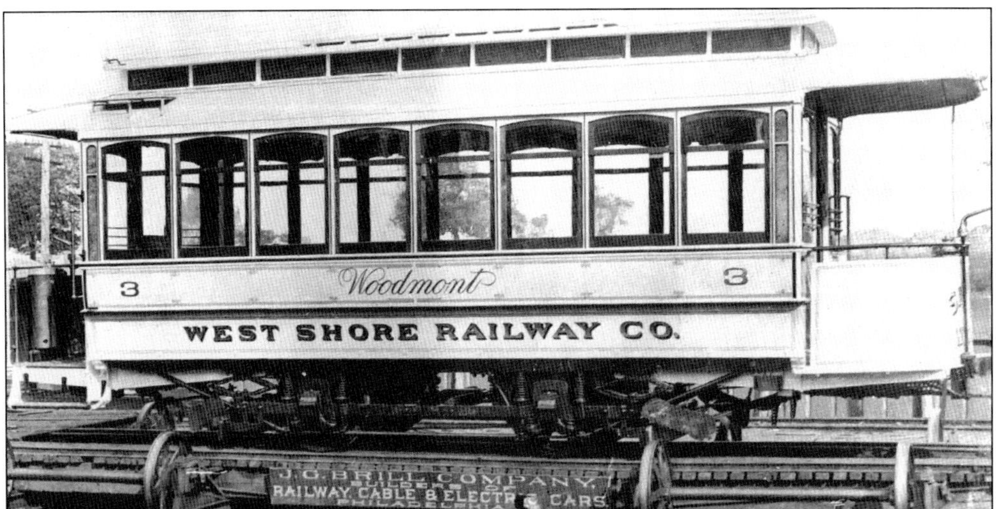

THE WOODMONT. This was the handsome Woodmont car, in a photograph taken at the J. G. Brill factory in Philadelphia. The West Shore Railway extended the trolley line of the New Haven and West Haven Horse Railroad west from Savin Rock to Milford, passing right through Woodmont. (Courtesy of Shore Line Trolley Museum Library Collection.)

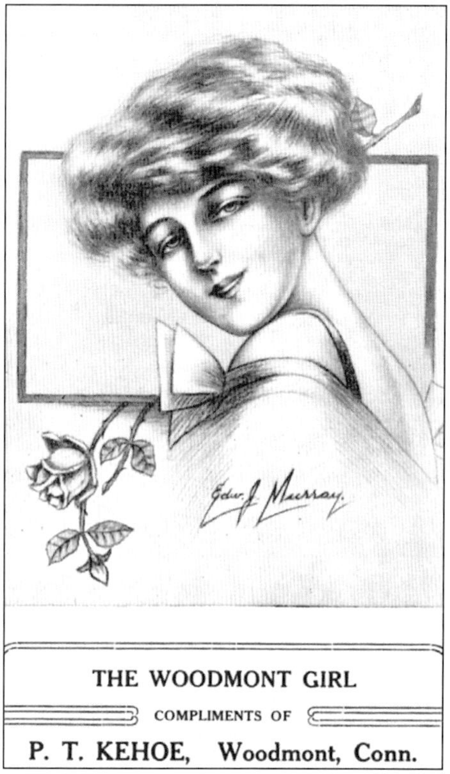

THE WOODMONT GIRL. In the early part of the 20th century, commercial postcards such as this enticed vacationers to come to Woodmont on the trolleys, supporting the new industry of tourism.

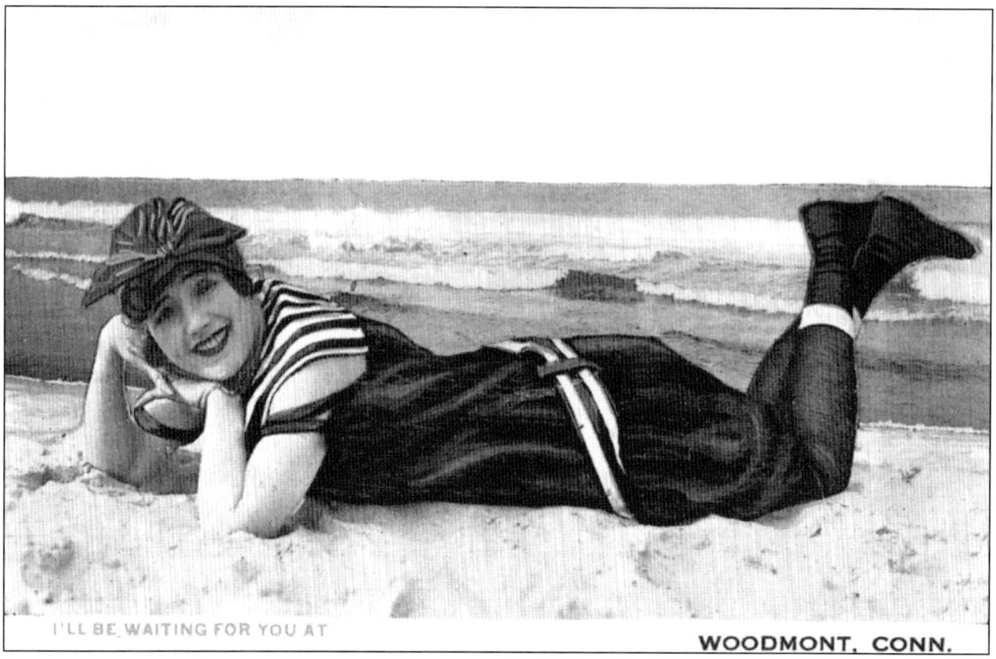

"I'LL BE WAITING FOR YOU AT WOODMONT, CONN." This postcard was probably mass-produced, with the name of the town and state added after the fact. This same postcard could well have been sold from Maine to Florida, promoting tourism in beaches from Woodmont to Miami Beach.

CENTRAL AVENUE TROLLEY STATION. Woodmont had several trolley stops, including this one at Central Avenue (at what is now the intersection of Dunbar Road and New Haven Avenue). The trolley trip from New Haven to Woodmont took about 45 minutes, and from Bridgeport to Woodmont took about an hour and 15 minutes. (Courtesy of Photography by Joseph.)

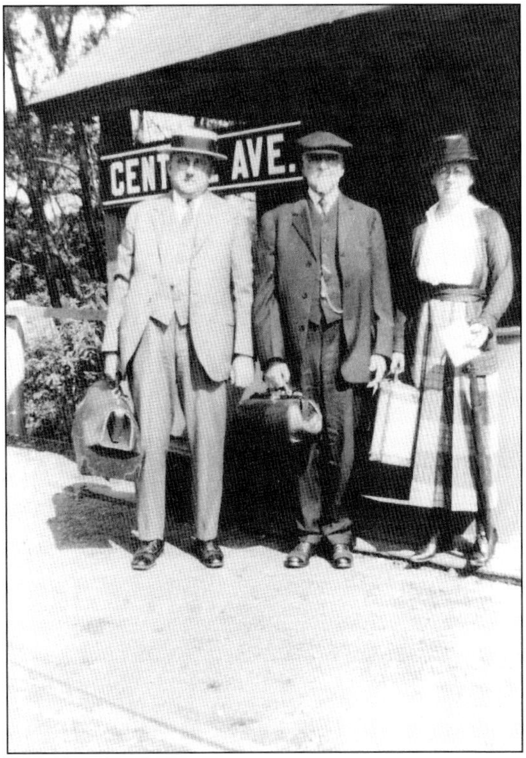

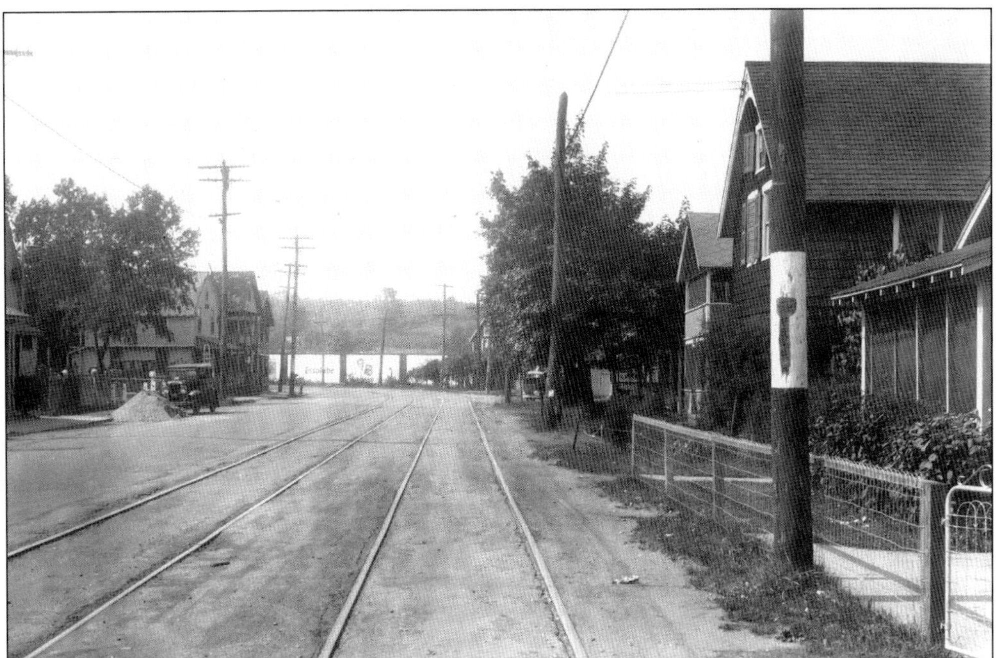

MERWIN AVENUE TROLLEY STOP. As trolleys left Woodmont, they traveled west down Merwin Avenue. This photograph, taken at the Merwin Avenue trolley stop on September 21, 1932, shows three billboards in the distance, including one advertising Essolube. (Courtesy of Shore Line Trolley Museum Library Collection.)

FOR SALE

Ideal country home, twelve rooms, all-year house with two baths, fireplaces, city water, gas, and electricity.

Located on high ground, two short blocks from Long Island Sound, with bathing privileges and good view of the water, in the select residential resort of Woodmont, Conn., seven miles from New Haven and Yale College.

The house is very well built, having slate roof and copper valleys and leaders and is situated on good concrete road leading to New York and New Haven.

The grounds, about three acres, have large shade trees, flower and vegetable gardens and an orchard, furnishing several kinds of large fruit and berries.

Country club and golf links nearby. Price, $20,000.

Additional land and gardener's cottage can be purchased with it if desired.

WOODMONT COTTAGE FOR SALE. Around the beginning of the 20th century, the trolleys, or the "electric street railways" as they were first called, started a housing boom in Woodmont. Before that, a horse-and-buggy trip could take a day or more from other towns. This 12-room house, which was advertised in 1920 for $20,000, still exists at the corner of Kings Highway

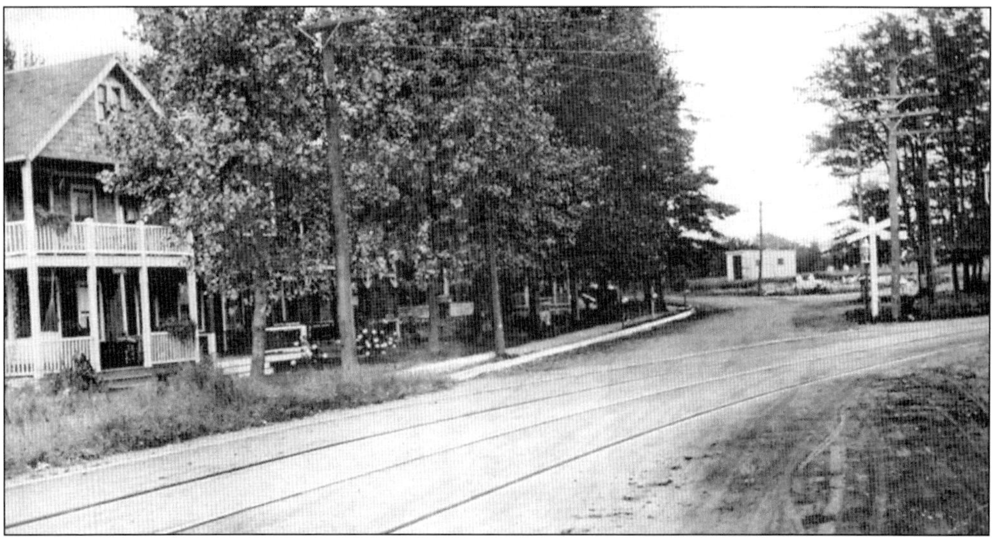

MERWIN AVENUE, LOOKING EAST. This postcard, dated 1917, shows the trolley tracks on Merwin Avenue that fork to the right onto Mark Street. At that intersection, where the white trolley crossing sign stands, the Villa Rosa Trolley Stop would be built 10 years later.

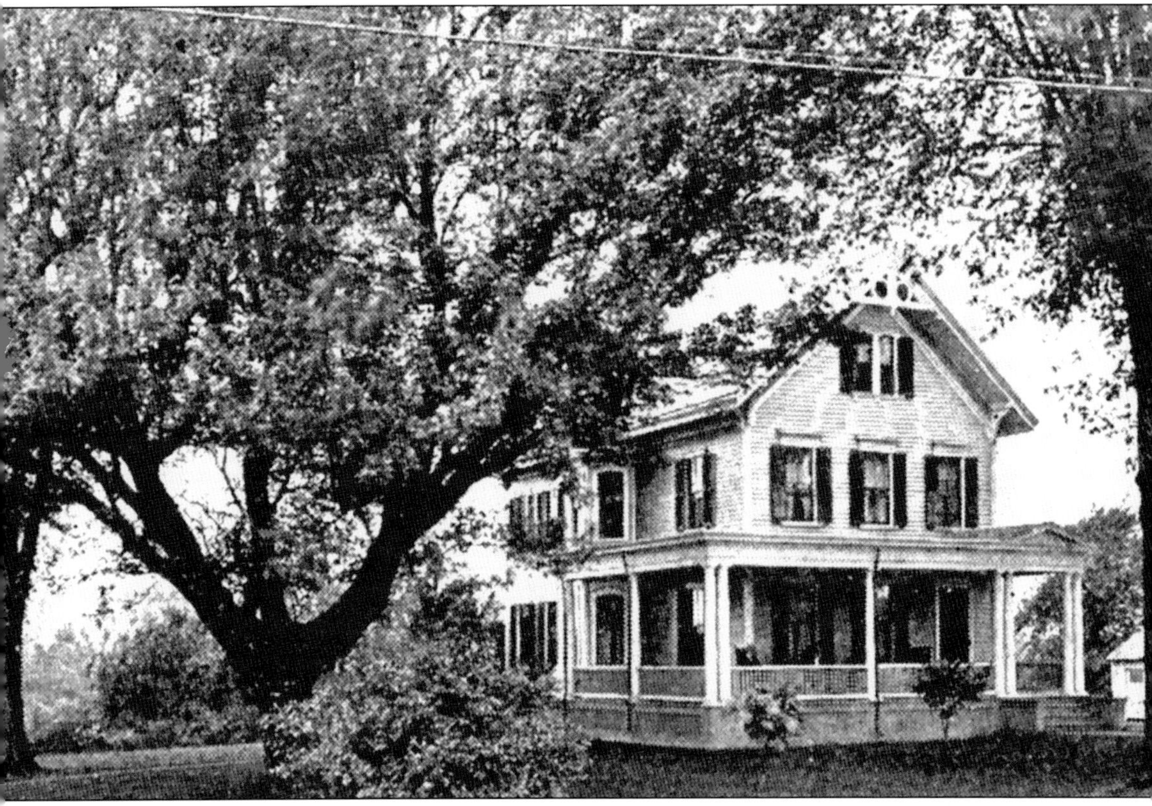

and Dunbar Road, and looks nearly as it did over 85 years ago. In 1920, however, it came with three acres of land, including an orchard and gardens—the gardener's cottage was optional. (Courtesy of George Peacock.)

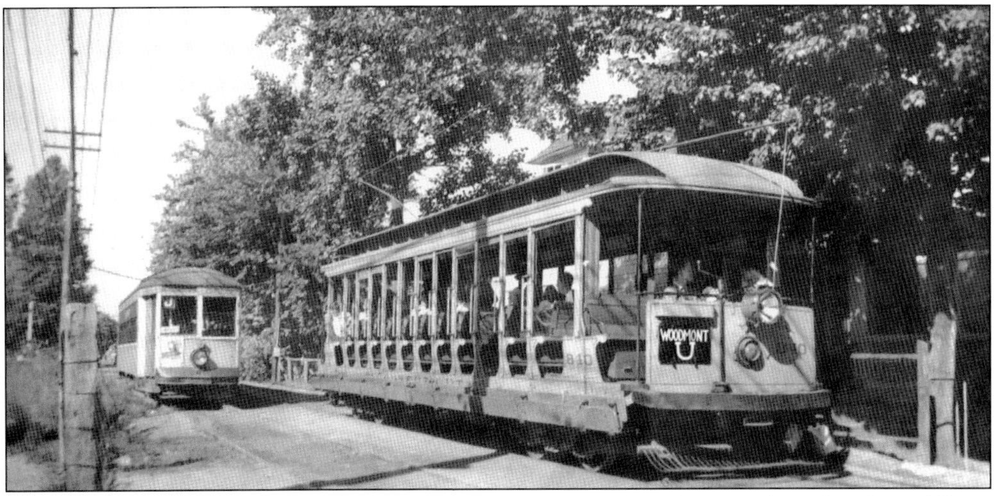

OPEN AND CLOSED TROLLEY CARS IN WOODMONT. In this photograph, a closed car follows an open car on the line from West Haven through Woodmont. November 20, 1937, was the day the last trolley to Woodmont ran. By September 1948, the last of the New Haven trolleys stopped running, and they were the last to exist in Connecticut. (Photograph by Al Gilcher; courtesy of Shore Line Trolley Museum Library Collection.)

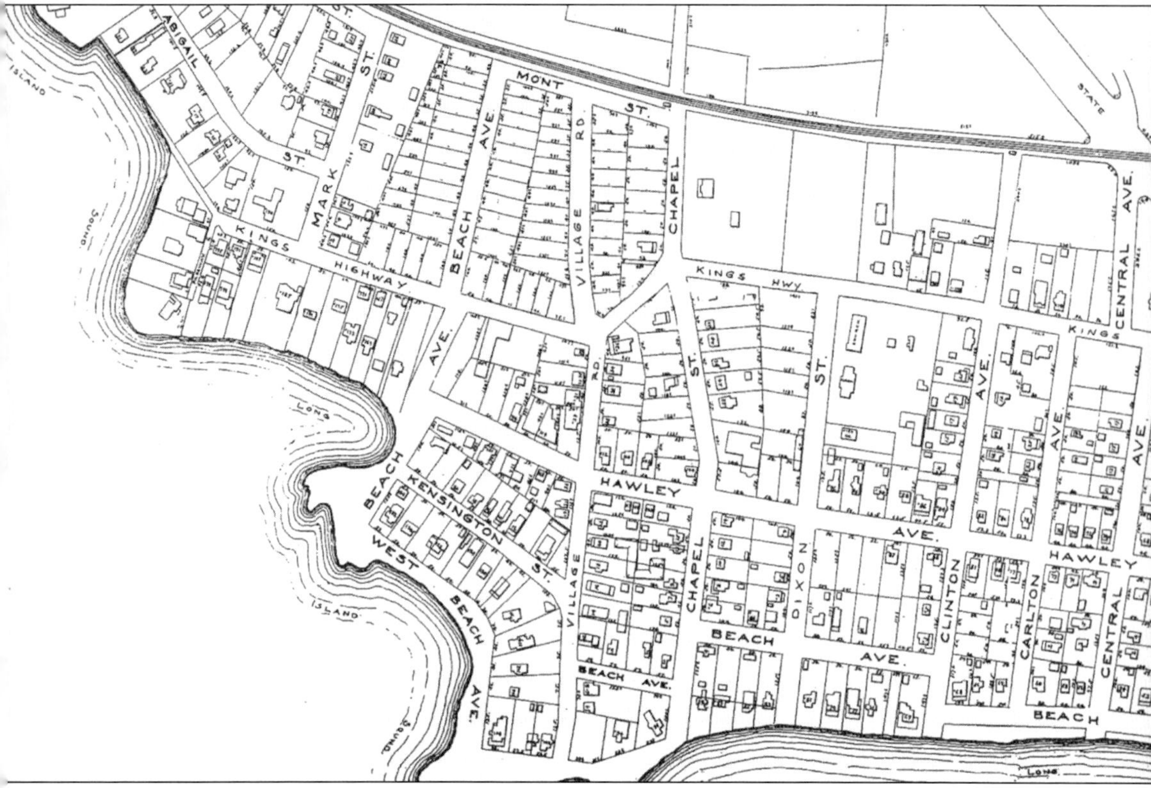

THE TROLLEY LINE IN WOODMONT, *C.* 1930. The Woodmont trolley line went from Oyster River in the east to the Villa Rosa area in the west. The solid line near the top of this map shows the trolley route, which also designates most of the northern border of Woodmont. Coming from West Haven, the trolley right-of-way crossed a bridge over Oyster River, crossed Anderson Avenue, went through about a half mile of woods, and emerged on Central Avenue (now Dunbar

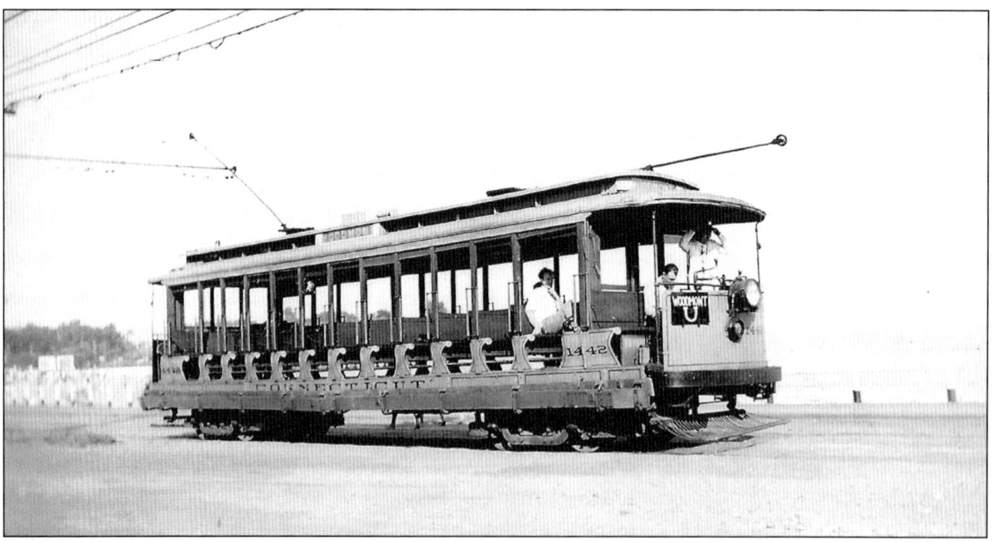

FROM SAVIN ROCK TO WOODMONT. This trolley has just left the Savin Rock amusement park and is heading toward Woodmont along the West Haven shoreline.

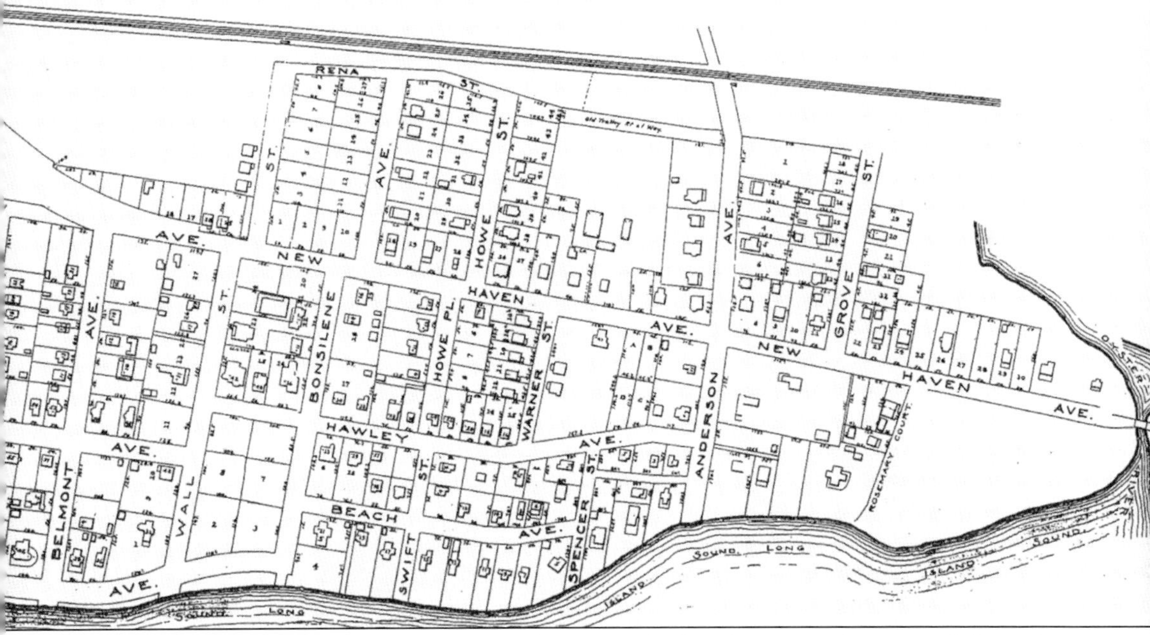

Road) where it met New Haven Avenue. It then crossed Chapel Street and continued through another wooded area, emerging once again alongside Mark Street by the Villa Rosa Trolley Stop, heading toward Morningside. There were trolley stops at Anderson Avenue, Clark Street (now Wall Street), Central Avenue (now Dunbar Road), Clinton Street, Chapel Street, and, after 1927, the Villa Rosa.

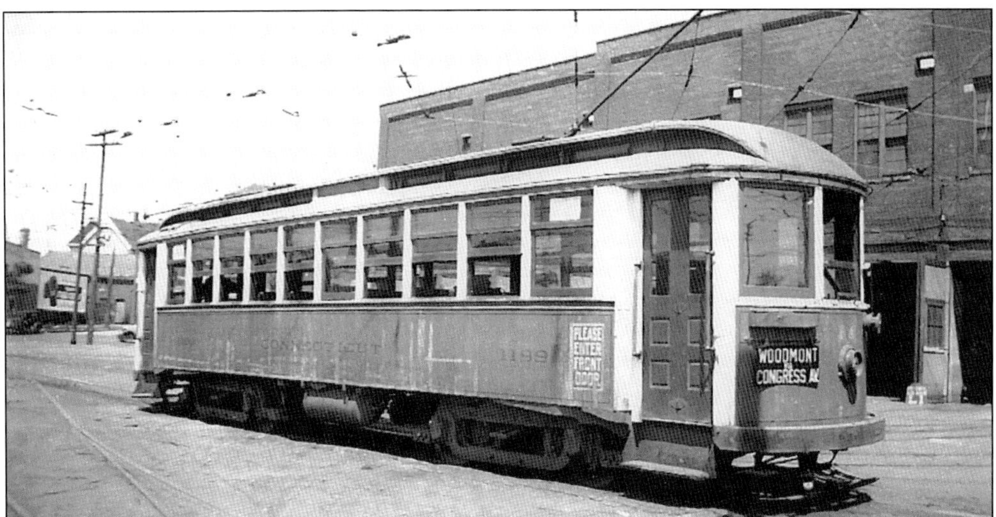

Leaving New Haven. This Connecticut Company trolley is leaving the trolley barn on James Street in New Haven, headed to Woodmont.

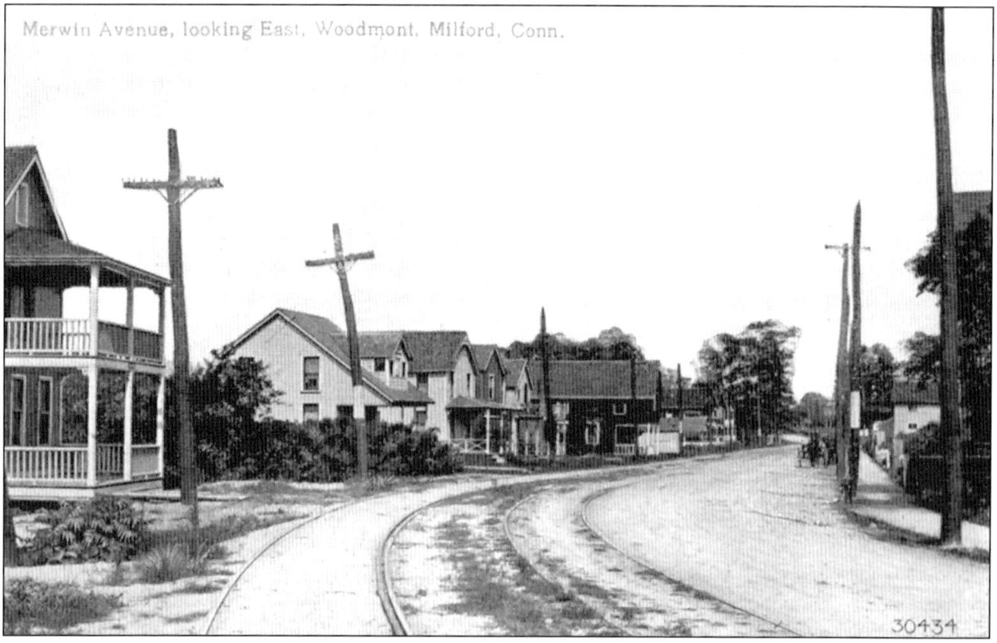

MERWIN AVENUE TROLLEY TRACKS. After stopping at Merwin Avenue (note the white marking on utility pole signifying a trolley stop), the trolley continued along the upper end of Merwin Avenue taking passengers to Merwin's Beach, just outside of the borough of Woodmont. Woodmont was where the Connecticut Company and the Connecticut Railway and Lighting Company (CR&L) met, and passengers had to change trolleys at that point. This postcard is postmarked 1922.

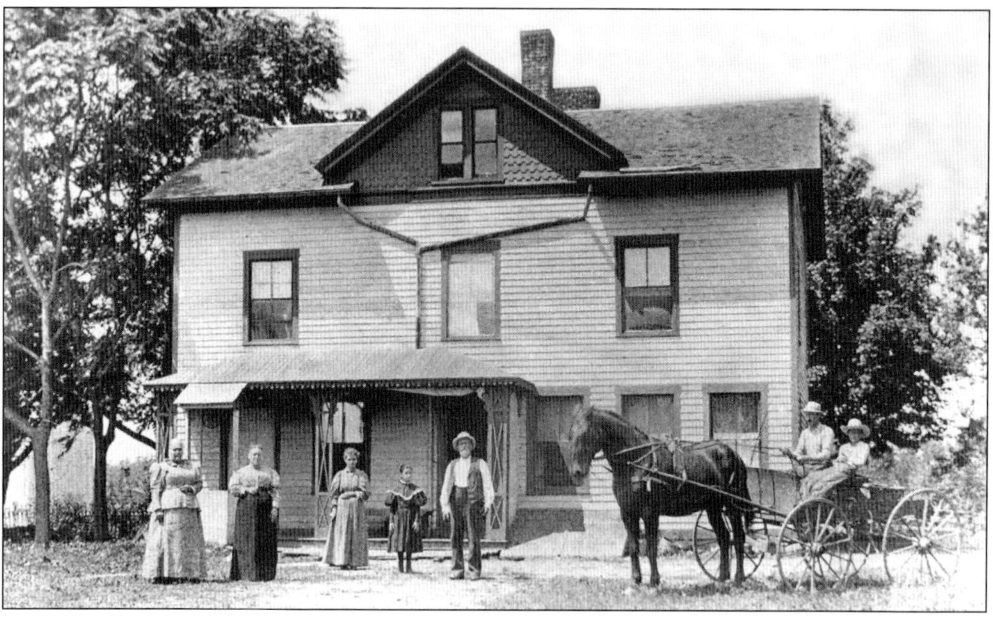

AN EARLY HOMESTEAD. The people who lived in Woodmont year-round relied on horses and buggies for family transportation. The majority of Woodmont houses had barns; many of them can be seen today, although they were converted into garages long ago. (Courtesy of Photography by Joseph.)

Three

A Cottage Industry

After trolleys made Woodmont easily accessible around the beginning of the 20th century, builders and developers bought property and carved out dozens of small lots for summer cottages. People came for all or part of the summer from numerous Connecticut towns—Waterbury, New Haven, Bridgeport, Meriden, Hartford, Derby, and Ansonia. According to the *Saturday Chronicle*, "there would have been a much larger delegation from Waterbury had not the farmers put such a high price on the land, that they went instead to Madison and formed what became known as the Waterbury settlement there."

The earliest cottages were not built along the water but on the hillside on the dirt road that was called Vue de L'eau Avenue, as the view of the water was spectacular, with gently sloping meadows between the houses and the water. Of course, it was not long before developers realized they could place houses on the long grassy knoll between Vue de L'eau Avenue and the water.

Later, perhaps because subsequent development blocked the views of the early cottage owners, Vue de L'eau Avenue was renamed Hawley Avenue, after one of its notable residents. Joseph Roswell Hawley, a Hartford resident who served in the Civil War, had a summer home in Woodmont. Hawley was a U.S. senator for 24 years and a two-term member of the House of Representatives, as well as governor of Connecticut in 1866.

Just as the trolley first brought crowds to Woodmont, the automobile made it even easier for people from all around the state to travel to Woodmont. When Henry Ford installed moving assembly lines in his factory in 1913, cars started to become affordable. The following year, Ford raised the minimum wage of his workers to $5 a day and he cut the work week to five days a week and eight hours a day. With more leisure time and better wages, he figured his employees would become huge customers. They proved him right. By achieving his goal of creating "a motor car for the great multitude," Ford forever changed the character of the country.

If ever there was a location suited for leisure time, it was Woodmont. And now it was no longer limited to the wealthy.

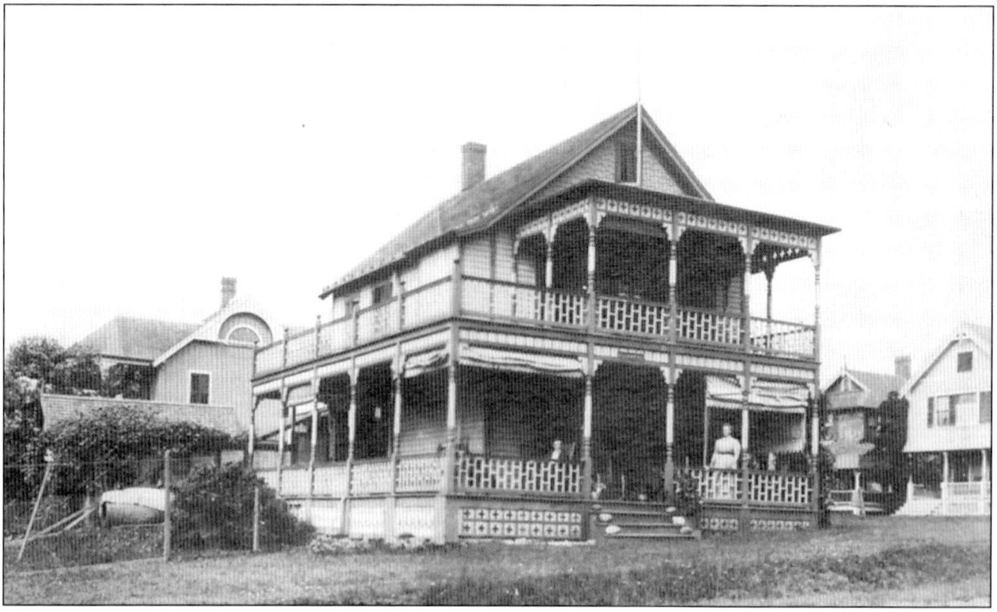

GINGERBREAD COTTAGE. This cottage was typical of the gingerbread style once popular in Woodmont and other beach communities, most notably Oak Bluffs on Martha's Vineyard. Once located at the corner of Hawley Avenue and Dunbar Road, this house was torn down for the construction of a large modern house in the 1980s.

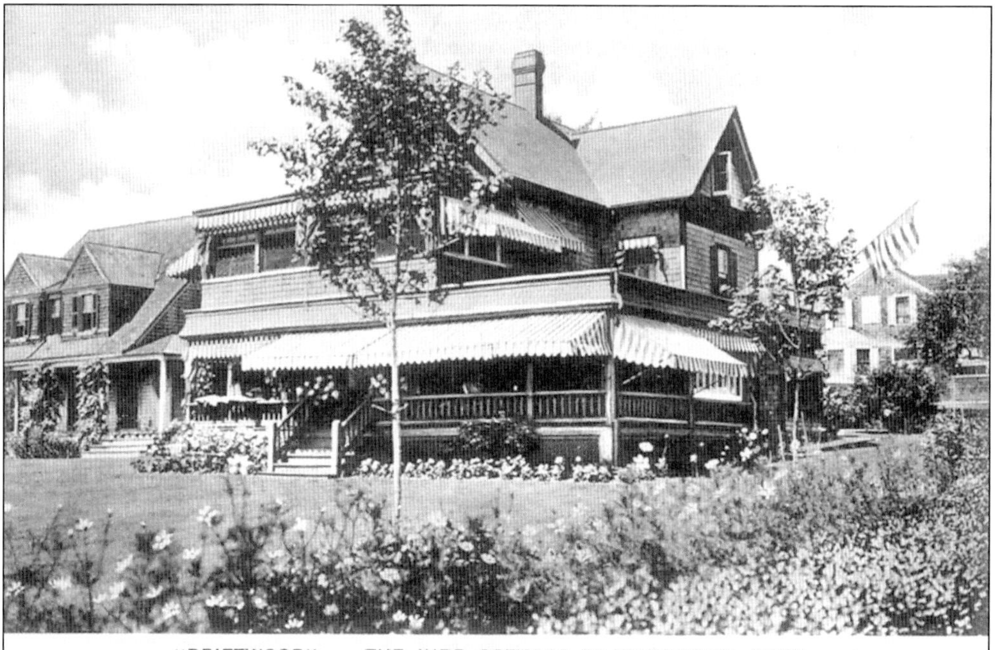

"DRIFTWOOD". THE JUDD COTTAGE AT WOODMONT, CONN.

THE JUDD COTTAGE. Many of the Woodmont cottages had names, such as Driftwood, the Judd family home. The Judd cottage was a large sprawling cottage with a wraparound first-floor porch and striped awnings. On September 30, 1916, the borough board voted "to grant J. A. Hall a permit to move the Brown cottage between Mrs. Cowles and Mr. Judd's to the corner of Center and Beach Avenue."

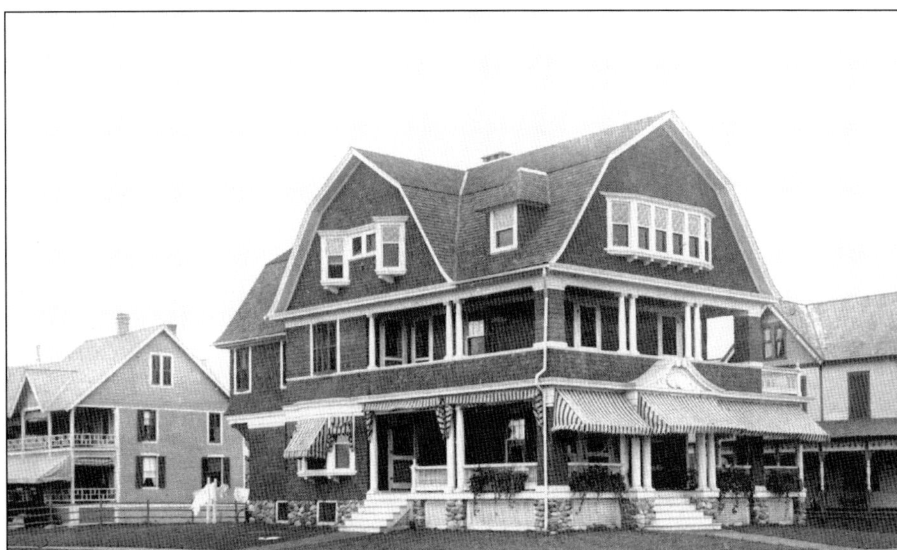

THE BLAKESLEE COTTAGE. The Blakeslee cottage was owned by Charles Wells Blakeslee, who established a construction business in New Haven in 1844. Said Clarles in 1865, "It is my creed to build for the future—to build quality and permanence." Theodore R. Blakeslee, one of his sons, became a Woodmont burgess in 1913. The cottage still exists today at 108 Beach Avenue.

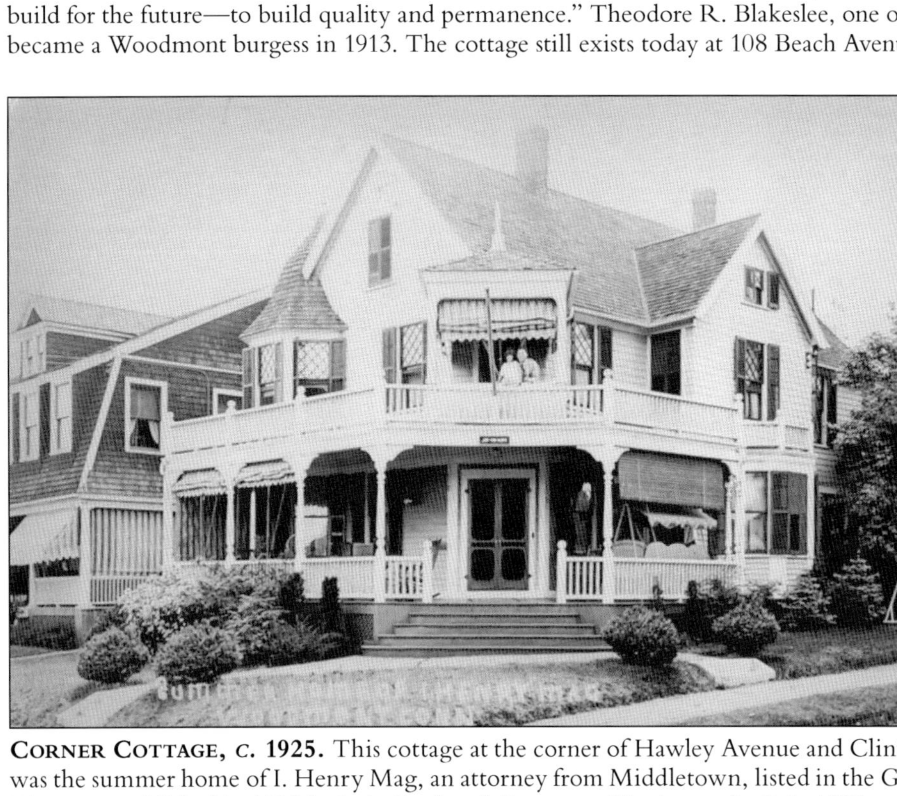

CORNER COTTAGE, *C.* 1925. This cottage at the corner of Hawley Avenue and Clinton Street was the summer home of I. Henry Mag, an attorney from Middletown, listed in the Graft Legal Directory published in 1908 by J. A. Graft and Company. The house, built in 1906, exists today and has been impeccably maintained. The sign over the door reads, "Jay—Wm—Hope," the names of their first three children.

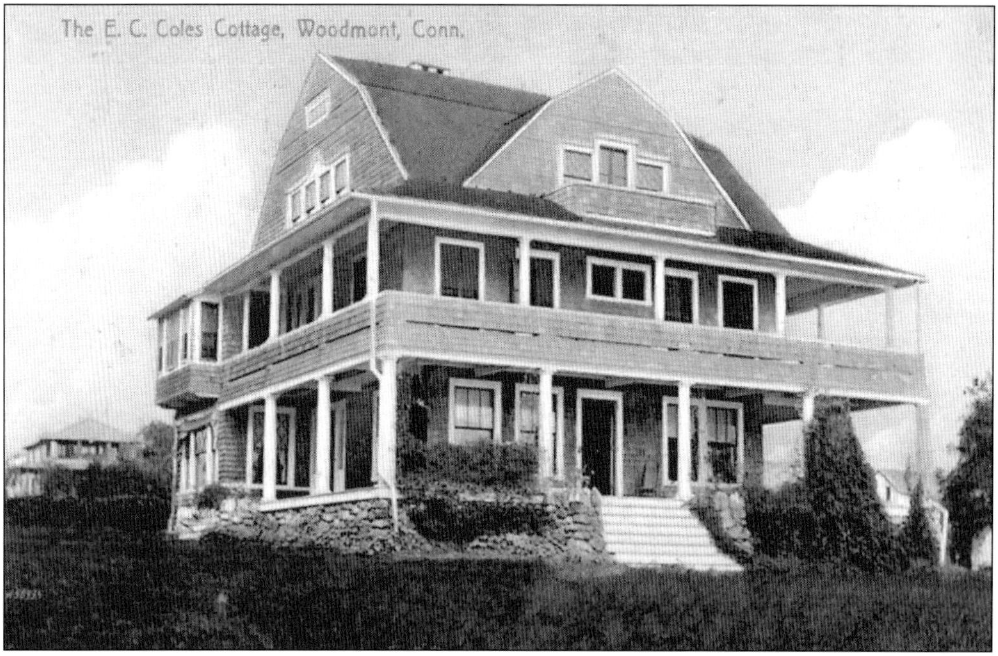

THE E. C. COLES COTTAGE. Located at 21 Beach Avenue, at the corner of Beach Avenue and Bonsilene Street, the E. C. Coles cottage was typical of the grander cottages in Woodmont, most of which were on beachfront property. The three-floor house, almost 5,000 square feet, has eight bedrooms, seven bathrooms, and a butler's pantry. This is one of the few Victorian cottages in Woodmont that remains in almost pristine condition. This postcard is postmarked 1908.

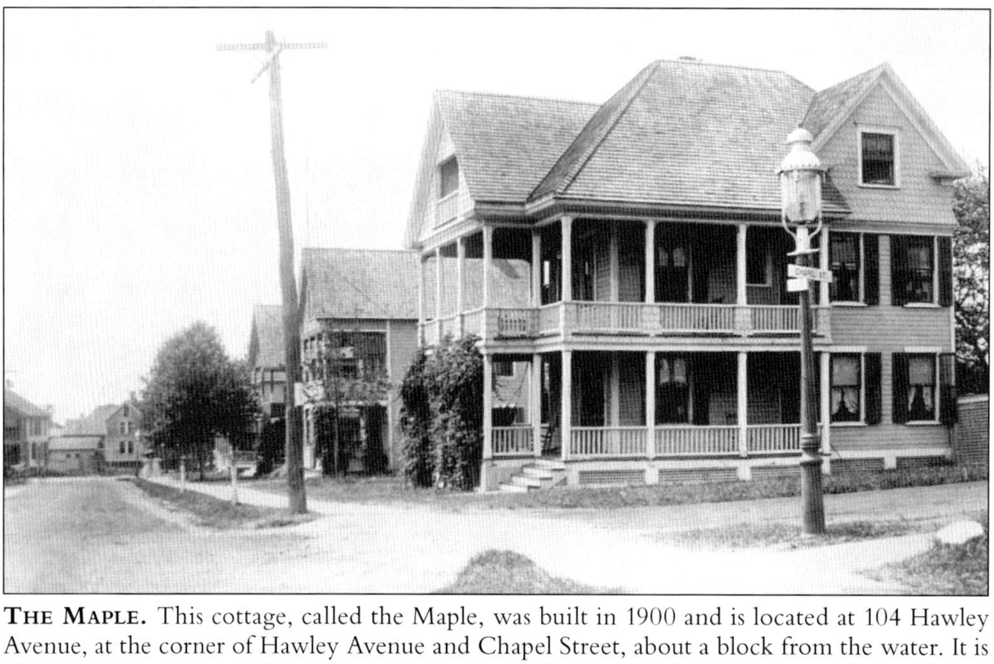

THE MAPLE. This cottage, called the Maple, was built in 1900 and is located at 104 Hawley Avenue, at the corner of Hawley Avenue and Chapel Street, about a block from the water. It is directly across the street from what was the Pembroke Hotel and used to house the maids and butlers who worked at the Pembroke. It is a single-family residence today.

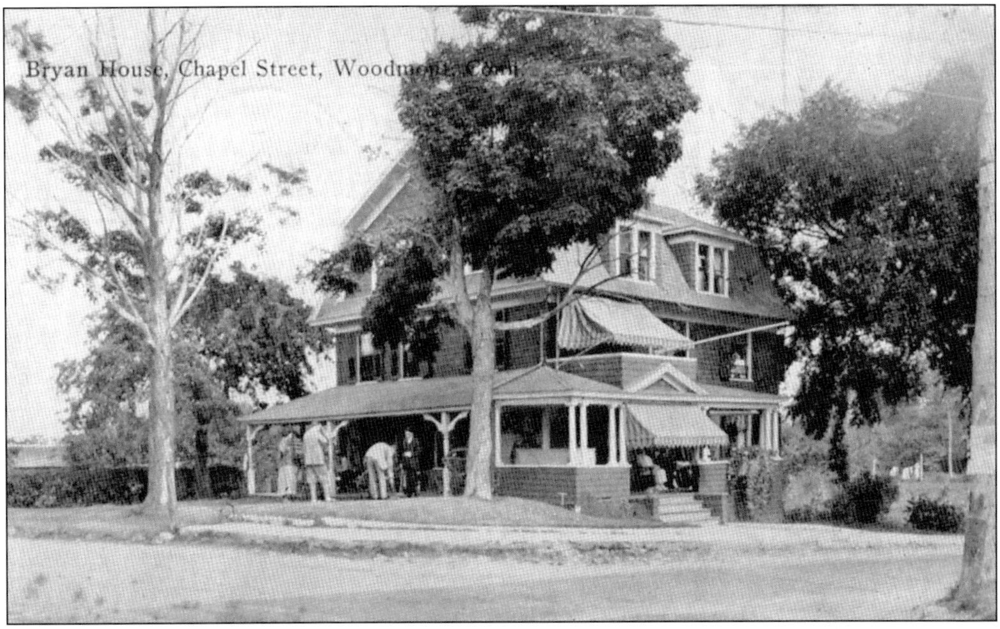

The Bryan House. This house, at 158 Chapel Street, was originally owned by the Bryan family and is located right across the street from the original Bryan House, which had been built in 1790. In this postcard, dated 1924, a couple staying here invited their friend Nancy Malone from Brooklyn to come join them for the weekend in this bungalow, diagonally across the street from the Woodmont Chapel.

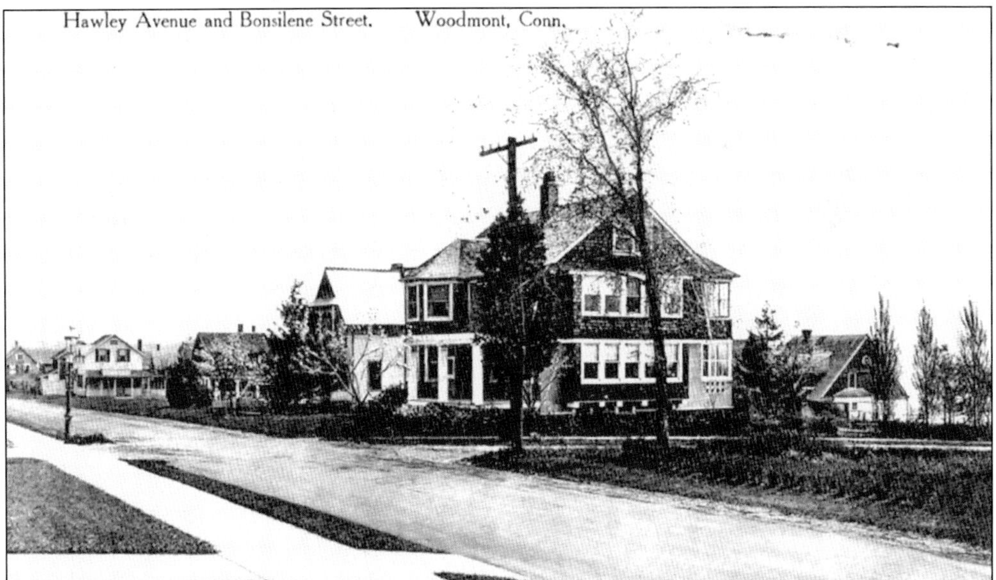

Corner of Hawley Avenue and Bonsilene Street. According to city land records, this house at 33 Hawley Avenue was built in 1920 next to the Hawley Avenue playground. In this postcard, postmarked in 1924, a woman writes to her mother in French, thanking her a thousand times for sending money and telling her she went to the Palace Theatre in New Haven to see a light comedy and that she heard from Louis, who was at the Saratoga race track. This house still exists today.

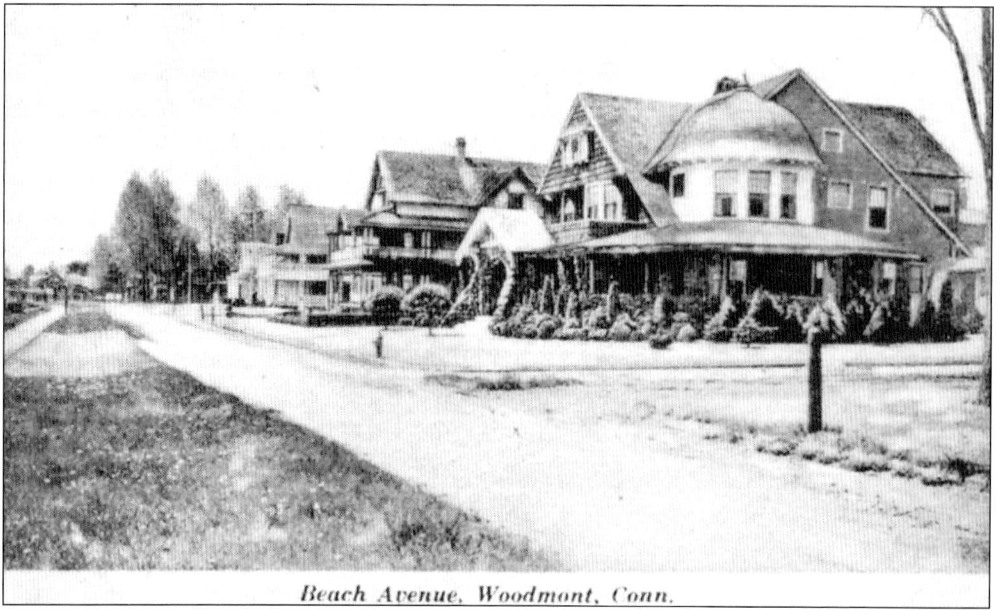

THE STONE HOUSE. The stone house at 40 Beach Avenue has long been one of Woodmont's most admired houses. The house has changed ownership only once in nearly 100 years. Built in 1910, it has been owned by the same family since 1927, when Esedor Derecktor, a red-headed immigrant from Russia who settled in Connecticut, purchased the house from a German immigrant named Charles Niklas, who made his fortune from his brewery business. This postcard is postmarked 1924.

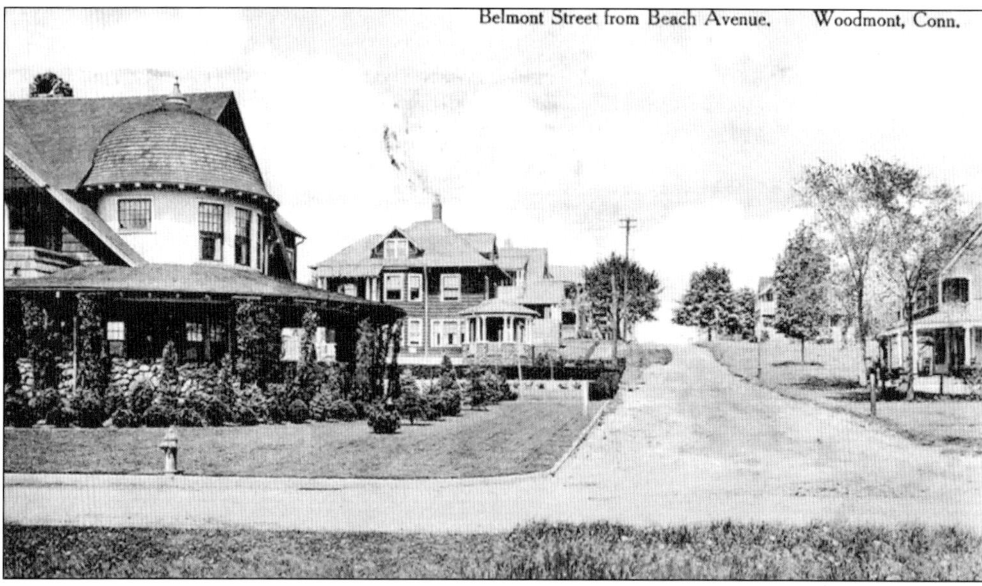

CHARLES NIKLAS'S HOUSE. According to the current owner Richard "Red" Schwartz (Esedor Derecktor's grandson), "The story was that during Prohibition, Mr. Niklas was approached by rumrunners who were preparing to deal with prohibition by engaging in illegal activities. They asked Niklas to join them, but Nicklas reportedly said, 'No, I would never do such a thing. I would not betray this wonderful country.'" This postcard was mailed in 1926, the last year Niklas lived in his house.

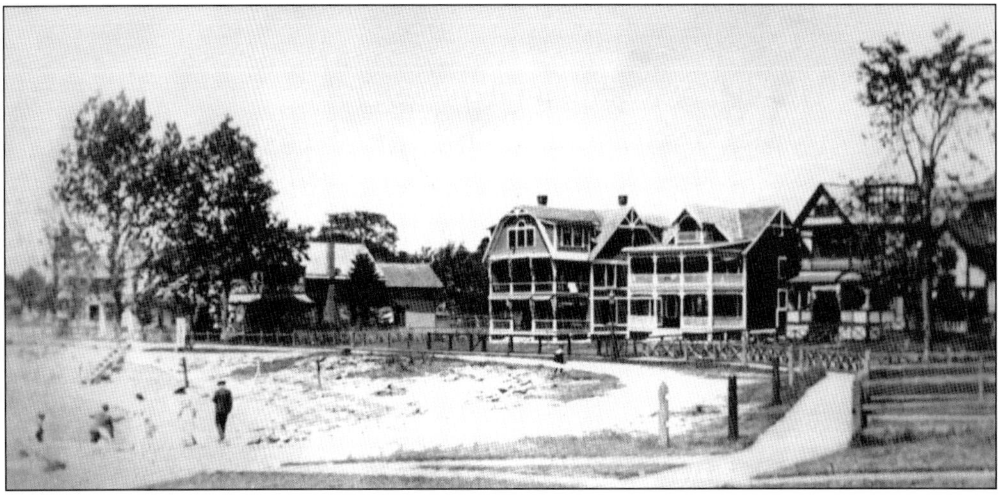

Crescent Beach Cottages, 1894. The two large cottages in the center of this photograph are the three-story Blackall Cottage and the cottage in the photograph below. Both still exist today. (Courtesy of Photography by Joseph.)

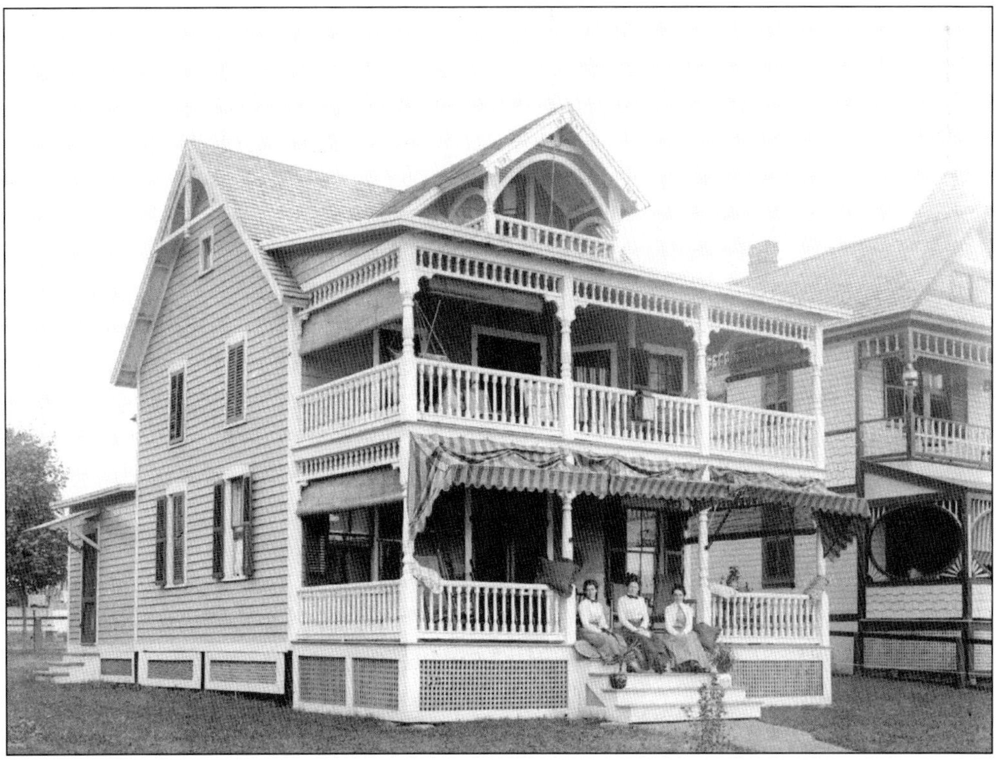

Cottage at the Crescent. The porches on this house at 120 Beach Avenue have been enclosed over the years, and the tiny rooftop porch has been turned into a full front dormer, but the same basic house can be seen today, across from Crescent Beach.

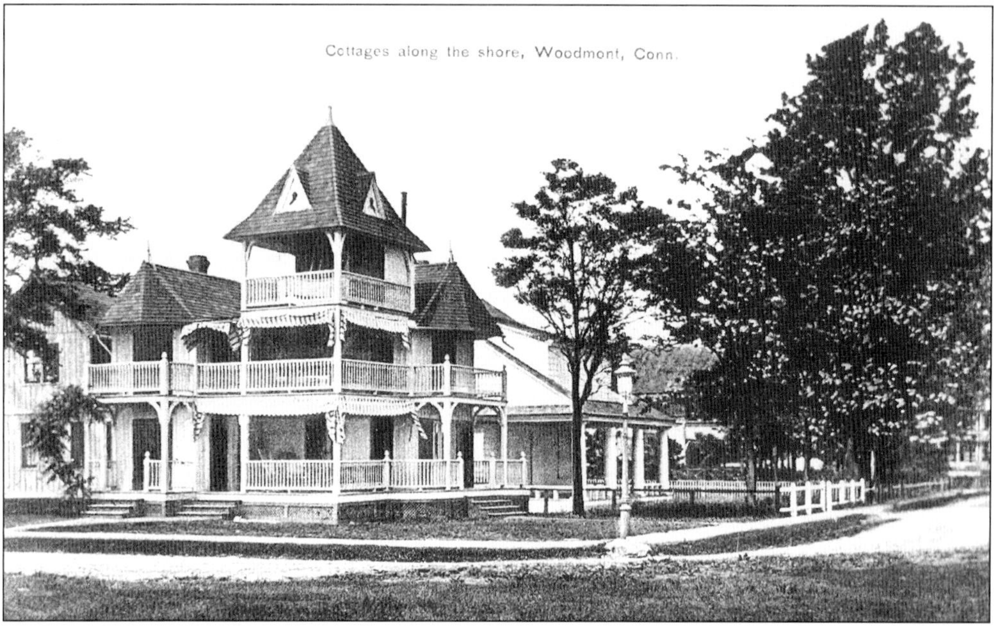

Cottage at Randall's Point. This was one of Woodmont's most charming cottages, built around 1900 and located at 132 Beach Avenue. Years later, the three-story gable and its porch were removed, and today this is a three-story, two-family house. (Courtesy of Photography by Joseph.)

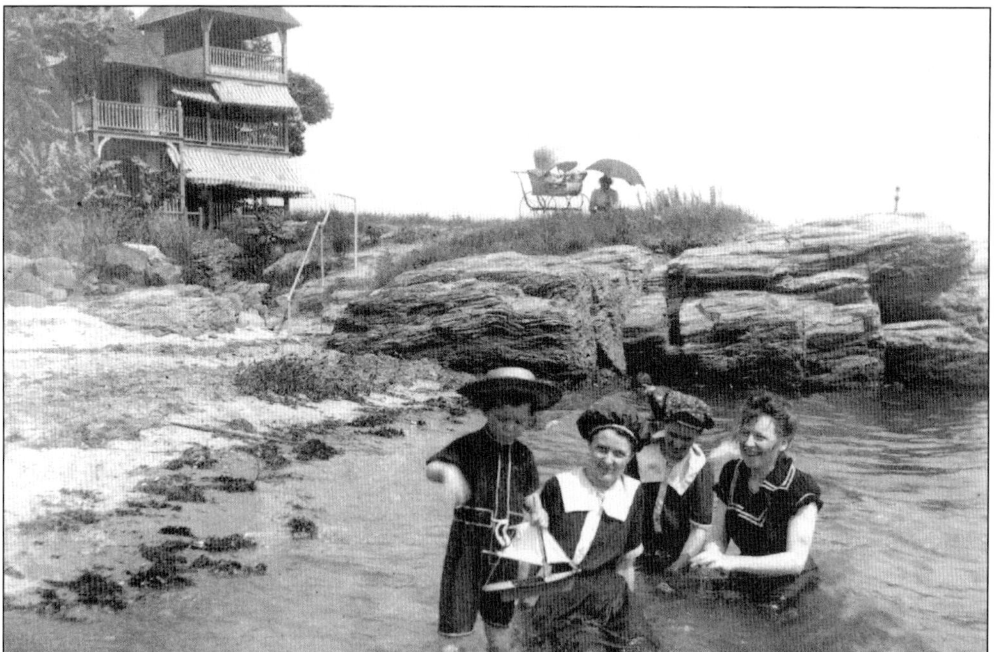

Boy with a Boat, c. 1900. Three women and a little boy launch his toy sailboat right in front of the three-story cottage at Randall's Point. The average water temperature in Woodmont during July and August is about 68–73 degrees; the average air temperature during the day in the summer is about 80 degrees.

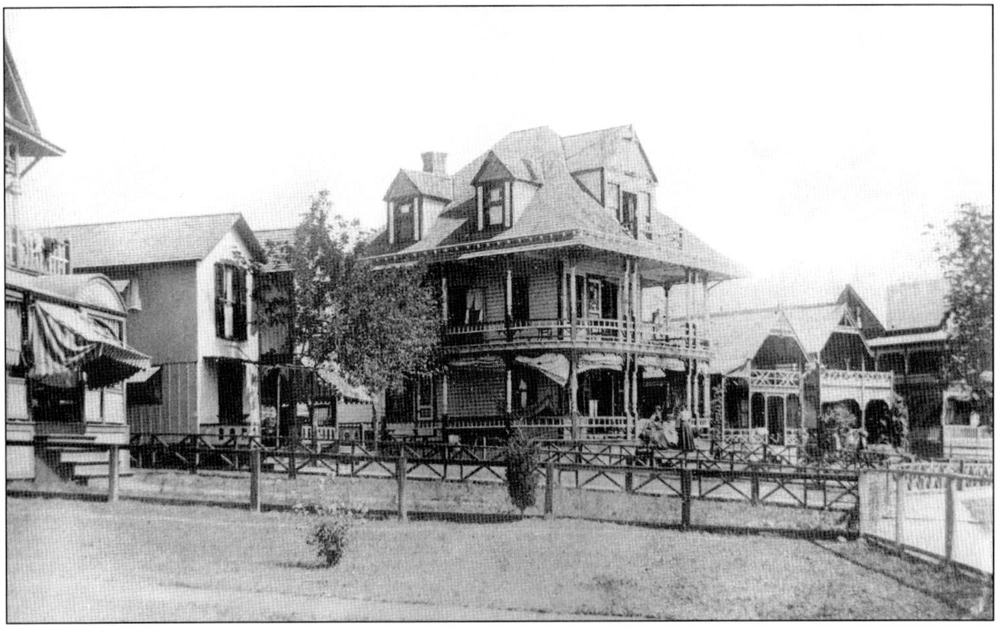

MAJESTIC COTTAGE AT THE CRESCENT. Built around 1910, this cottage at 116 Beach Avenue has been remodeled numerous times and no longer resembles the charming cottage that once graced Beach Avenue along Crescent Beach. As Woodmont cottages became winterized and insulated, siding covered the wooden shingles and sheet rock was placed over the wainscoting. After years of remodeling, many beautiful cottages are no longer recognizable. (Courtesy of Photography by Joseph.)

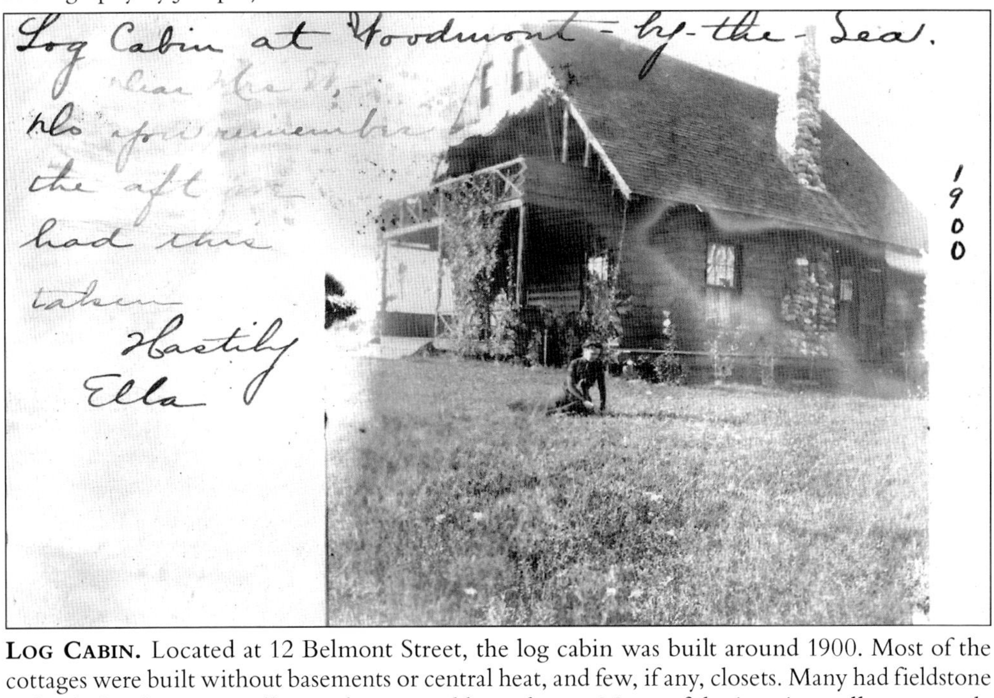

LOG CABIN. Located at 12 Belmont Street, the log cabin was built around 1900. Most of the cottages were built without basements or central heat, and few, if any, closets. Many had fieldstone or brick fireplaces, as well as outhouses and horse barns. Many of the interior walls were made of wainscoting, and floors were pine or Douglas fir. This postcard is postmarked 1906.

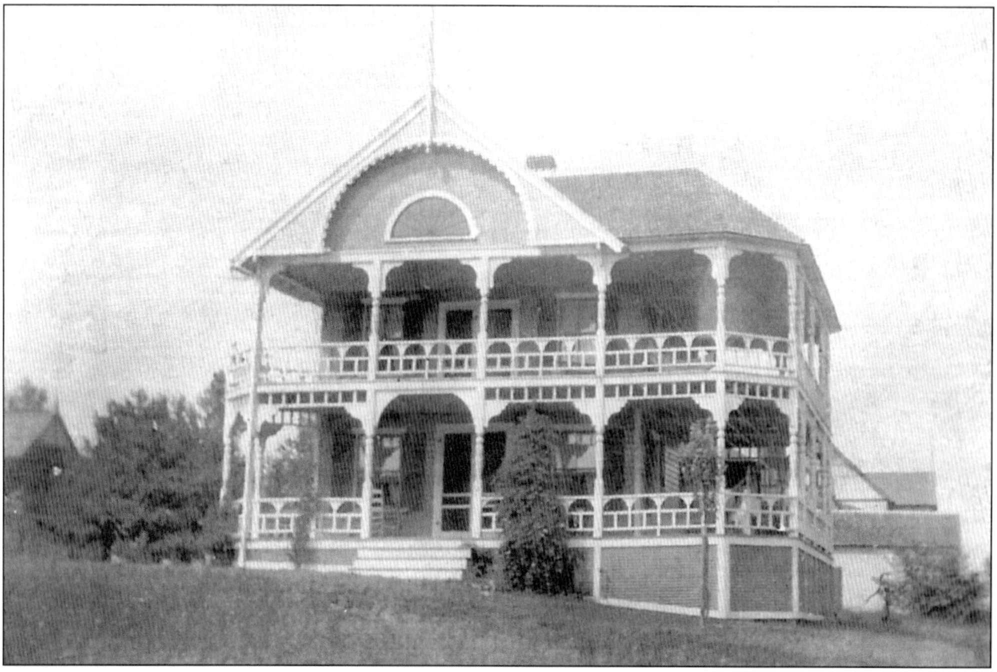

GINGERBREAD GALORE. This cottage, at the corner of Hawley Avenue and Usher Street, has retained its original charm and still has wraparound porches on both floors. The borough voted on July 31, 1916, "to change the name of Carlton St. to Usher St. Voted to instruct the sheriff to remove Mrs. Bradley's cow to the pound in Milford."

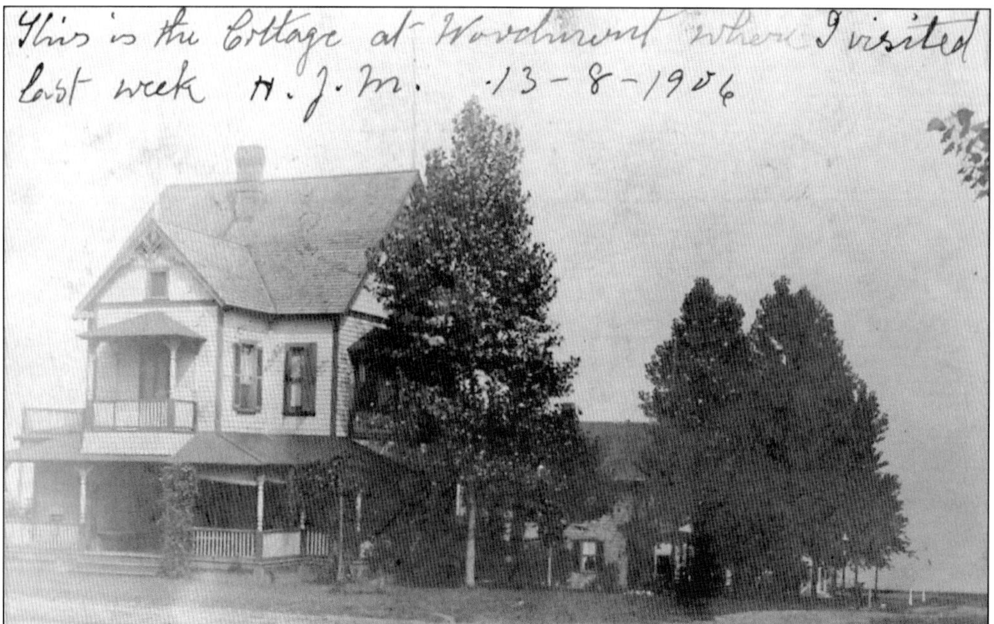

CORNER OF HAWLEY AND CENTRAL. Today this house at 67 Hawley Avenue hardly resembles the quaint cottage in this postcard, mailed in 1906. The front porch has been enclosed; the second-floor porch has been enclosed; and a dormer and three decks have been added to the rear.

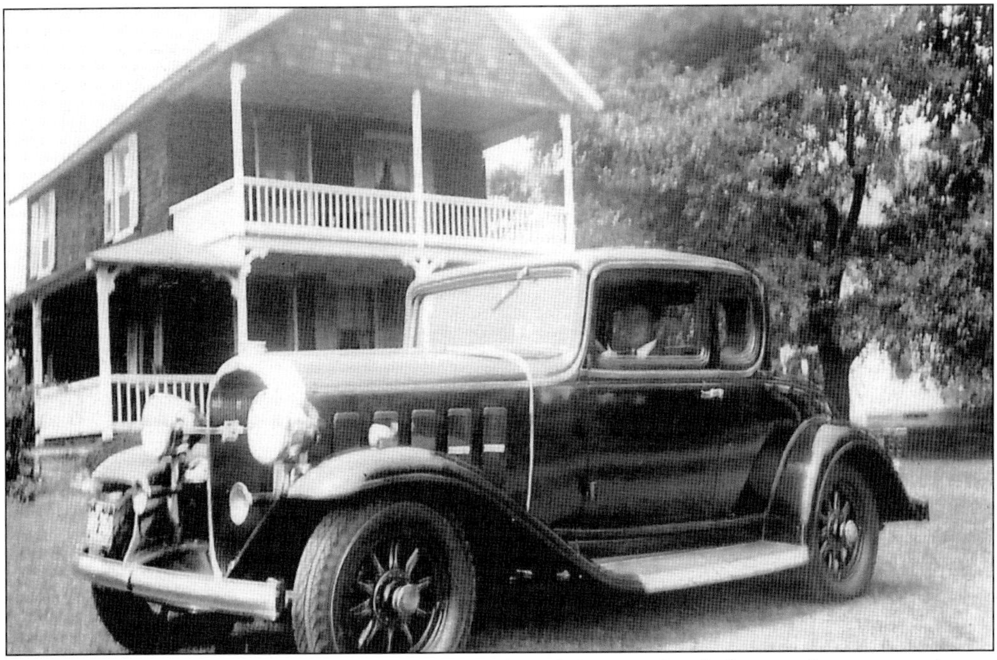

No. 5 Hawley Avenue. This cottage, built by Elisha Beach Clark, was the summer home of Helen Clark Prageman, Elisha's granddaughter. A high school teacher, Helen summered in this cottage from her birth, sometime before 1900, until her death in 1982. The car in front of her house is the Buick coupe that took her and some of her friends across the country in 1935, from Woodmont to California and back, for a total of 11,353 miles.

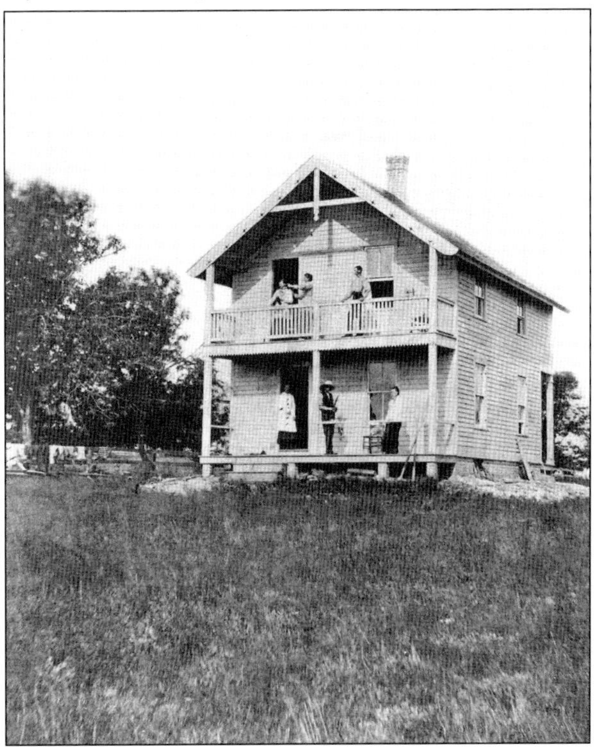

No. 3 Hawley Avenue. This cottage was one of seven cottages built by Elisha Beach Clark for his family members during the 1890s. Three were on the water, three were on Hawley Avenue, and one was landlocked in the middle. This view shows the side of the cottage facing the water. (Courtesy of Photography by Joseph.)

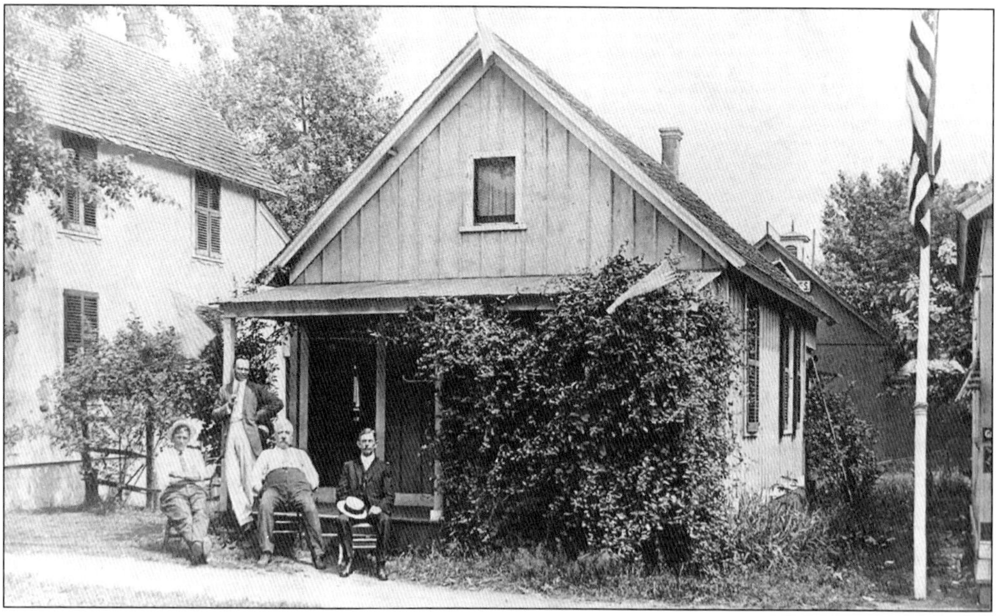

CHERRY STREET COTTAGE. By 1906, Woodmont had about 150 summer cottages, many of which had names, such as Allythea, Buena Vista, Wooster Cottage, Rosemary Cottage, Brewster Cottage, the Bandbox, Sterling Cottage, I Love View, Solana, and Cherryhurst. (Courtesy of Photography by Joseph.)

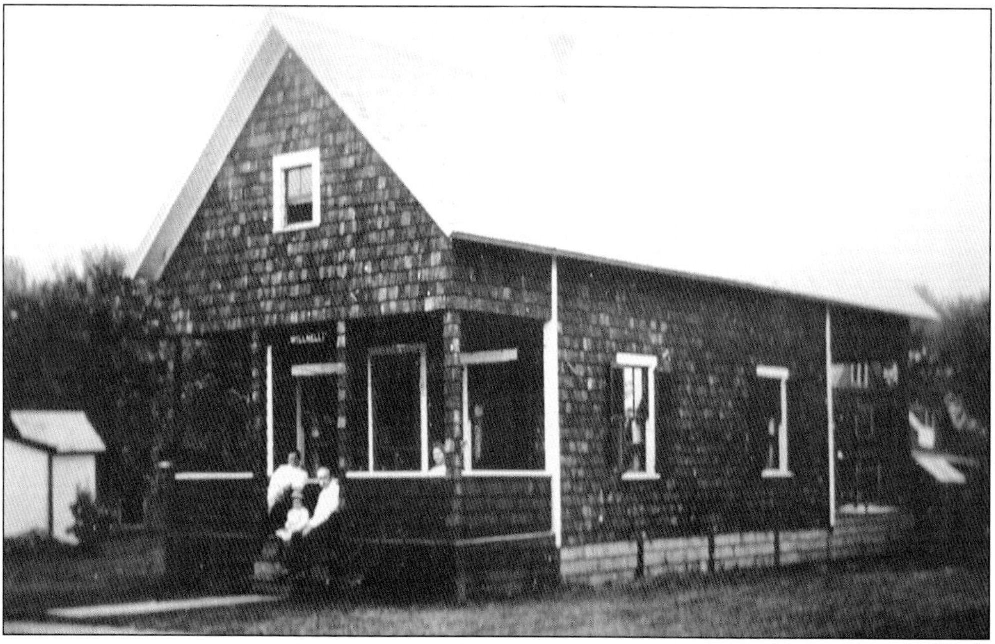

THE DUNBAR COTTAGE. Formerly Central Avenue, Dunbar Road was renamed for longtime Woodmont residents William A. and Carolyn Dunbar in the 1960s. William A. Dunbar's parents, William H. and Nellie Adams Dunbar, of Bristol, Connecticut, built a summer cottage in 1909 and named it WillNell. A second story was added in the 1920s. The cottage has been occupied by Dunbars ever since. In 1994, Nancy, daughter of William A., replaced the original cottage with a winterized house very similar in design.

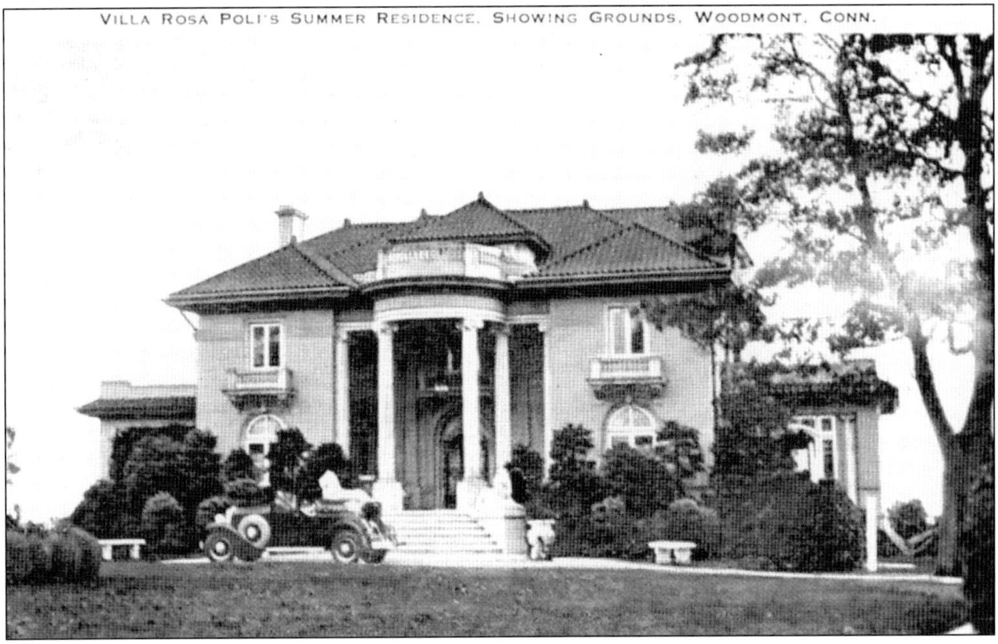

THE VILLA ROSA. Sylvester Z. Poli of New Haven built and named this Mediterranean mansion for his wife, Rosa. Sylvester, who came to the United States in 1881 at the age of 23, went on to found the Poli Theater as part of a chain of 28 vaudeville and movie theaters, which he operated for 18 years, from 1907 to 1925. The Villa Rosa is on Abigail Street. This postcard is postmarked 1934.

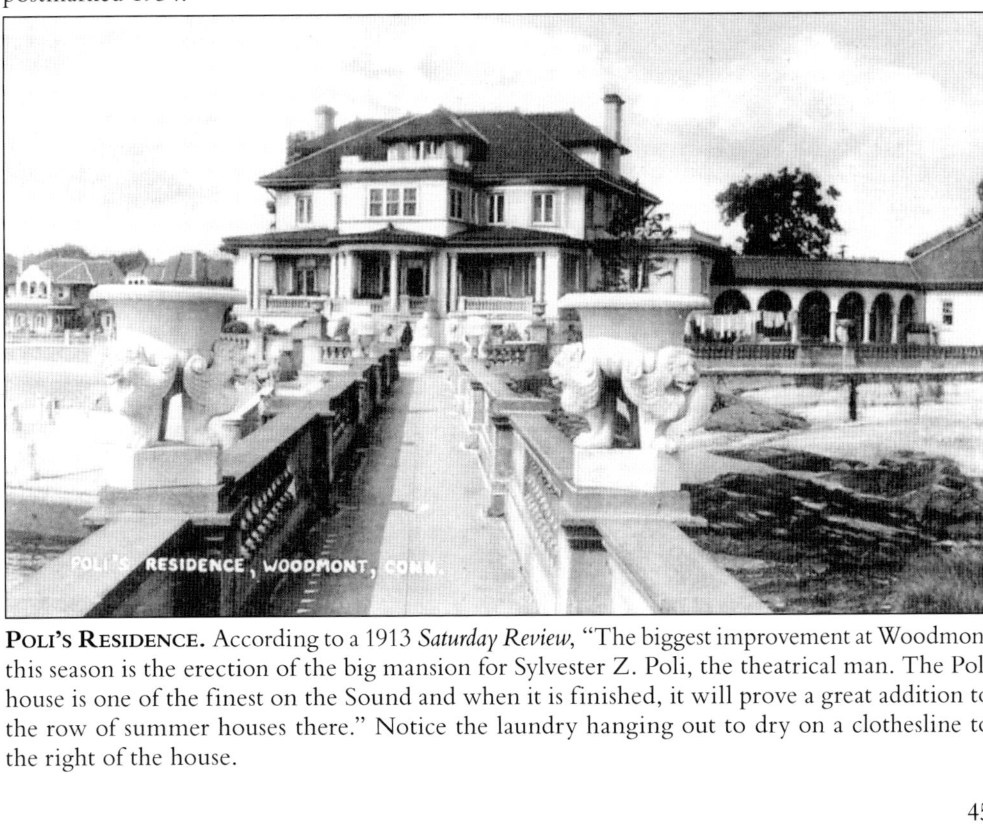

POLI'S RESIDENCE. According to a 1913 *Saturday Review*, "The biggest improvement at Woodmont this season is the erection of the big mansion for Sylvester Z. Poli, the theatrical man. The Poli house is one of the finest on the Sound and when it is finished, it will prove a great addition to the row of summer houses there." Notice the laundry hanging out to dry on a clothesline to the right of the house.

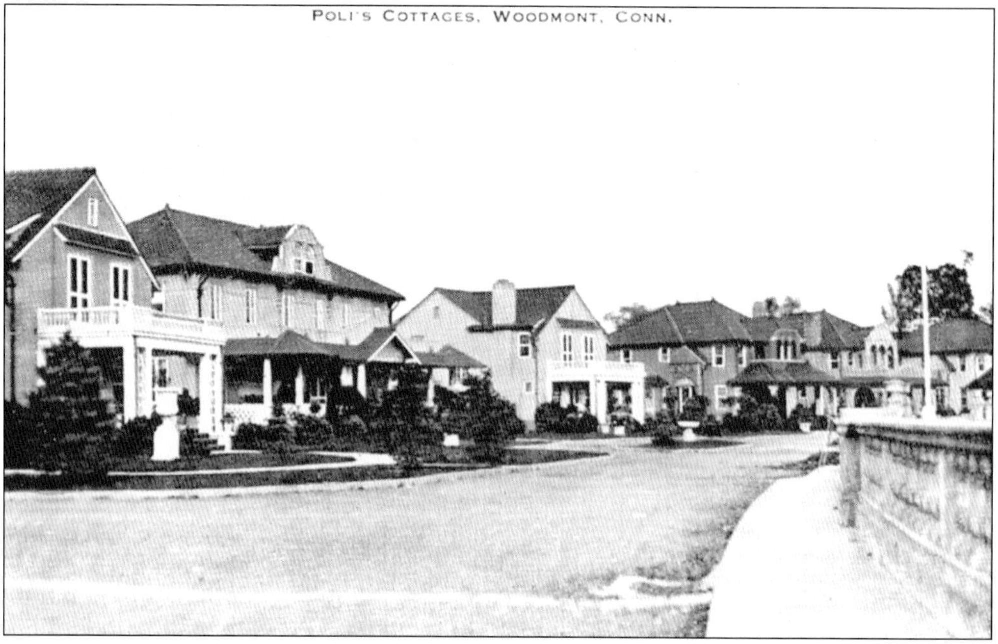

POLI'S COTTAGES. Between 1912 and 1932, Sylvester Z. Poli had a complex of 10 other "cottages" (spacious residences with up to 14 rooms) constructed for visiting family members. Like the main mansion, they were constructed of stucco with terra-cotta-tiled roofs and stained-glass windows. This Italianate style was typical of the mansions of silent-film stars and was a popular choice of millionaires at the time.

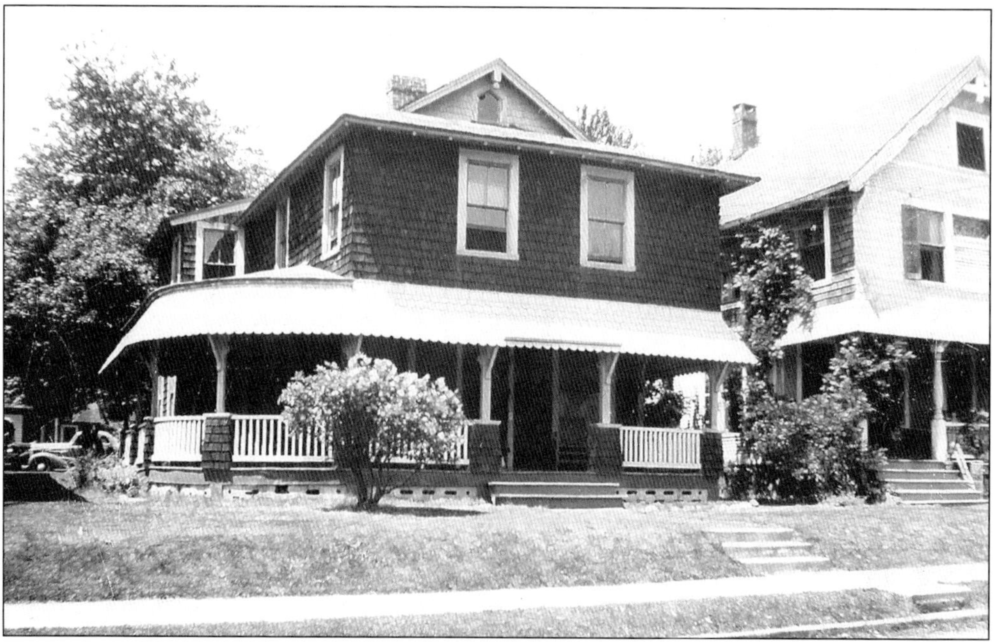

THE DONNELLY COTTAGE. This cottage is one of the few true cottages left in Woodmont without central heat. It has been in the Donnelly family for almost 75 years, purchased by the author's great-uncle John Donnelly. This photograph was taken in 1946, when the author's parents lived there for three years, right after World War II.

Four

Grand Hotels

Woodmont was a summer resort from the late 1890s until World War II, with the peak of its popularity between about 1900, when trolleys provided easy access, and 1929, when the stock market crashed, setting off the Great Depression. Initially summer visitors to Woodmont were from upper-class families in other cities and states, but the arrival of affordable automobiles in the 1920s enabled the middle class to enjoy the sun and saltwater of summer.

According to the July 2, 1904, *Saturday Chronicle*, a New Haven–based, weekly society newspaper, "The majority of the shore places are by no means, populated by New Haven people alone. Representatives from all over the state, as well as from other states are to be found during the summer. This place [Woodmont] is one of the many attractive spots on Long Island Sound, and has been for several years one of the most popular. New cottages are being erected each year, and new streets are being cut so that it has the appearance of a small city."

There were at least five large wooden hotels—the Merwin Point House, the Sanford House, the Pembroke, the Bonsilene Hotel, and Bonsilene Towers—and numerous smaller inns and rooming houses that rented rooms for the week, month, or entire summer. Interestingly none of these hotels was directly on the waterfront—they were at least a block from the water.

Many of the summer visitors arrived in their own carriages with their servants.

The *Chronicle* regularly reported on the comings and goings of members of "high society" who were staying in Woodmont. For example, in the August 1, 1903, issue, readers found out that "Mayor Pikes, of Danbury, has taken the Baldwin cottage and will occupy it for the month of August with his family," and "Mr. Harvey Warren of Bridgeport is visiting Mr. Stewart Merwin for a few days," and Marion Emerson, daughter of J. M. Emerson, editor of the *Ansonia Sentinel*, "has been the guest of friends here for the past two weeks." Leaving Woodmont also made the news: "Mrs. Ella Batcheller, who has been at the Bonsilene, is in Plymouth for a short time, visiting friends."

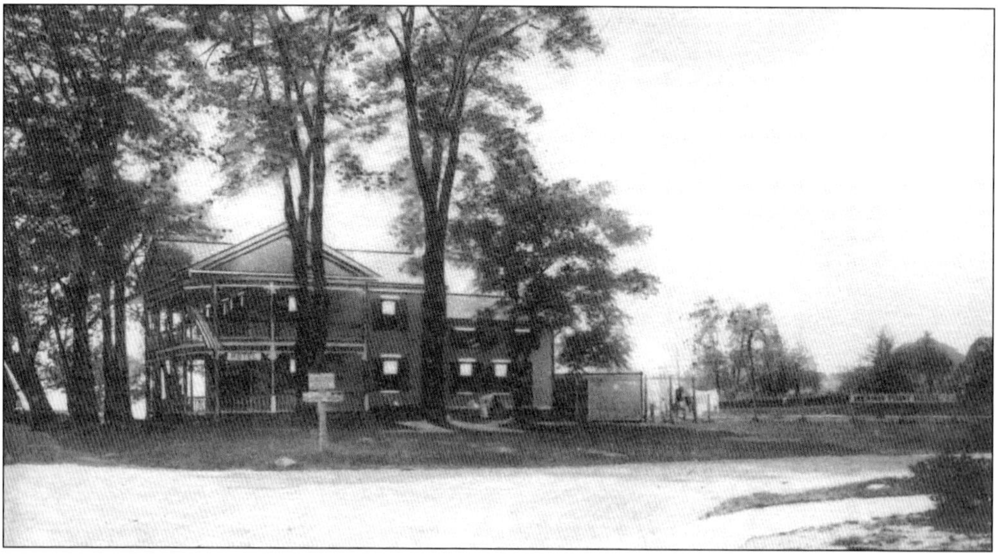

THE MARK MERWIN HOUSE. In the 1880s, the Mark Merwin House was the hotel in Woodmont for the upper class. Located near Merwin's Point, it later became known as the Merwin's Point House and then the Woodmont Lodge. It later was managed by a relative, John W. Merwin, and by G. W. Sanford, who went on to open the nearby Sanford House. Today it is the Woodmont Condominiums at 182 Kings Highway. (Courtesy of Cable Postcard Collection, Antiquarian and Landmarks Society.)

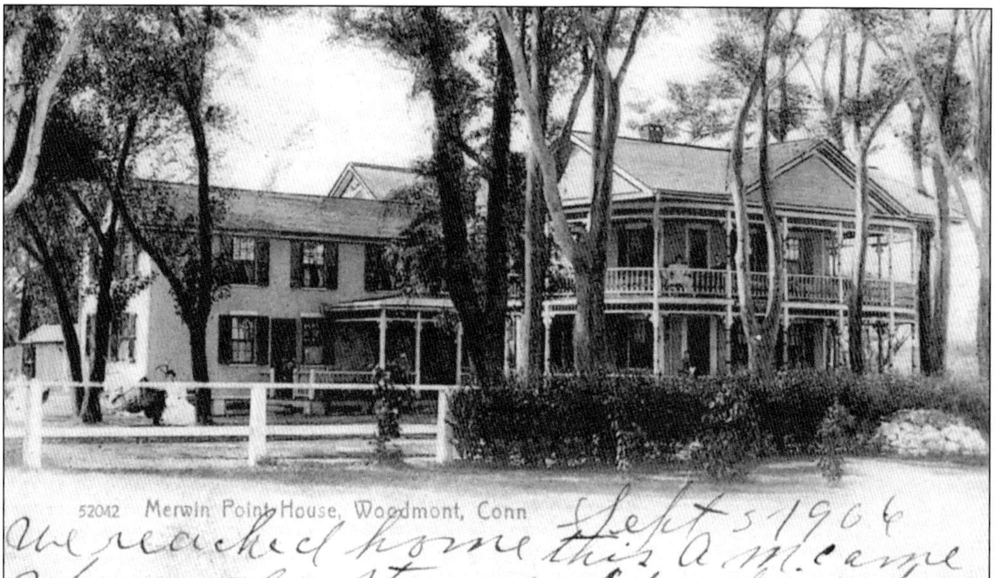

MERWIN'S POINT HOUSE. J. S. Rood, proprietor, placed an advertisement in the newspaper in 1884 saying, "Merwin's Point House, Woodmont, Conn. will open for the reception of guests June 4, 1884. For diversity of scenery, grassy lawns, rocky cliffs, abundant shade and beautiful sandy bathing beach, this point is unsurpassed. Seafood a specialty. Also a good stock of groceries, fish, clams, lobsters constantly on hand. Good stabling for horses. I also have a few cottages to rent at reasonable rates. Hotel stage meets every train. Telephone connection will be completed early in the season." This postcard is postmarked 1906.

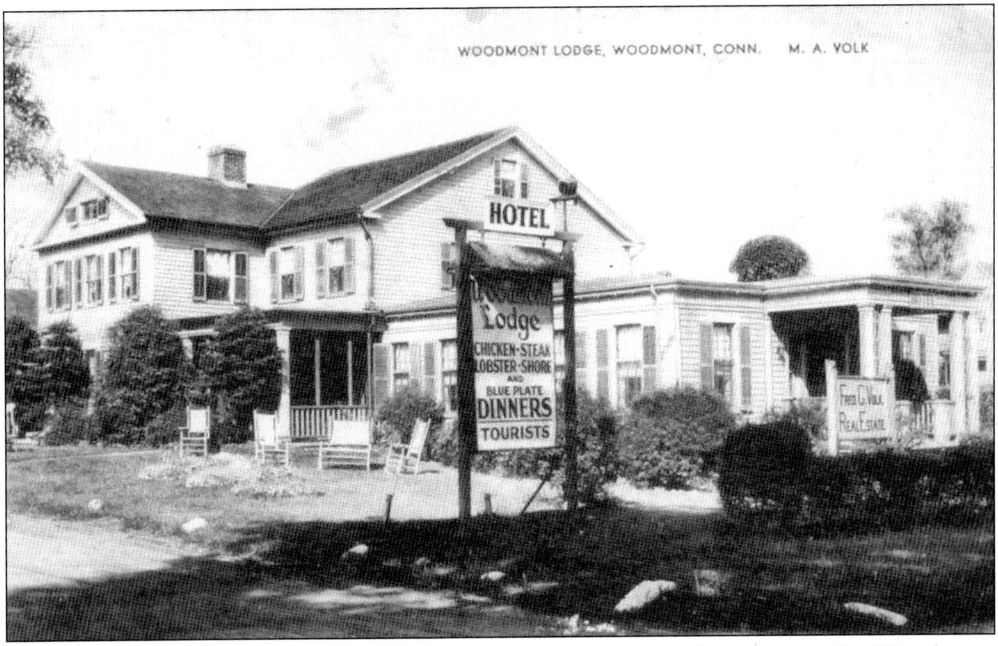

THE WOODMONT LODGE. Today the site of Woodmont Condominiums, the Woodmont Lodge was managed by George and Molly Volk, whose grandson John still lives in Woodmont. According to John, his grandparents owned the Hotel Volk in New Haven before the Depression and bought the Woodmont Lodge shortly after. He remembers his grandfather telling him that Albert Einstein came to the Woodmont Lodge for several summers because he liked the way his grandfather cooked mackerel. This postcard is postmarked 1939.

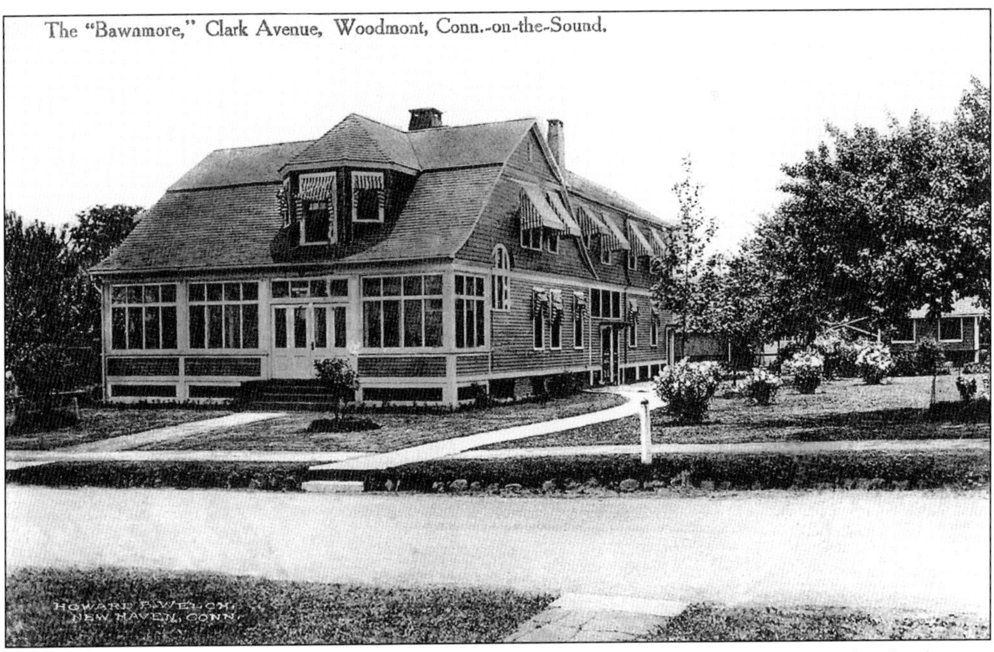

THE BAWNMORE. This hotel was located on Clark Street (now 11 Wall Street) and today houses six apartments. The Bawnmore was right across the street from Bonsilene Towers.

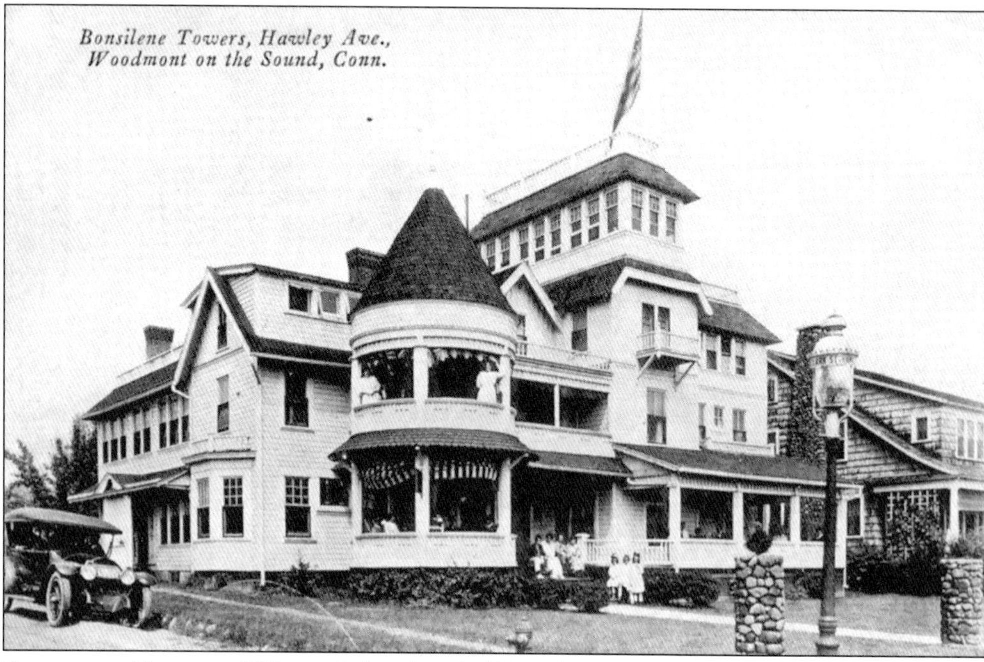

BONSILENE TOWERS. This stately hotel, called Bonsilene Towers, was located two houses from the Bonsilene Hotel, most likely at what was then 42 Hawley Avenue and what is now 4 Wall Street. It was destroyed by fire in 1950s.

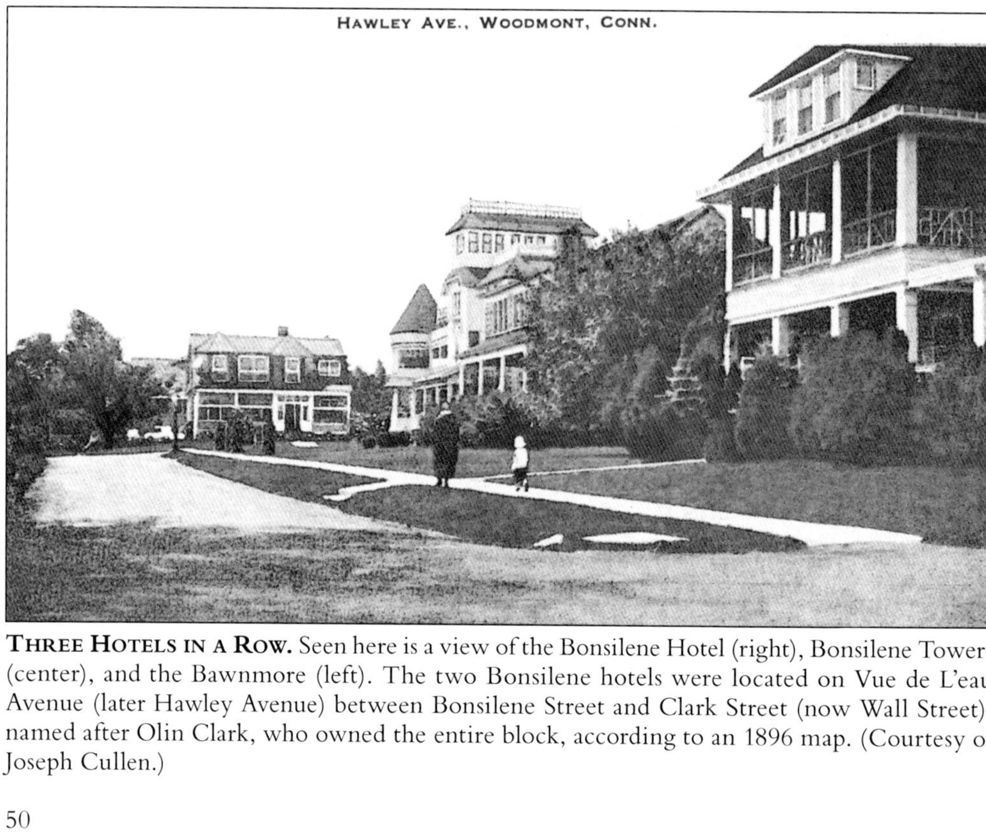

THREE HOTELS IN A ROW. Seen here is a view of the Bonsilene Hotel (right), Bonsilene Towers (center), and the Bawnmore (left). The two Bonsilene hotels were located on Vue de L'eau Avenue (later Hawley Avenue) between Bonsilene Street and Clark Street (now Wall Street), named after Olin Clark, who owned the entire block, according to an 1896 map. (Courtesy of Joseph Cullen.)

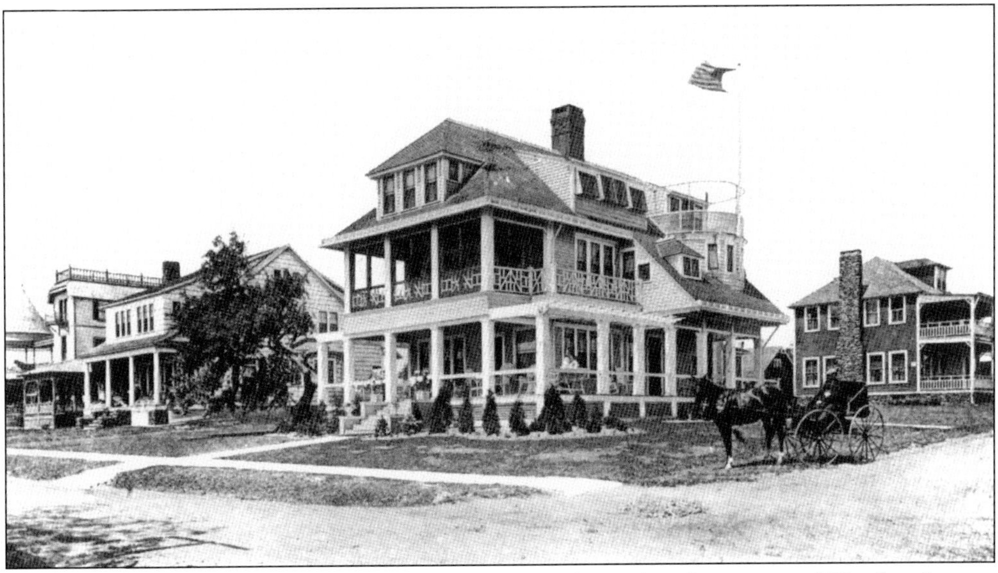

THE BONSILENE HOTEL. The Bonsilene Hotel was located at the corner of Hawley Avenue and Bonsilene Street. It was started by Olin H. Clark of Hartford, who was also given credit for having laid out Howard Park in front of the hotel. "The regular weekly hop, which has became just a social affair of the week at Woodmont, will be given this evening in the dining room of the Bonsilene," read the August 26, 1905, edition of the *Saturday Chronicle.*

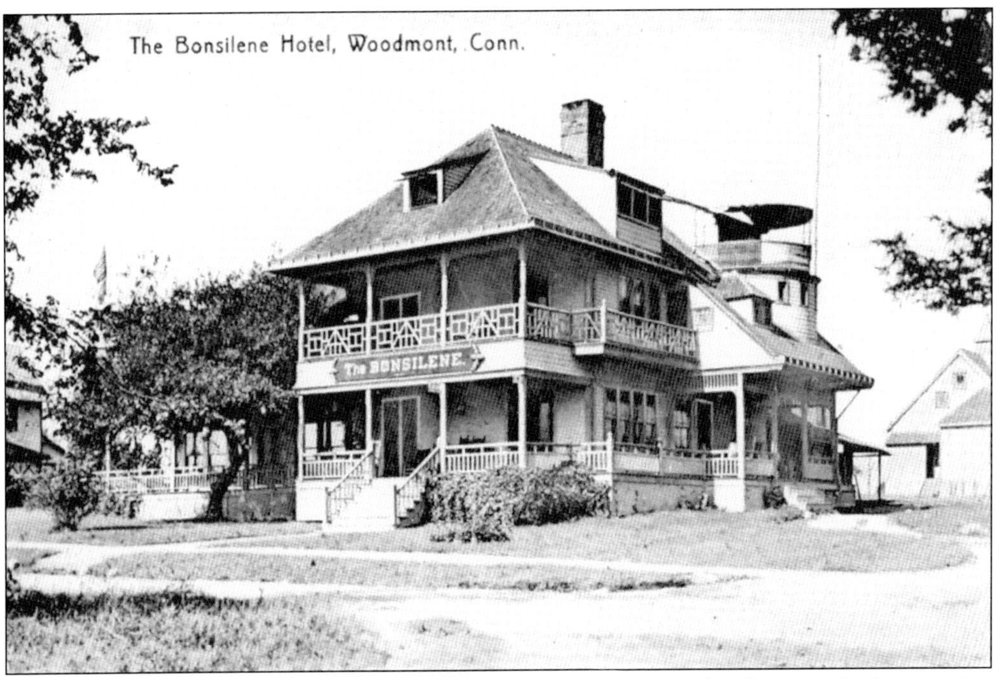

THE BONSILENE HOTEL. Built before 1893 and located at 36 Hawley Avenue, the intersection of Hawley Avenue and Bonsilene Street, the Bonsilene was one of Woodmont's smaller hotels and is one of the few that have survived, although it is now a multifamily house at the head of the Hawley Avenue playground. This postcard is postmarked 1908.

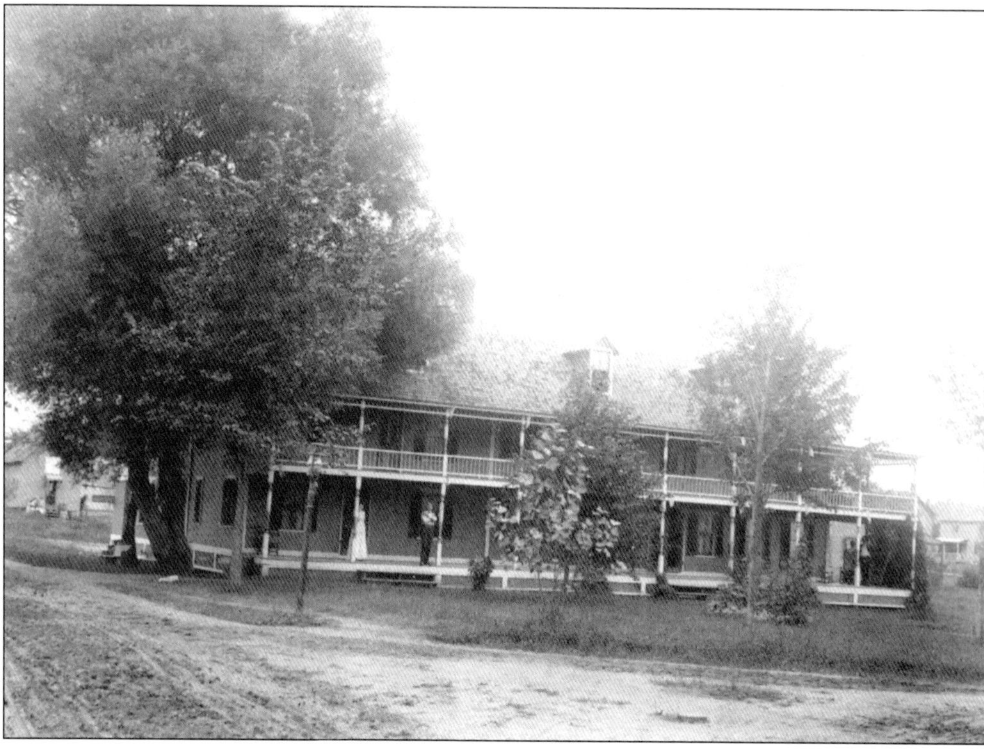

THE SANFORD HOUSE, *c.* 1900. One of Woodmont's two largest and most well-known hotels, the Sanford House was located on Beach Avenue across from Anchor Beach.

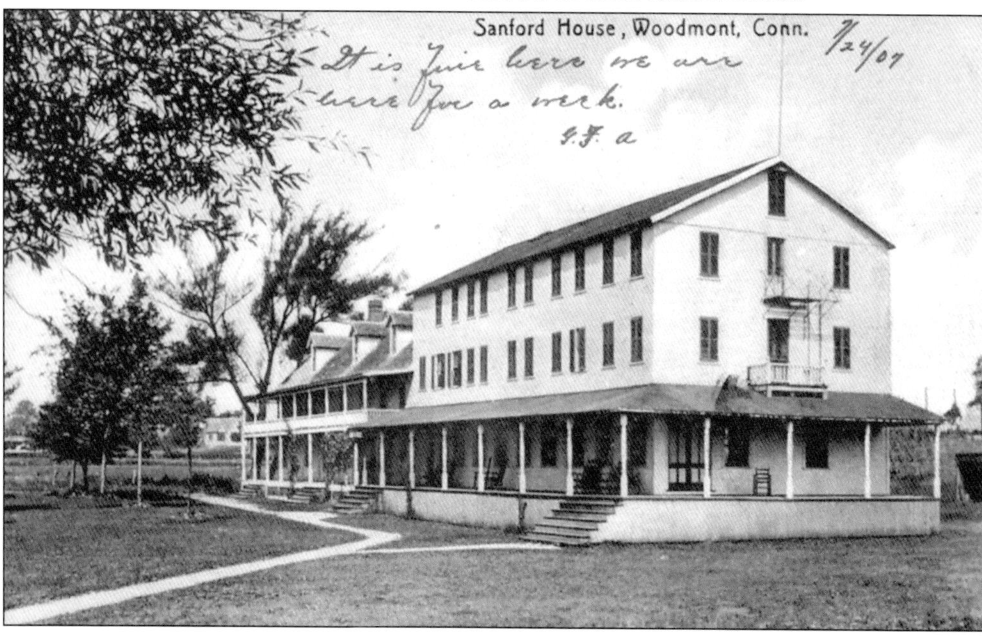

THE SANFORD HOUSE, *c.* 1907. A large white addition was constructed to the right of the original structure to accommodate more guests. According to the borough minutes, on September 30, 1916, "Voted to have the clerk notify Mrs. Sanford by registered letter to clean up her property in the rear of the hotel."

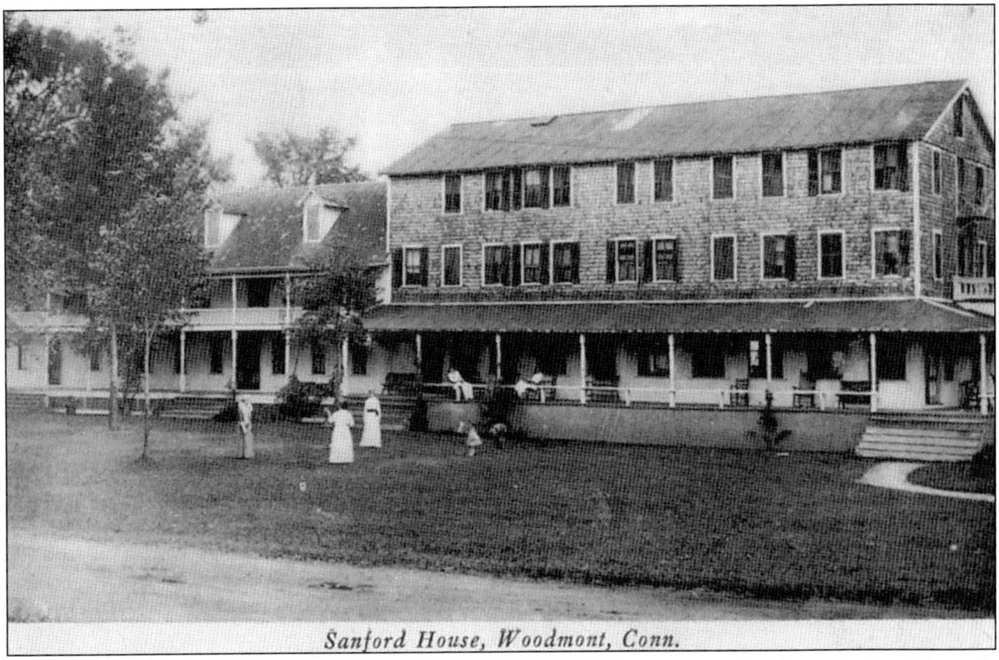

THE SANFORD HOUSE, c. 1917. As written in the July 2, 1904, edition of the *Saturday Chronicle*, "Hops are given at the several hotels during the season, on an average of about one a week. The golf links have been much improved during the past two seasons, and interest in the game has increased in a marked degree. Several tournaments were arranged and played last year by both men and women." The Sanford House sponsored numerous social and sporting activities.

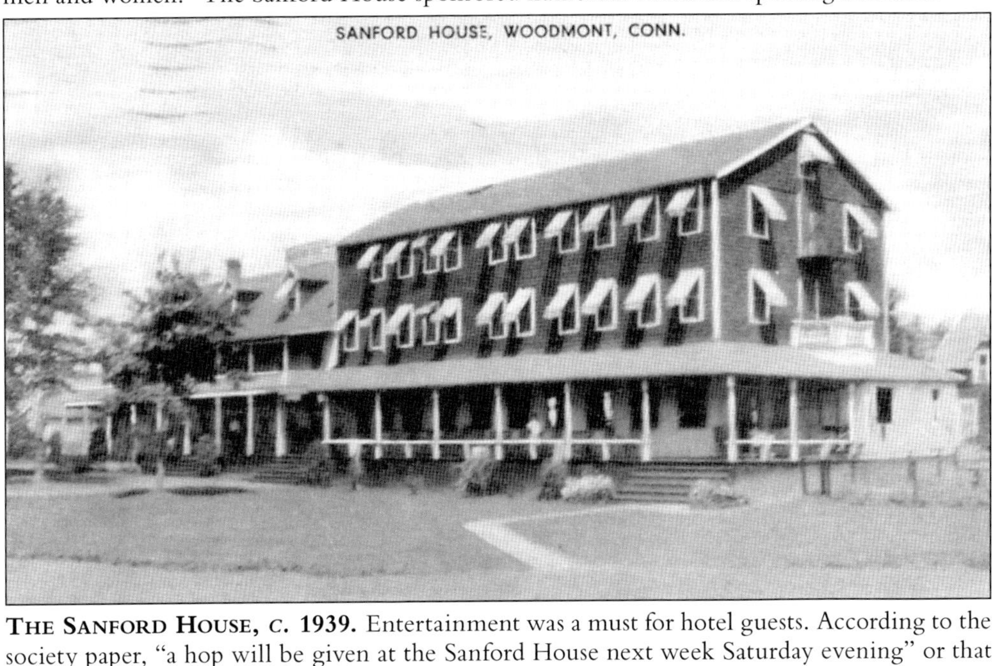

THE SANFORD HOUSE, c. 1939. Entertainment was a must for hotel guests. According to the society paper, "a hop will be given at the Sanford House next week Saturday evening" or that "a large whist was given at the Pembroke last evening by a number of ladies who are staying there. It was the first large whist to be given this summer and a large number of the cottagers were present."

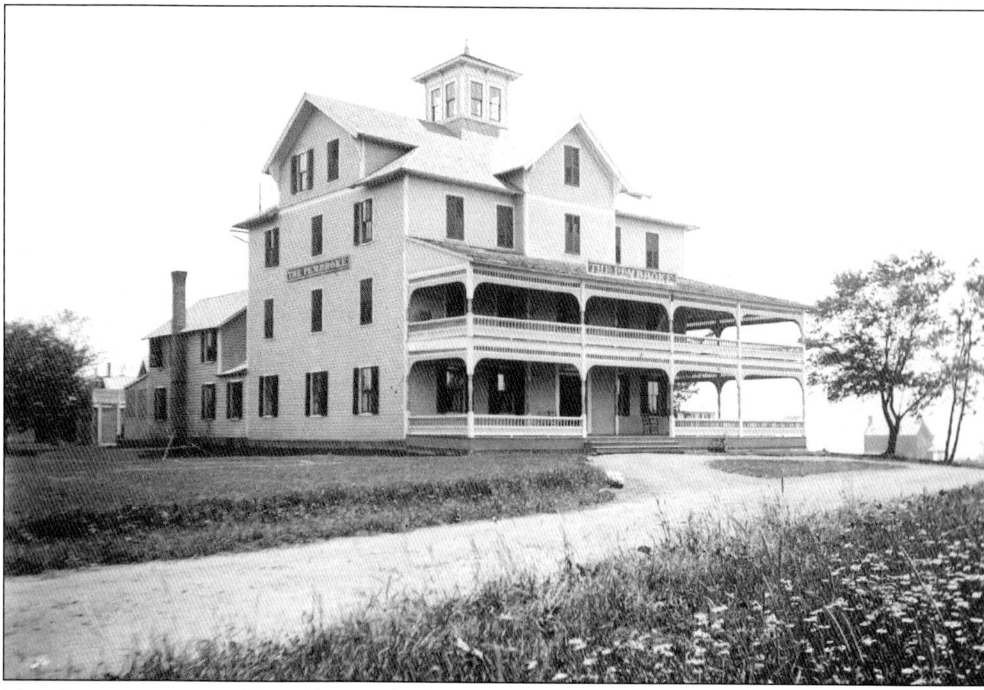

The Pembroke, c. 1900. The Pembroke may have been Woodmont's second hotel, after the Mark Merwin House. It is estimated to have been built around 1875.

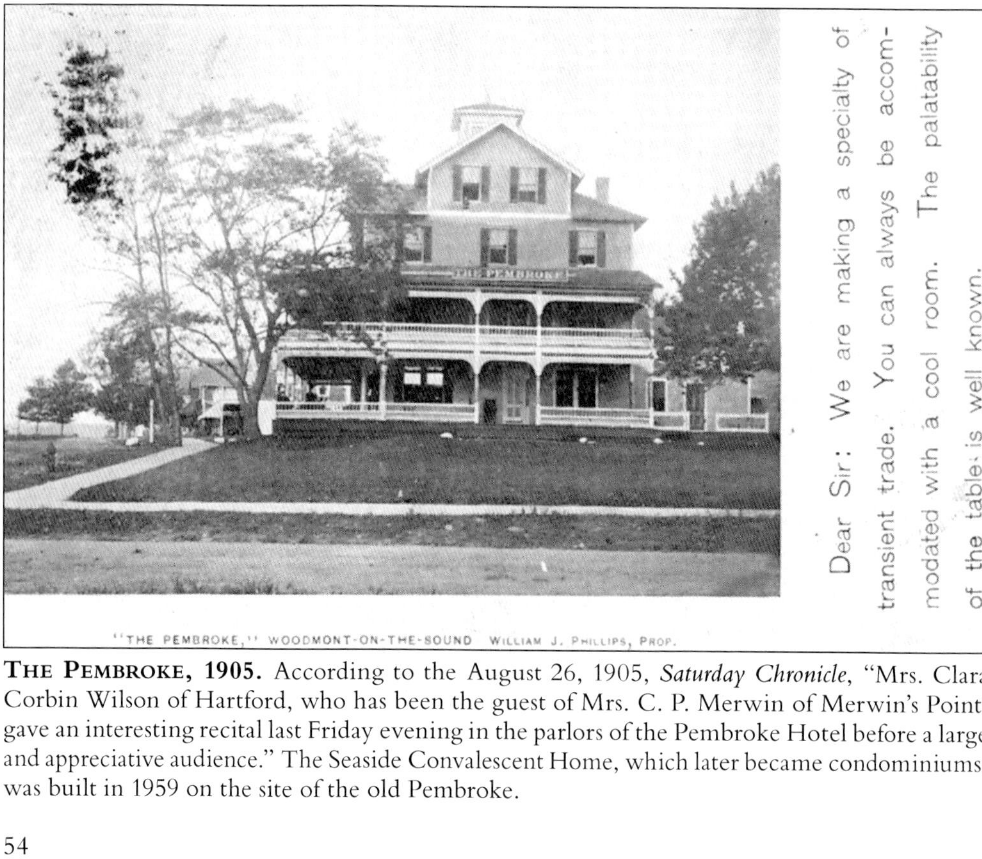

The Pembroke, 1905. According to the August 26, 1905, *Saturday Chronicle*, "Mrs. Clara Corbin Wilson of Hartford, who has been the guest of Mrs. C. P. Merwin of Merwin's Point, gave an interesting recital last Friday evening in the parlors of the Pembroke Hotel before a large and appreciative audience." The Seaside Convalescent Home, which later became condominiums, was built in 1959 on the site of the old Pembroke.

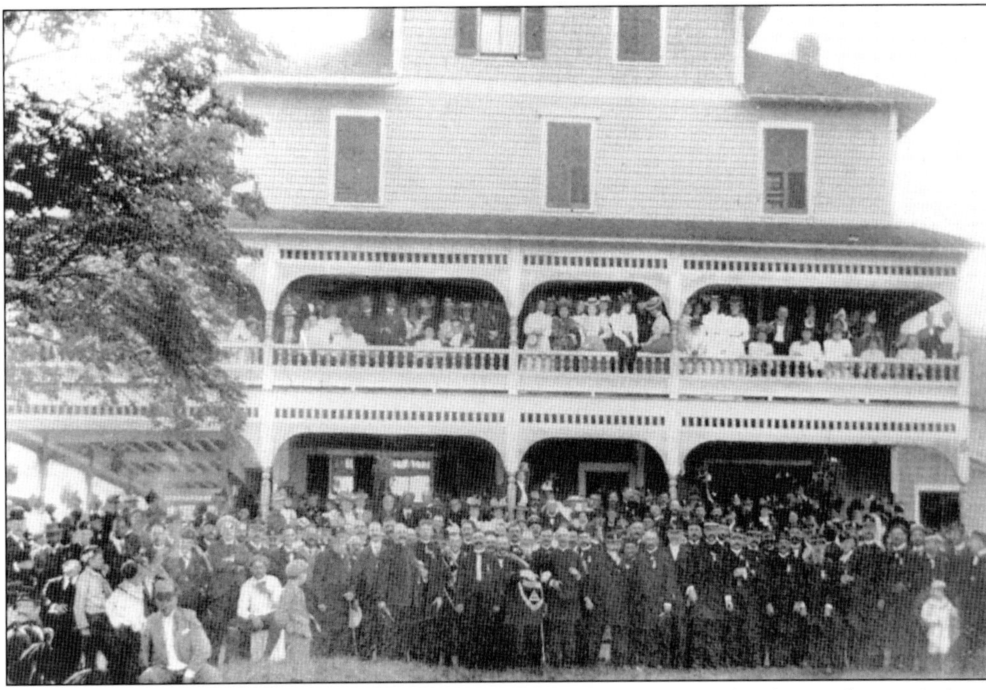

The Pembroke Guests. According to a *New Haven Register* article (date unknown) about the Pembroke Hotel, "Those coming by rail used to get off at the old Woodmont Station at the end of Woodmont Road about a mile-and-a-half from the hotel, where they were picked up by Fritz Chaffler, who met the train with a horse and wagon to pick up the mail and transport the hotel guests." (Courtesy of Photography by Joseph.)

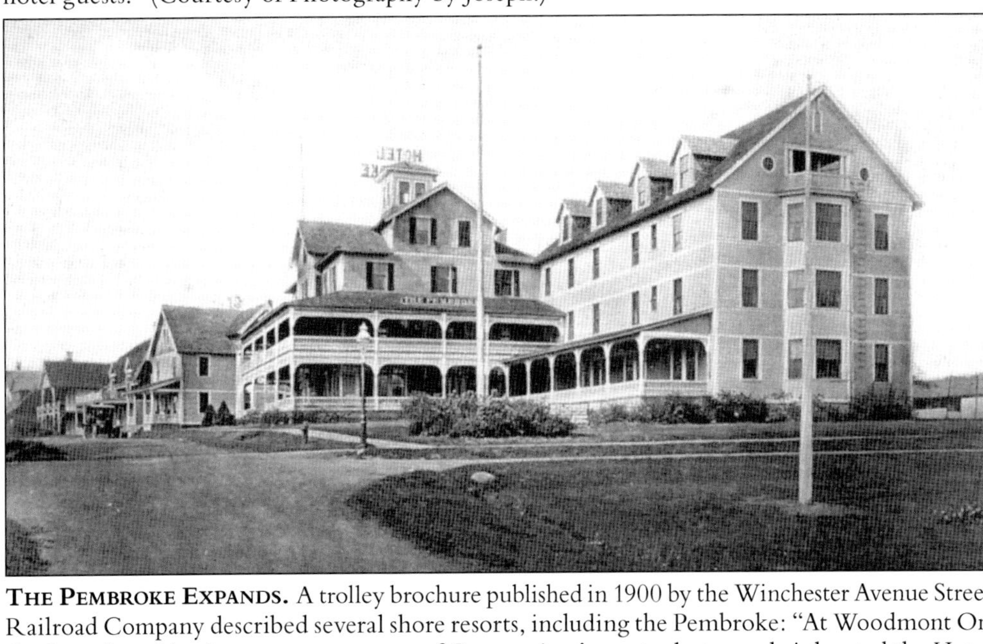

The Pembroke Expands. A trolley brochure published in 1900 by the Winchester Avenue Street Railroad Company described several shore resorts, including the Pembroke: "At Woodmont On the Sound, amidst the summer cottages of Connecticut's most select people is located the Hotel Pembroke. There are accommodations for 100 guests. All rooms are large and well ventilated." A large addition was added to the Pembroke in 1906, increasing its capacity even further.

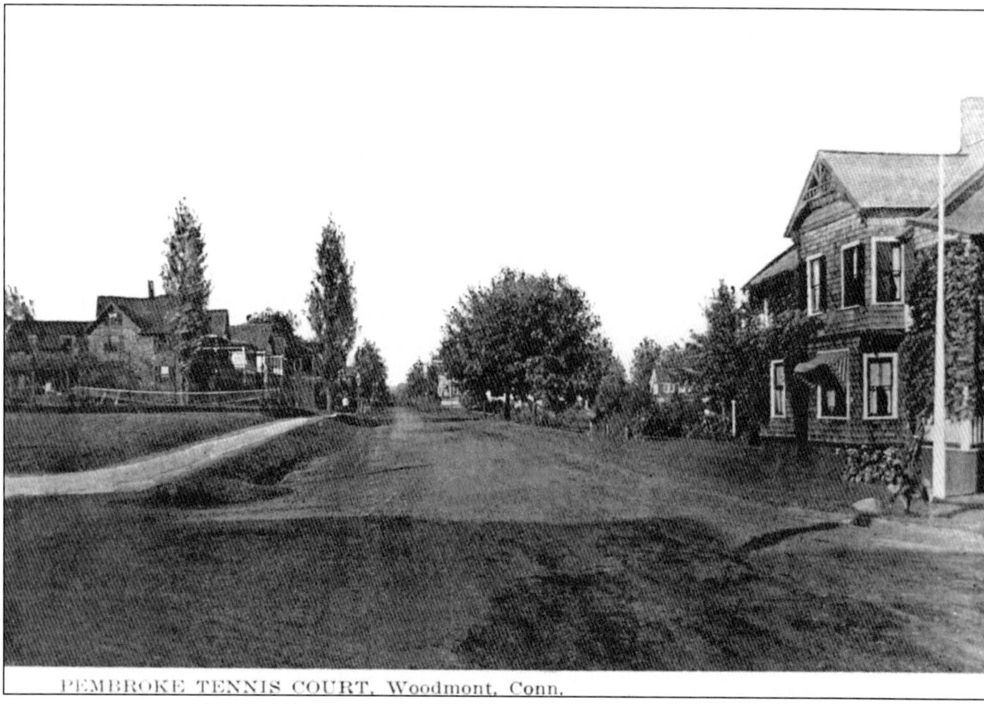

THE PEMBROKE TENNIS COURTS. On the lawns to the right of the hotel were tennis courts for the guests. For many years, the Pembroke was managed by Mr. and Mrs. William Phillips. Mrs. Phillips's brother was Charles Templeton, governor of Connecticut from 1923 to 1925, who had a summer home across the street from the Pembroke, at the corner of Hawley Avenue and Center Street, visible at the left of this photograph. (Courtesy of Photography by Joseph.)

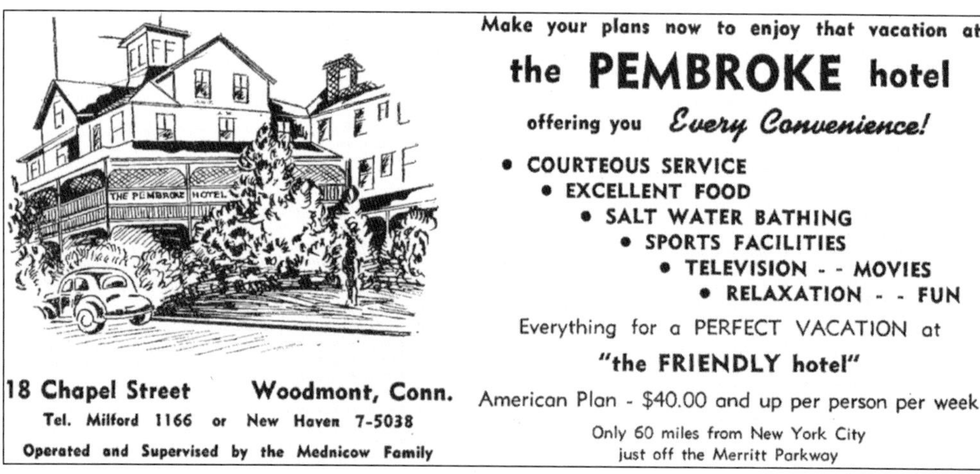

PEMBROKE ADVERTISEMENT, LATE 1940S. A much earlier advertisement in the *New Haven Evening Register* on September 13, 1901, read, "Hotel Pembroke, Woodmont On the Sound. Rates for September, $1 and $1.50. Come on down on the trolley and try one of our shore dinners. Wm. J. Phillips, Proprietor." After Labor Day, many hotels and restaurants began to close for the season, although the Pembroke, and local residents, knew that September was the loveliest month in Woodmont.

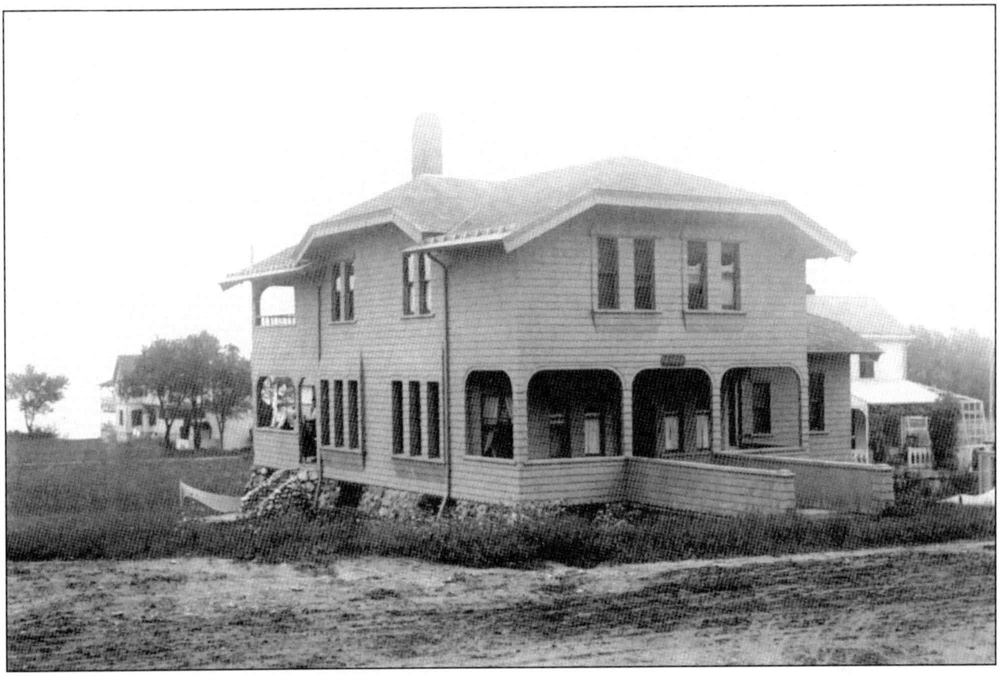

AN EARLY GUESTHOUSE. At 83 Hawley Avenue, at the corner of what is now Hawley Avenue and Clinton Street, was a small guesthouse that had a clear view of Long Island Sound. Today the house looks almost exactly as it did when this photograph was taken, around 1900.

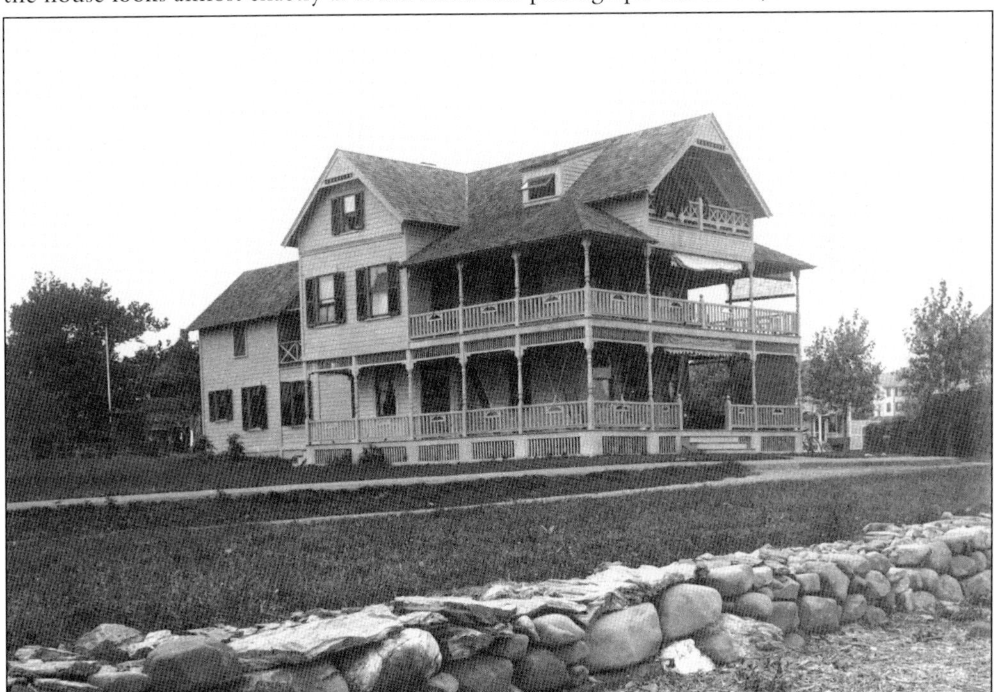

THE SILVER BOW. Located at 90 Beach Avenue, this guesthouse was built around the beginning of the 20th century and was recently meticulously restored to its original condition. This photograph was taken around 1900.

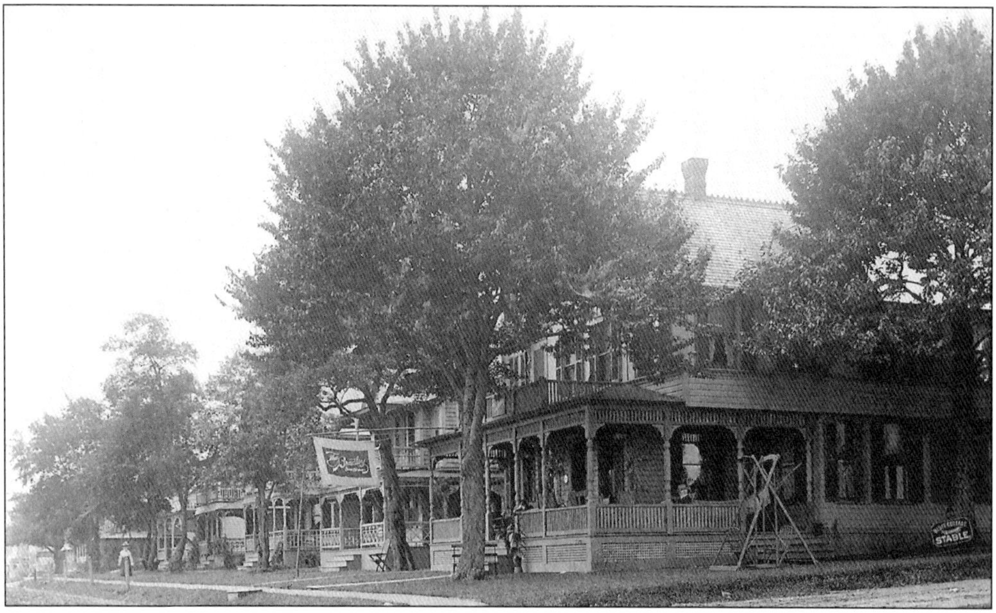

THE BRADLEY BLUFF COTTAGE. Built around 1900, the Bradley Bluff on Hawley Avenue was one of the early hotels in Woodmont. According to a 1903 *Saturday Chronicle*, "The Bradley Bluff Cottage had the following guests arrive during the week: Mrs. Charles E. Blackmore of Winona, Minn.; Mrs. Henry D. Upson of Hartford; Mr. Frank N. Rodman of New York; Mrs. M. E. Austin of Stamford; and Mr. and Mrs. John S. Wolfe of Pittsfield, Mass."

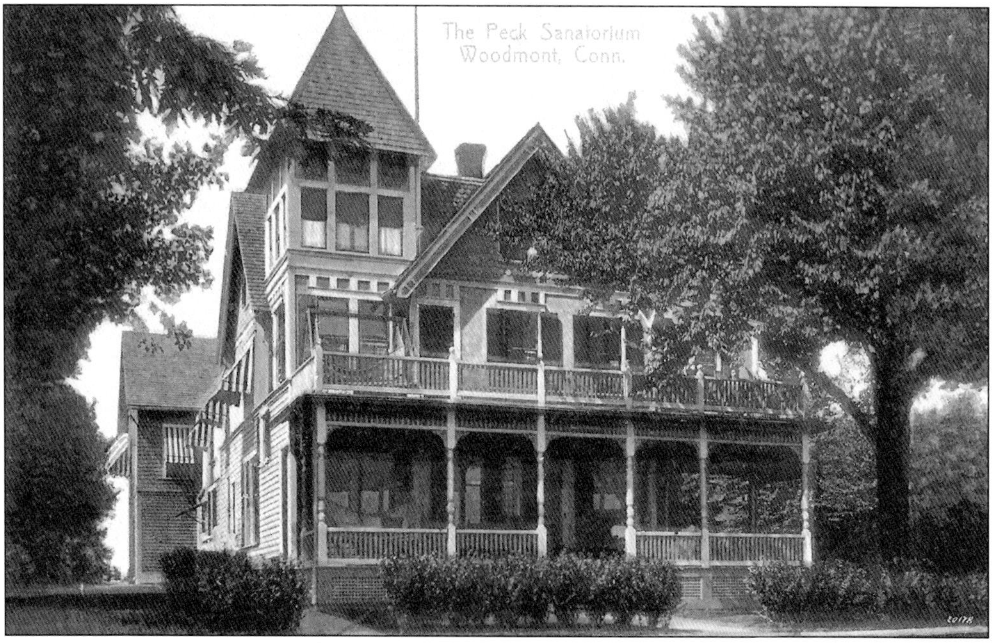

THE PECK SANATORIUM. The Bradley Bluff became a private hospital for the treatment of nervous disorders. The advertisement on the reverse of this postcard read, "The Peck Sanatorium, a rest resort on the shores of Long Island Sound, fully equipped with modern apparatus for the treatment of nervous disorders and other invalids. (No mental cases received.) Robert E. Peck, M.D., Vernon M. Boothby, R.N., Superintendent." This postcard is postmarked 1912.

RULES AND REGULATIONS OF THE PECK SANATORIUM. An advertisement in the August 14, 1915, *Saturday Chronicle* read, "The Peck Sanatorium, Woodmont. A quiet home situated on Long Island Sound, combining the features of both seashore and country, with delightful views, pleasant walks and abundance of sunshine. Nervous cases, convalescents and such medical cases as require treatment away from home are received. Facilities for hydrotherapeutic, including carbon dioxide (Anaheim) baths, and electrotherapeutic treatment, massage, gymnastics, etc." The building that started out as the Bradley Bluff Cottage became the Peck Sanitorium and later, Woodmont Hall. (Courtesy of Photography by Joseph.)

The Peck Sanatorium, Inc.

General Information and Rates

Money, jewelry and other valuables should be deposited in the office and a receipt taken therefor. The Institution will not be responsible for articles when other disposition is made of them.

Patients desiring meal service for guests are requested to notify the office beforehand.

Breakfast is served at 8 A. M., to all patients in their rooms; Dinner at 1 P. M., and Supper at 6 P. M., in the dining-room.

Patients are requested to be in bed, with the lights out, at 9:30 P. M.

Any patient having cause for complaint of any sort will confer a favor upon the management by immediately notifying the Superintendent.

Patients are not allowed to visit other patients in their rooms except as a special privilege.

Smoking is not allowed in the house, except in the billiard-room.

VISITORS

Patients may receive visitors during the hours of 3 and 6 P. M., subject to the physician's orders.

Not more than two visitors are permitted to see a patient at a time unless by special permission of the Physician in charge.

CHARGES

Bills are due and payable one week in advance, and no patient will be received for a period of less than one week.

The fixed weekly charge for room and board include the general attention of the regular nursing staff, but not special nursing, special treatments, personal laundry, consultation, or medical attention other than by the Physician in charge.

Room and board are furnished to patients' relatives and friends for five dollars a week less than is charged patients. An extra charge of twenty-five cents is made for serving meals to patients in their rooms when able to go to dining-room. Single meals are served to patients' guests in the dining-room for Dinners, Weekday $.75 Sunday $1.00

Arrangements may be made with the Superintendent for personal laundry work.

SPECIAL NURSES

The wages of special nurses vary from seven to twenty-five dollars per week, according to the grade of attendance required by the individual case, and are payable to the nurse, not to the Sanatorium.

A charge twelve dollars per week, ~~or one dollar and twenty-five cents~~ per day, is made for the board of a special nurse.

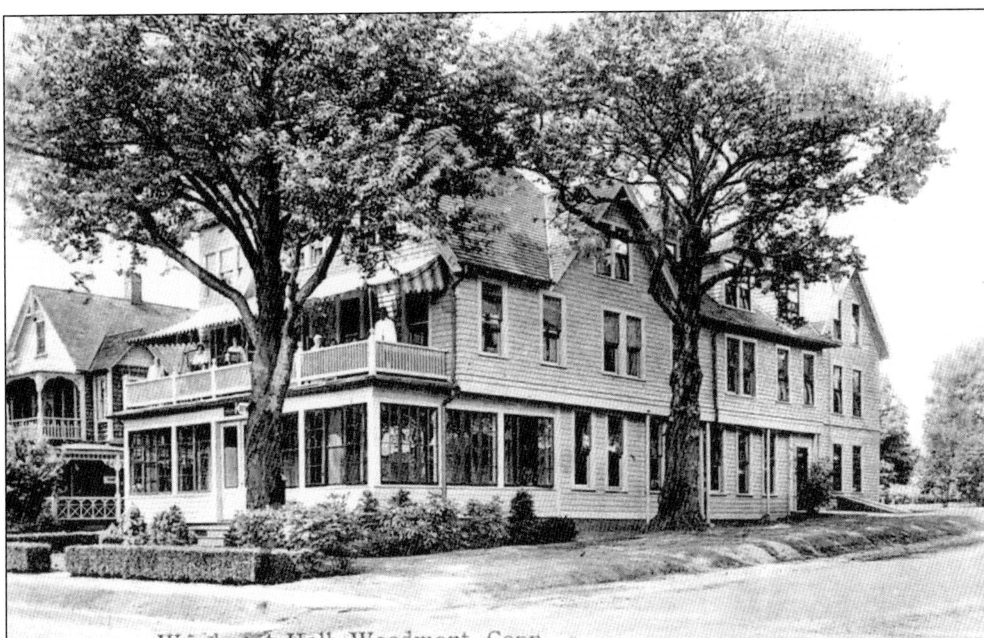

WOODMONT HALL. By 1939, the building had come full circle—no longer a health care facility, but once again a guesthouse. It still stands today as a 12-unit apartment house at 60 Hawley Avenue.

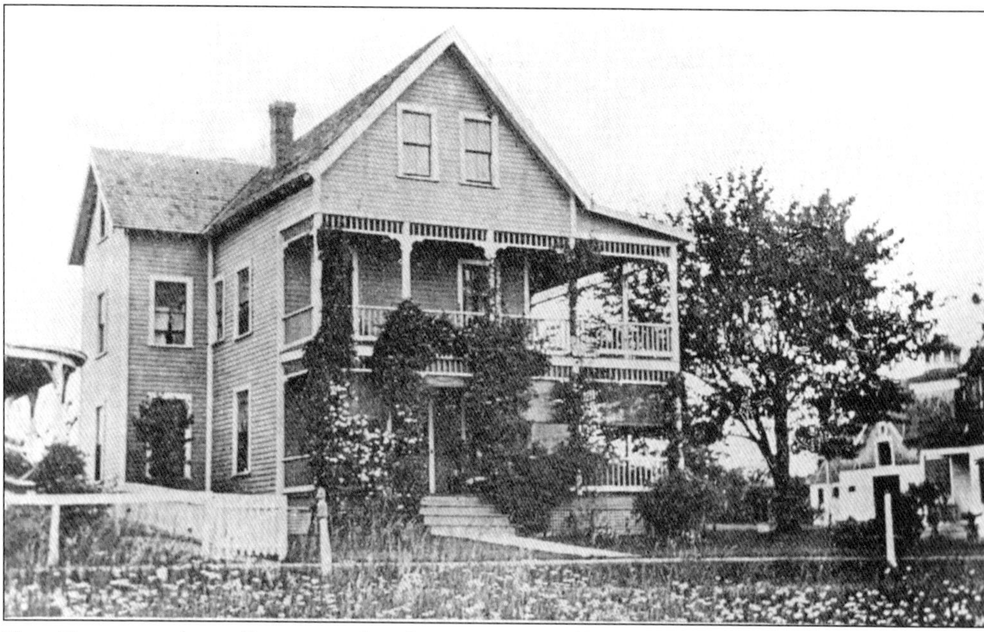

THE ELLAMAY. According to an advertisement in a cookbook sponsored by the New Haven Gas Light Company, the proprietor of the Ellamay around 1910 was Mrs. F. A. Stockin, who offered "summer board and rooms." In the *Saturday Chronicle* of August 22, 1903, "A very enjoyable whist party was given Tuesday evening at the Ellamay cottage. The first gentleman's prize, an inkstand, was won by Mr. Ernest Dillon. The ladies prize went to Miss Gall of Chicago who won a very handsome handkerchief." (Courtesy of Photography by Joseph.)

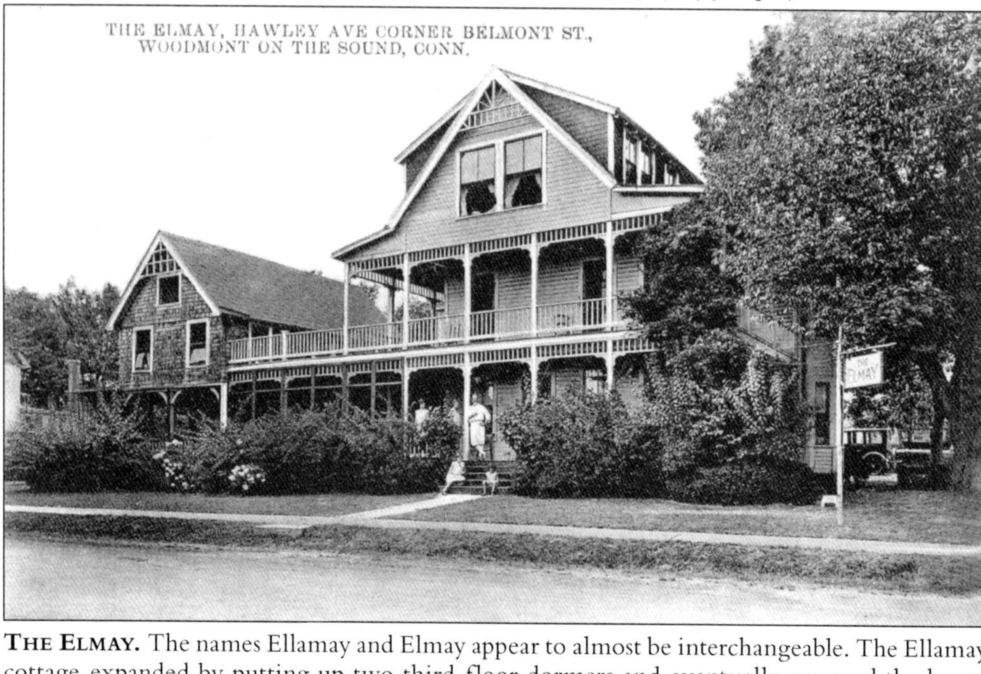

THE ELMAY. The names Ellamay and Elmay appear to almost be interchangeable. The Ellamay cottage expanded by putting up two third-floor dormers and eventually annexed the house next door to it. Today the building, at 54 Hawley Avenue, has 10 apartments. (Courtesy of Photography by Joseph.)

Five

A Borough is Born

By the beginning of the 20th century, the neighborhood was growing fast and becoming fairly organized. In 1901, residents formed the Woodmont Association, a community improvement organization. Two years later, the association requested and was granted a charter from the Connecticut legislature. Although it was still referred to as the Woodmont association for many years, Woodmont became an official borough within the town of Milford on June 18, 1903.

By then, Woodmont was attracting a few hundred residents in the summer, and the borough needed to provide many of the same services as a full-time community—places of worship, education, recreation, and public safety. A schoolhouse, a nondenominational church, and a fire house all existed before the borough was formally established.

The first school to serve the area had been in operation since at least the mid-18th century when Milford's initial school districts were established near the town's four major farms: Amity, Wheeler's, Bryan's, and Burwell's farm. Each of these districts had a one-room schoolhouse. Woodmont's, in the Burwell's farm district, was on the Road to New Haven.

Since Milford had been founded by a group of men and women seeking religious freedom, it was no surprise that the first community building erected in Woodmont was a church. The Woodmont Union Ecclesiastical Society organized on May 5, 1885, at the schoolhouse, where Sunday school and evening church meetings had been held for several years. The land on which to build the new a nondenominational church was donated by local farmers Mortimer P. Treat and the Bryan family. The people of Woodmont worked tirelessly until the chapel was constructed in 1886.

In 1897, the Woodmont Fire Company was established, housed in a barn on Center Street (now Dixon Street). In 1906, St. Agnes Chapel, a Roman Catholic church, opened at the intersection of Center Street and New Haven Avenue (now Kings Highway) for the summer months only. The Woodmont Hebrew Congregation, while not technically within the borough of Woodmont, opened across from Sloppy Joe's in 1926, serving many Jewish Woodmont residents with an orthodox synagogue, and later, a social hall. Both are still standing, and the synagogue is still operational on a seasonal basis and is listed in the National Register of Historic Places.

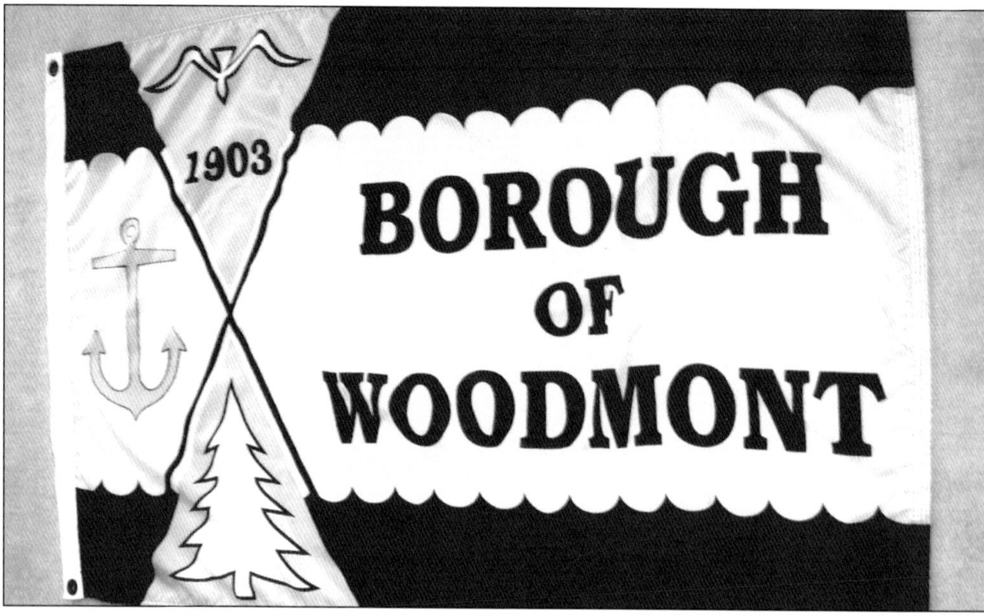

The Borough Flag. It is not known who designed the Borough of Woodmont flag, but it is a colorful depiction of what makes Woodmont Woodmont. The flag is a blue-white-blue horizontal tricolor; on the upper triangle is a seagull and the date of the borough's incorporation, 1903; on the lower triangle is an evergreen tree. Near the hoist is a gold anchor. Each Woodmont Day, the borough flag leads the Woodmont Day parade.

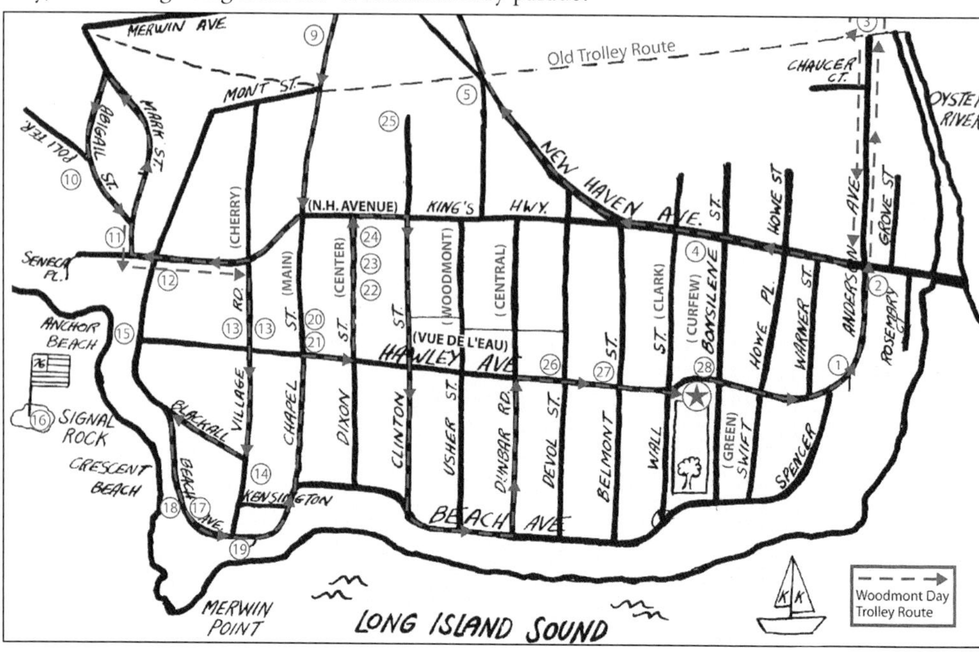

Map of the Borough. This map was drawn by the author for the 1976 Woodmont Day program booklet, and updated for the Woodmont Day 2003 (which celebrated the 100th anniversary of the borough) program booklet. A special attraction that day was gasoline-driven trolley rides around the borough and guided tours of the sites of various landmarks, including old farms, hotels, the country club, and other highlights.

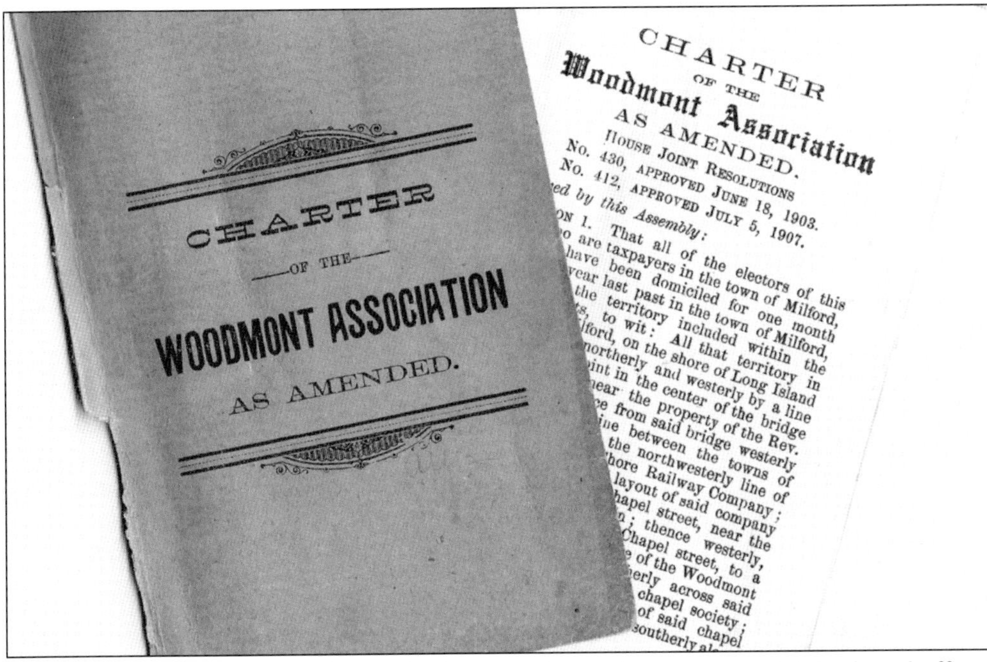

Woodmont Charter. The borough adopted a charter that empowered duly elected officers to collect taxes; control health and sanitation; build roads, sidewalks, and drains; appoint special police; and do anything to improve the borough that did not specifically encroach upon the authority of the City of Milford. In addition, Milford was required to pay Woodmont a share of the town taxes for public works. The back of the charter says, "Cunningham Printers, Clinton Street, Woodmont."

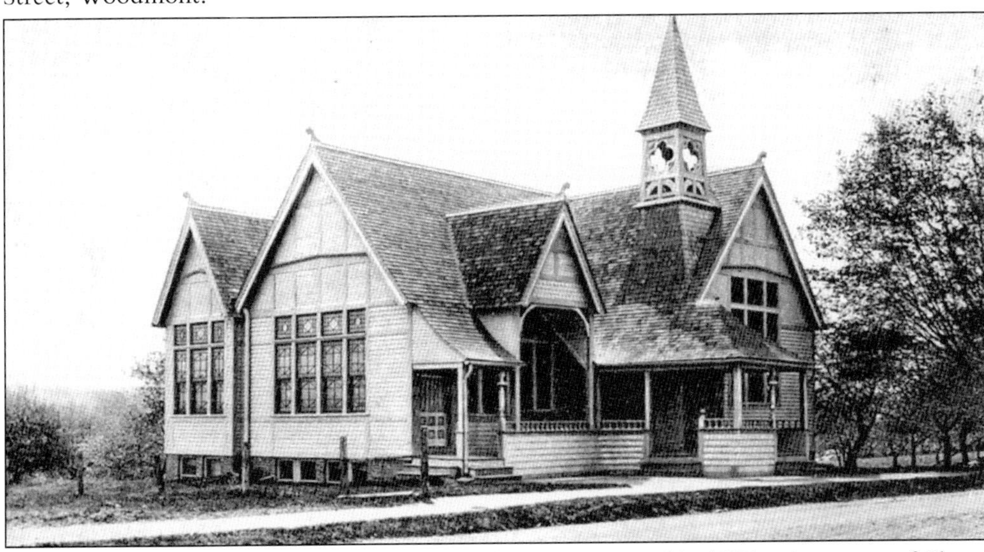

Woodmont Chapel. The Woodmont Chapel was constructed in 1887 at the corner of Chapel Street and Merwin Avenue. An addition, including a kitchen and dining room, was added in 1896. In 1969, it became Woodmont United Church of Christ, and shortly after, moved to New Haven Avenue. The Woodmont Library rented the abandoned chapel for several years until the City of Milford closed the branch in 1981. Today the building at 160 Chapel Street is once again a church—Mission Good Shepherd Church.

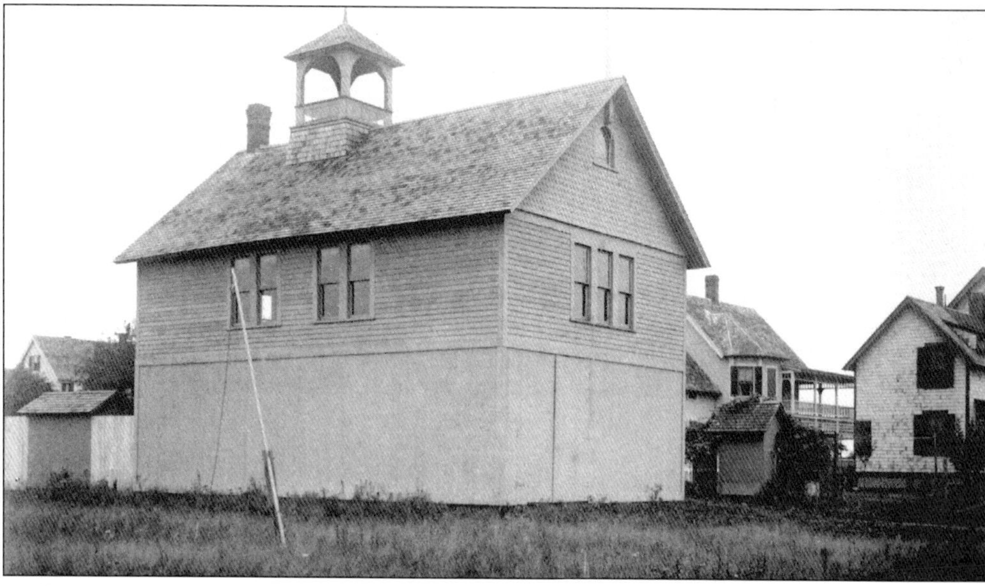

E. B. Little's Barn, c. 1900. Milford had established a fire department in 1838, but a disastrous fire in Woodmont in 1886 demonstrated the need for a fire company in that end of town, and a volunteer fire department petitioned the state for a charter and the Woodmont Fire Company was formed in 1897. It was first housed in E. B. Little's barn on Center Street (now Dixon Street), since the fire equipment was horse-drawn at the time.

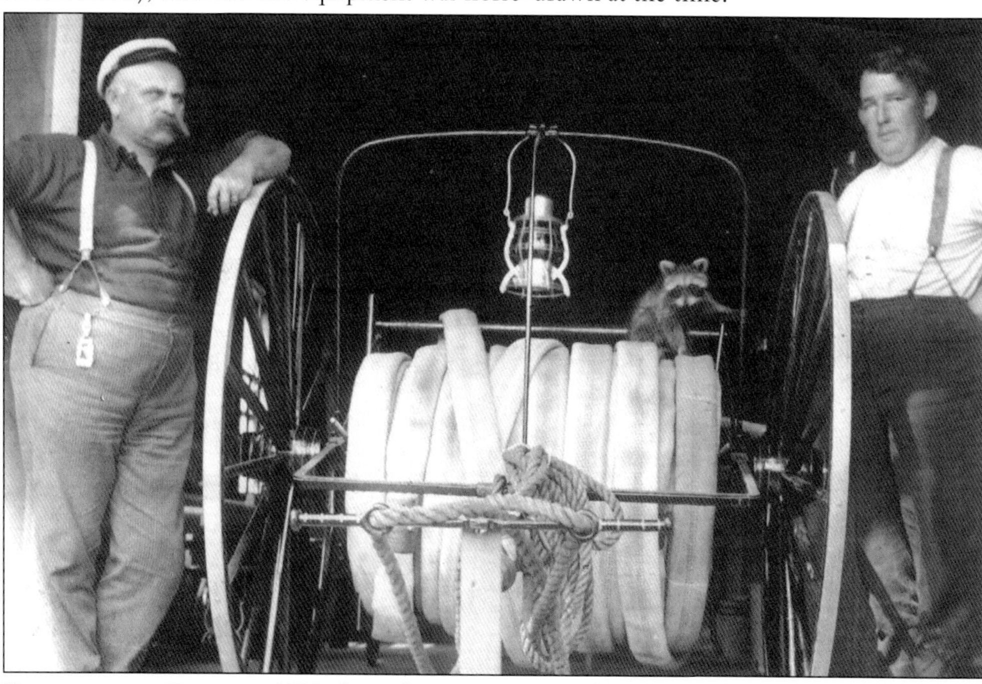

Firemen with Pumper, 1909. According to section 18 of the 1905 ordinances of the Woodmont Association, "The locomotive tire [steel wheel] suspended from the engine house of 'Fire Company, Number One' is hereby set and established in as the fire bell of the Association." The locomotive tire was later replaced with a steel bell, which was hung in the bell tower of the barn. (Courtesy of Cable Postcard Collection, Antiquarian and Landmarks Society.)

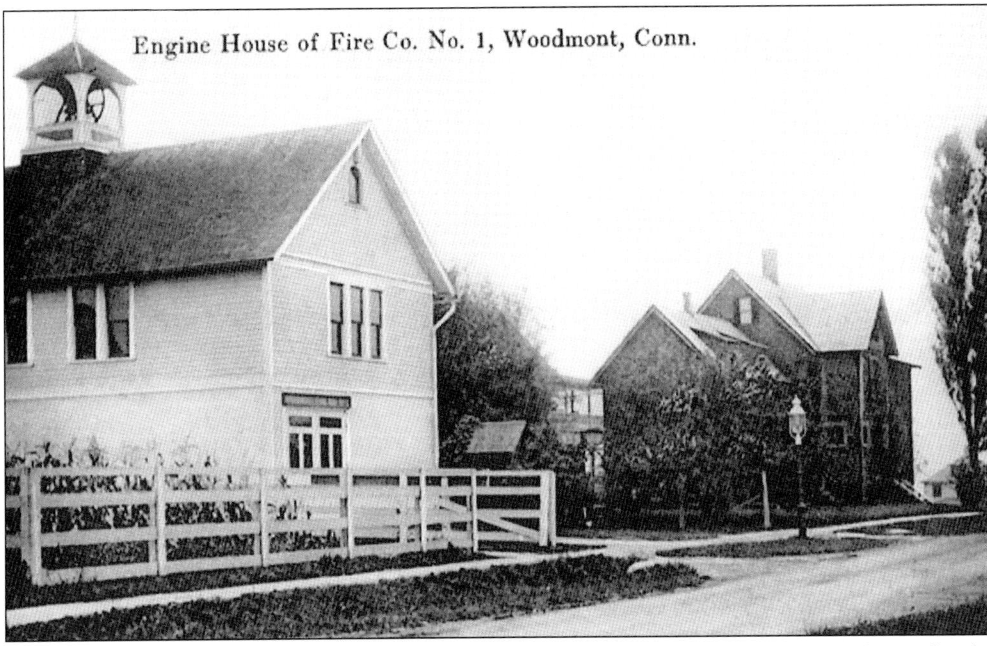

WOODMONT FIREHOUSE. In 1897, the Woodmont Fire Company was granted a charter by the State of Connecticut for the purpose of "the extinguishment of fires and the protection of life and property." An 1898 inventory for the firehouse included one engine with a 75-foot hose; one ax for one pump; two poles; four pails and four lanterns; one barrel lime; 100 pounds of aluminum; one-quarter barrel soda; two-thirds bag salt; and one empty barrel. (Courtesy of Photography by Joseph.)

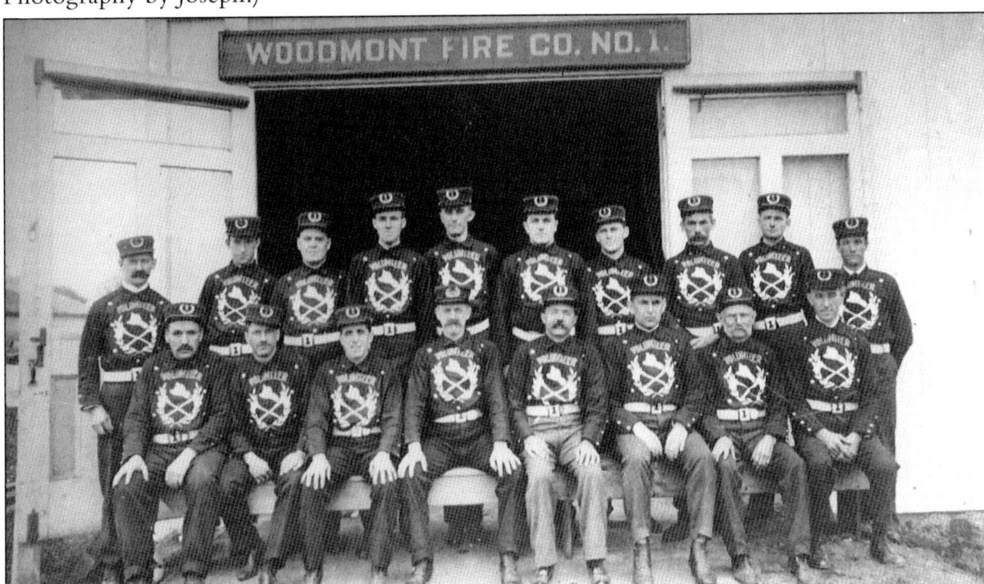

WOODMONT FIRE COMPANY NO. 1. In the early days, the members of the fire company held their meetings at the Woodmont Post Office. For its first 10 years, the Woodmont Fire Company borrowed a horse-drawn "chemical machine" from the town of Milford, but around 1907 upgraded to "force pumps" and "hose wagons." (Courtesy of Photography by Joseph.)

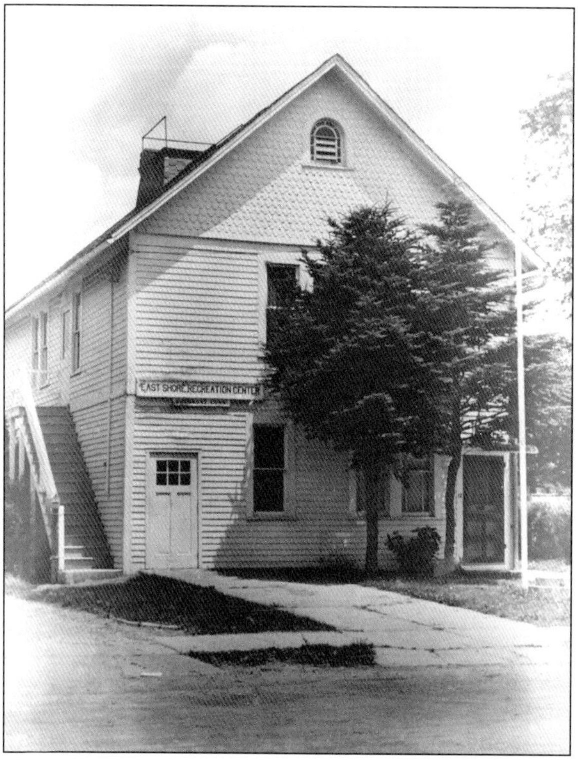

EAST SHORE RECREATION CENTER. The old firehouse was replaced with a larger brick structure on Kings Highway that opened on the Fourth of July, 1949. After this new brick firehouse opened at the end of Center Street (Dixon Street), the old wooden firehouse became a recreation center for the eastern side of town. It also served as the borough hall. (Courtesy of Photography by Joseph.)

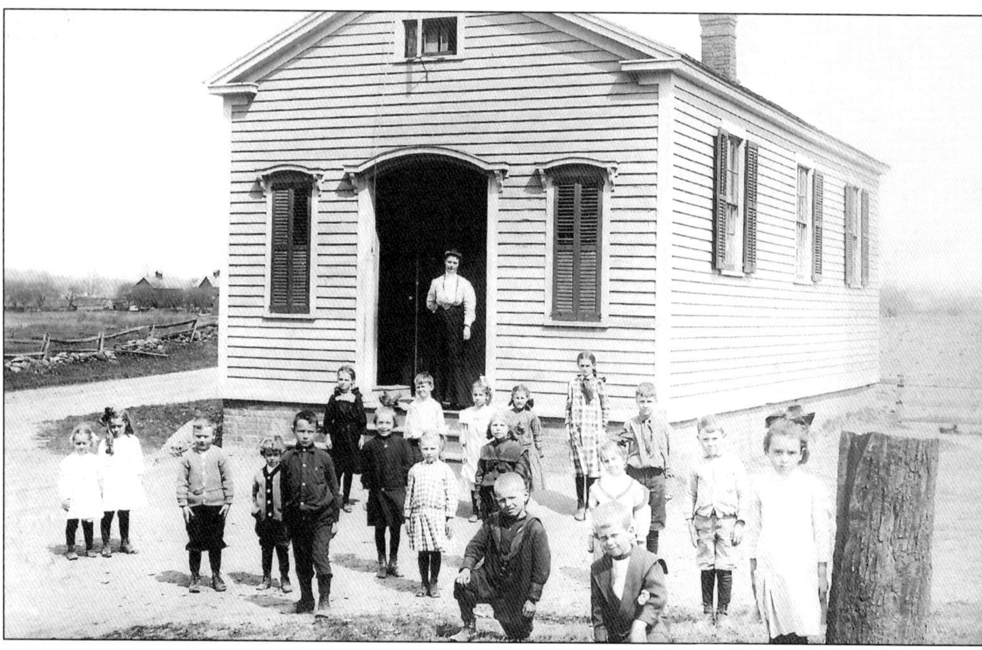

THE ONE-ROOM WOODMONT SCHOOL. This was the little one-room schoolhouse where generations of Woodmont students were taught. Milford land records estimate it was built in 1880. Today it is a tiny 886-square-foot, four-room private home at 233 Chapel Street, directly across the street from the East Shore Middle School (formerly Seabreeze School). (Courtesy of Lowell Beach Sykes.)

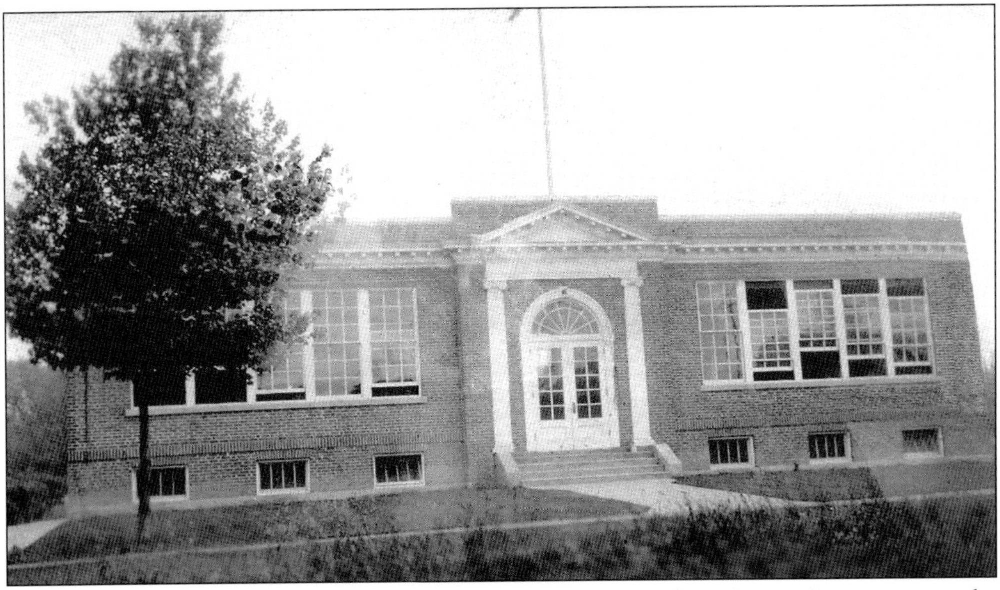

The New Woodmont School. A new brick school opened on Center Street, next to the firehouse, in 1918. After World War II, schools had become overcrowded and the city purchased a two-room portable classroom for the school. The portable was used until 1953 when Seabreeze School opened, ironically directly across the street from the old one-room schoolhouse. Today the portable serves as the Woodmont Borough Hall at the end of Clinton Street. In 2002, it was named the Richard J. Austin Borough Hall, in honor of Woodmont's longest-serving warden. (Courtesy of Lowell Beach Sykes.)

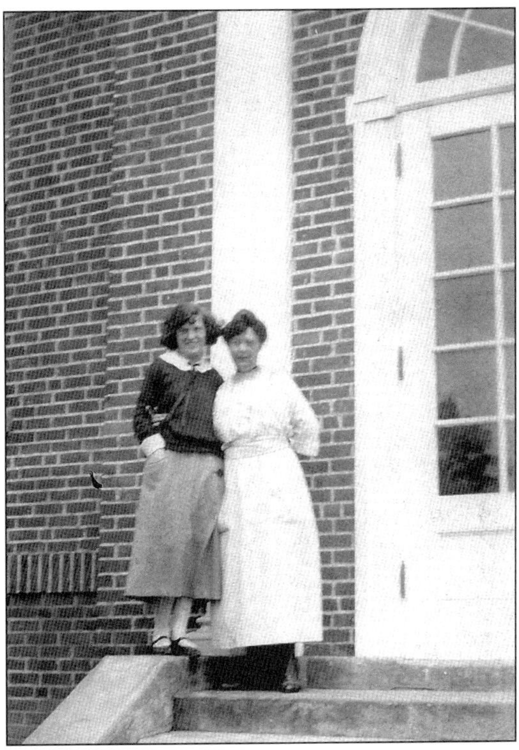

Miss Cody and Miss Fannie Beach. The Woodmont School served children from kindergarten through fourth grade. In 1970, it was renamed Fannie Beach Woodmont School, in honor of its most well-known teacher and principal, who taught first at the one-room schoolhouse, starting in 1891, and then in the new school, until she retired in 1934. The small school closed in 1979 because of declining enrollment, and today it houses the borough's volunteer library, a neighborhood center, and other community services. (Courtesy of Lowell Beach Sykes.)

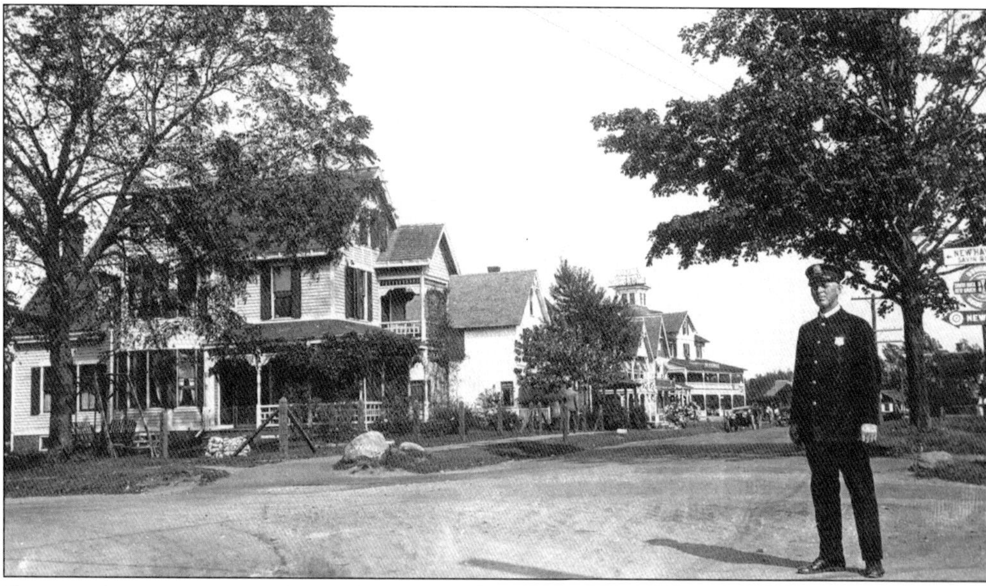

CHAPEL STREET COP. Police officer John Kingston Sullivan was the traffic officer stationed at the busy Chapel Street intersection in 1915–1916. It was apparently a traffic concern for many years since in 1927, the Woodmont Board "voted to write to the police commissioners of Milford asking for a policeman at the corner of Chapel Street and New Haven Avenue to protect the children going to and coming from school." (Courtesy of Cable Postcard Collection, Antiquarian and Landmarks Society.)

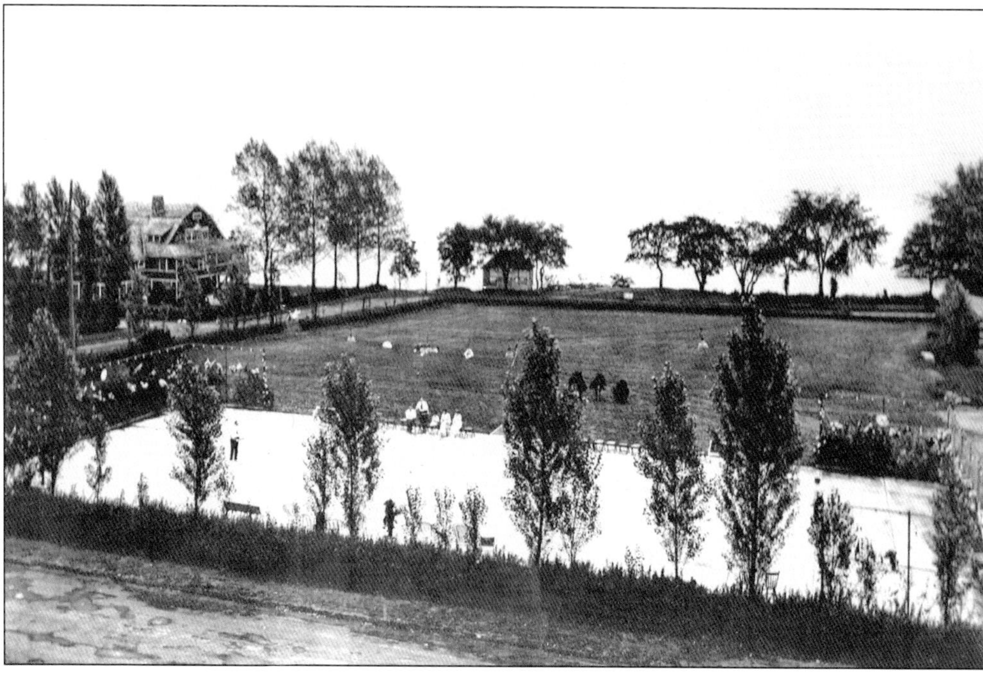

TENNIS COURTS. These tennis courts were located at the top of the Hawley Avenue playground, between Clark Street (now Wall Street) and Bonsilene. They were probably used by guests of the Bonsilene Hotel and Bonsilene Towers. There was also a gazebo, called the Bonsilene pavilion, at the foot of the playground, overlooking the sound. (Courtesy of Photography by Joseph.)

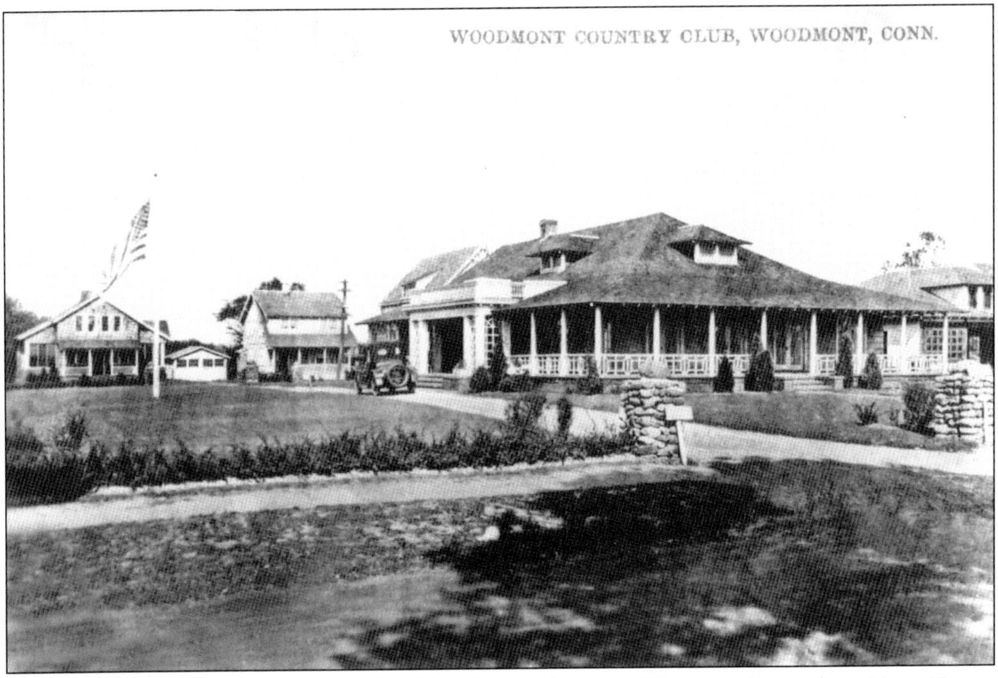

WOODMONT COUNTRY CLUB. The Woodmont Country Club was located on New Haven Avenue between Bonsilene and Wall Street (it later became St. Agnes Hall before it was razed in the 1990s). The country club had clay tennis courts across the street on the far side of New Haven Avenue. (Courtesy of Photography by Joseph.)

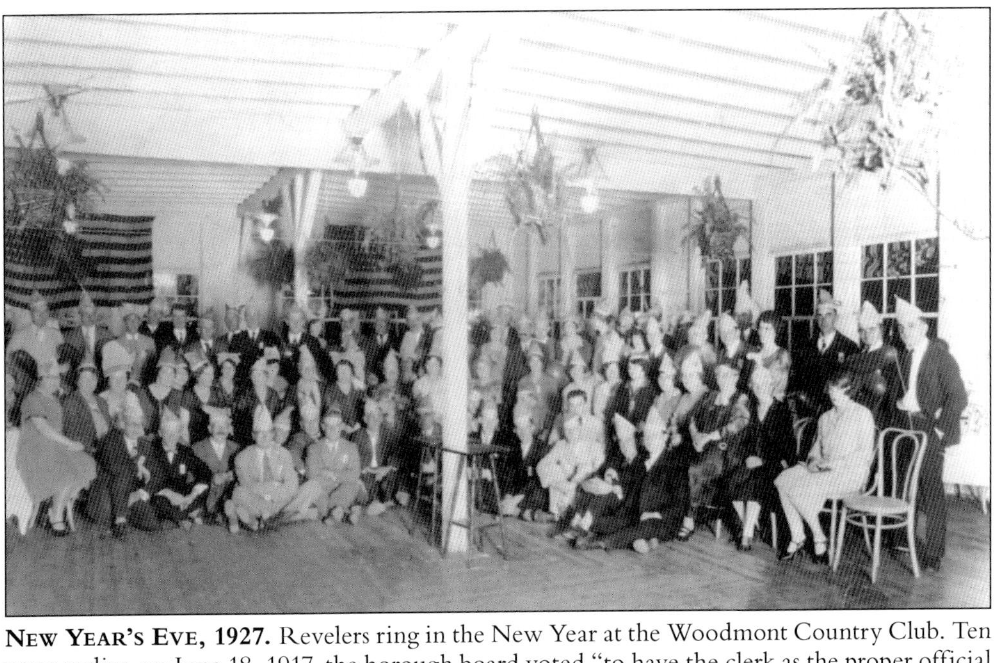

NEW YEAR'S EVE, 1927. Revelers ring in the New Year at the Woodmont Country Club. Ten years earlier, on June 18, 1917, the borough board voted "to have the clerk as the proper official at the Connecticut Company to change the name at the Bonsilene Station to the Country Club Station." (Courtesy of Photography by Joseph.)

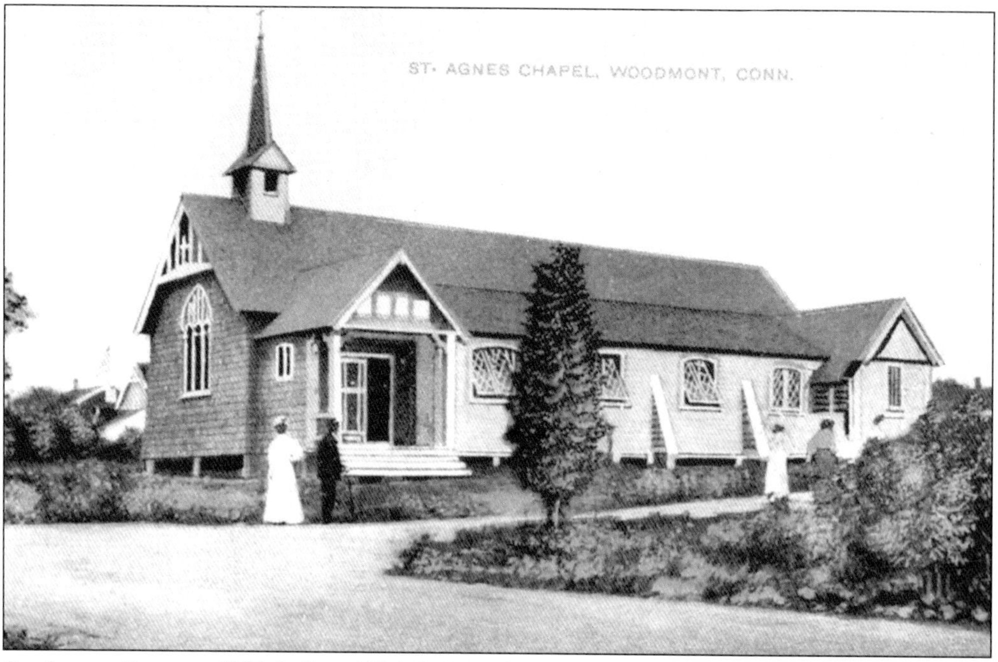

St. Agnes Chapel, 1909. In June 1906, St. Mary's Roman Catholic Church on Gulf Street opened St. Agnes Chapel for the summer parishioners in the eastern end of town. St. Agnes was located on Center Street (today Dixon Street) at the corner of New Haven Avenue (now Kings Highway). In 1951, it was winterized to remain open year-round. This card is postmarked 1909.

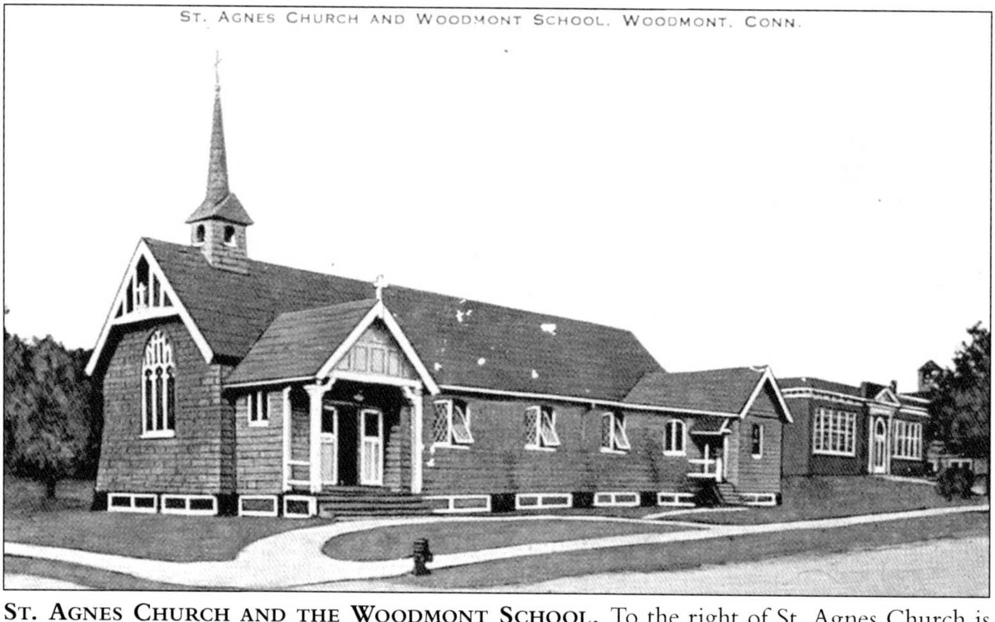

St. Agnes Church and the Woodmont School. To the right of St. Agnes Church is Woodmont's first "modern" school, which opened in 1918 and by 1927 had four rooms. On the other side of the school was the Woodmont Firehouse. Its bell tower is visible to the right of the school.

Six

Earning a Living

A commercial center of Woodmont began to develop on Cherry Street (now Village Road) in the 1890s, with the Woodmont Grocery store and a bicycle shop. There were two tinning, plumbing, and gas fitting establishments, one operated by Werner Gutenberg Sr., a Swiss immigrant, and another by J. A. Hall.

According to an advertisement in a cookbook sponsored by the New Haven Gas Light Company around 1912, the Woodmont Meat and Grocery Company, located directly opposite the post office, offered "choice meats, groceries, vegetables, and fruits, as well as boats and fishing tackle, a full line of kitchen utensils, newspapers, and periodicals." They also boasted a telephone.

The post office was in three different locations on Cherry Street at different times. In later years, Woodmont Meat and Grocery became Petersen's market (now the left side of Scribner's Restaurant), and Hall's plumbing became Clark-Hall Hardware (now the right side of Scribner's). To the right of the hardware store was Susman's department store, where local residents purchased their bathing suits, nose clips, swim masks, and bathing shoes. The local pharmacy, called Lowe's Sea Side Pharmacy, was also on Cherry Street, but closer to the water.

Miss M. A. Gage had a dry goods shop on the corner of Hawley Avenue and Cherry Street, offering fancy goods and notions, and furnishings for men and women. The Woodmont Linen Store on Bath Avenue sold art needlework and materials, gave lessons, and took orders for embroidery and stamping. At different times, Cherry Street had a barbershop, a beauty salon, a bakery, an A&P, a candy store, and a liquor store. Chapman's Sea Food Market in Woodmont advertised itself as a "dealer in all kinds of fresh and salted fish, oysters, and clams. Native lobsters and soft-shell crabs a specialty."

There were several restaurants in later years: the Anchor Restaurant (with Woodmont's only pinball machine), just across from Anchor Beach; Tobak's luncheonette at the corner of Cherry Street and New Haven Avenue (now Kings Highway); and just around the corner, on Hawley Avenue, Kitty Torpy's bar.

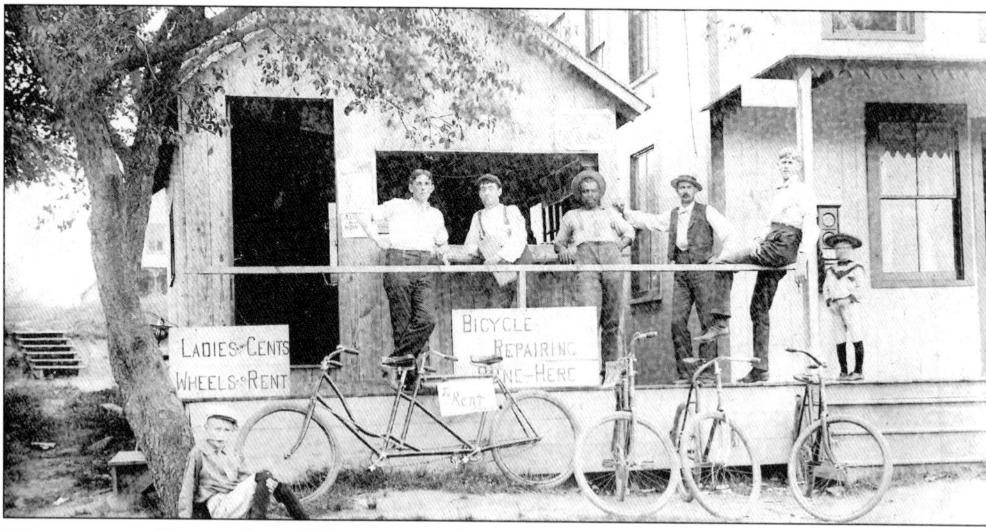

Wheels for Rent. This 1898 photograph shows a bicycle rental and repair shop on Cherry Street (now Village Road) near the corner of New Haven Avenue (now Kings Highway), owned by William S. Clark, then postmaster of Woodmont. "The bicycle was quite the popular thing in the way of transportation as well as a great reducing medium for anyone who might be a little overweight," said George Van Horn, in a letter to the *Milford News*, February 5, 1948. Standing left to right are Van Horn; Henry Hart; the blacksmith; William Clark; William Sturgess; and Tracy Clark, the older brother of Russell Clark. (Courtesy of Milford Historical Society.)

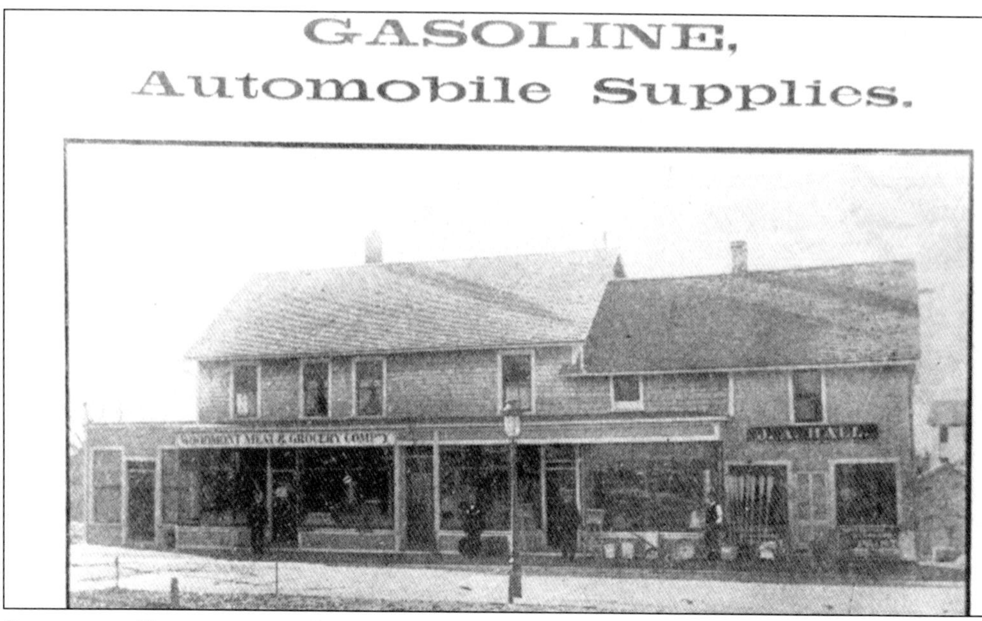

Plumbing, Tinning, and Gas Fitting. This is an advertisement for J. A. Hall Plumbing, Tinning, and Gas Fitting and the Woodmont Grocery and Meat Company, both on Cherry Street "Henry Hart supervised the distribution of the daily newspapers for Mr. John Hall who had a plumbing establishment across the street, and down a little way. Mr. Hart was allowed the use of the large opening and counter at the front of the bicycle shop for his paper business," wrote the February 5, 1948, edition of the *Milford News*. (Courtesy of Photography by Joseph.)

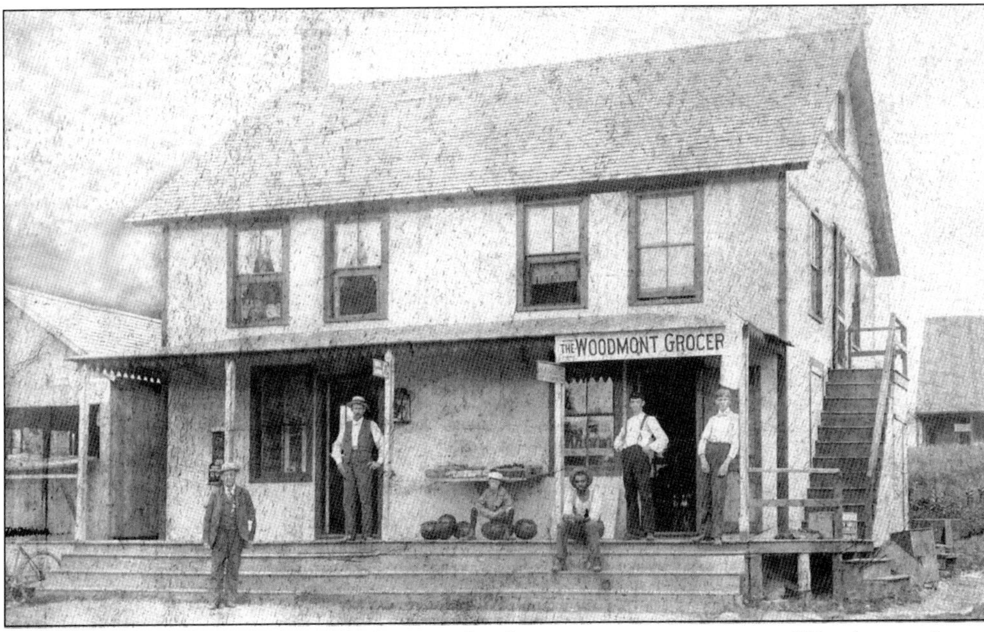

WOODMONT GROCERY, 1898. This was the first grocery store to serve Woodmont. It was located on Cherry Street across the street from what is today Scribner's Restaurant. Some of the same men who were photographed in front of the bicycle rental shop are in this photograph also. This building later became the telegraph and post office. To the left of this building is the bicycle shop. (Courtesy of Milford Historical Society.)

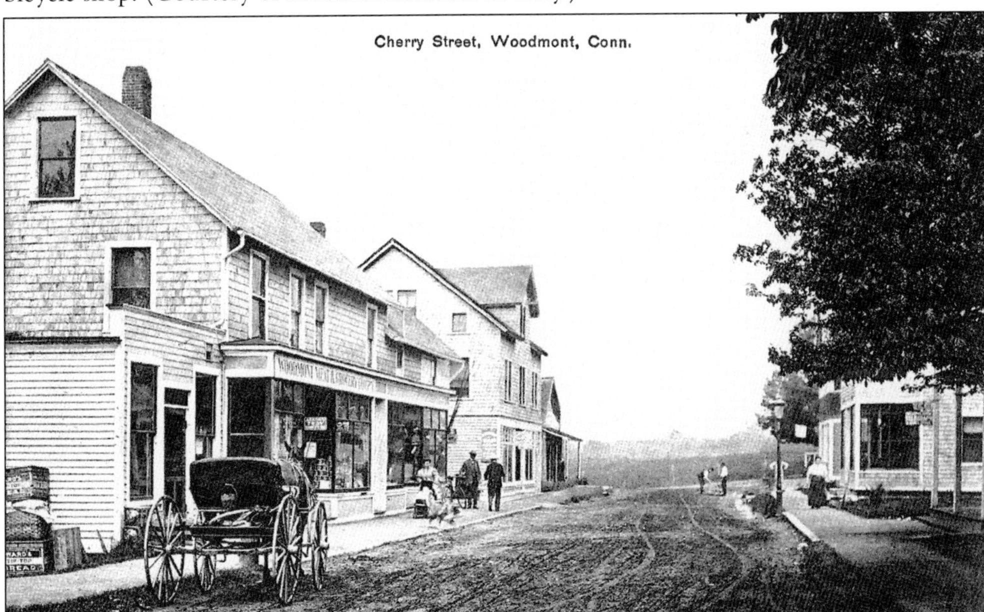

CHERRY STREET, LOOKING WEST. This view shows Cherry Street looking toward New Haven Avenue, with undeveloped fields and farms in the distance. The side-by-side buildings on the left are Woodmont Grocery and Meat and J. A. Hall Plumbing. Years later, Susman's department store was located in the last building on the left. Across the street, partially obscured by trees, is the post and telegraph office.

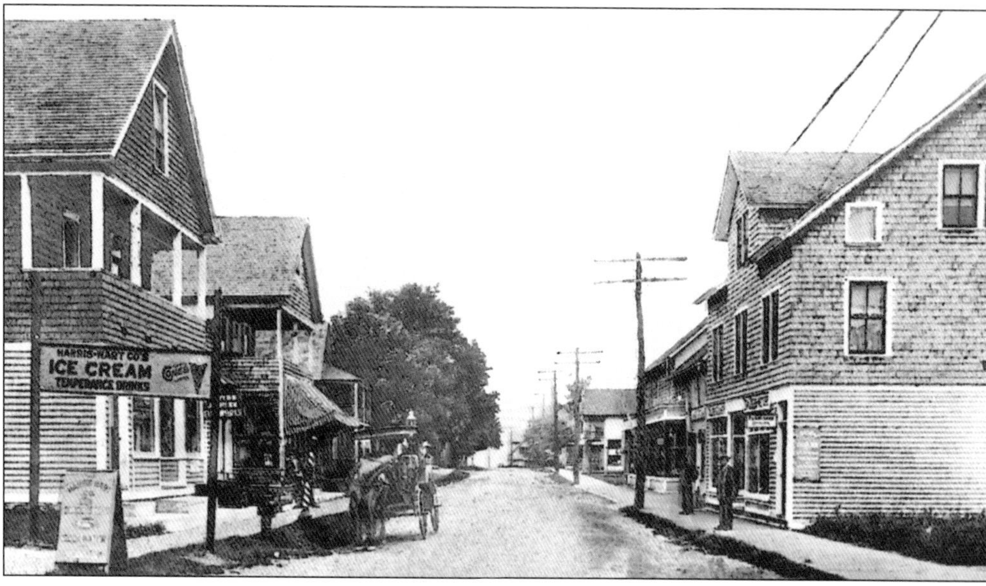

CHERRY STREET, LOOKING EAST. The commercial center of Woodmont was only one block long—Cherry Street (now Village Road) between Hawley Avenue and New Haven Avenue (now Kings Highway). In this photograph, probably around the beginning of the 20th century, Cherry Street had a post and telegraph office, an ice-cream store, a grocery store with a butcher, and a plumbing establishment. A sign on the ice-cream store says "Harris-Hart." In addition to ice-cream cones, they sold temperance drinks (early soft drinks). Today Scribner's Restaurant is located in the buildings that were once Peterson's Market and Clark-Hall Hardware. (Courtesy of Photography by Joseph.)

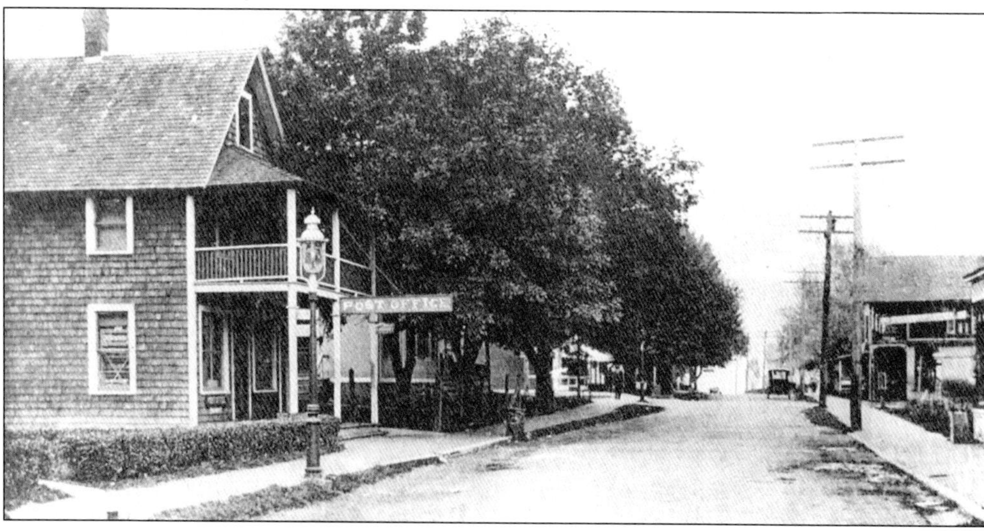

CHERRY STREET POST OFFICE. At the September 12, 1904, borough meeting, "The report of the Committee on Gas Lamps was accepted and it was voted that gas lamps be maintained until the beginning of the regular lighting season at the following places: the Post Office; at Doolittle's Merwin grove; corner of Chapel St and New Haven Ave; Clinton St near Mr. Little's; near Miss Alice Lockwood's; at Park opposite Lindley Bath Avenue–provided that the same be lighted and put out without expense to the Association." Today borough residents enjoy enhanced street lighting. (Courtesy of Photography by Joseph.)

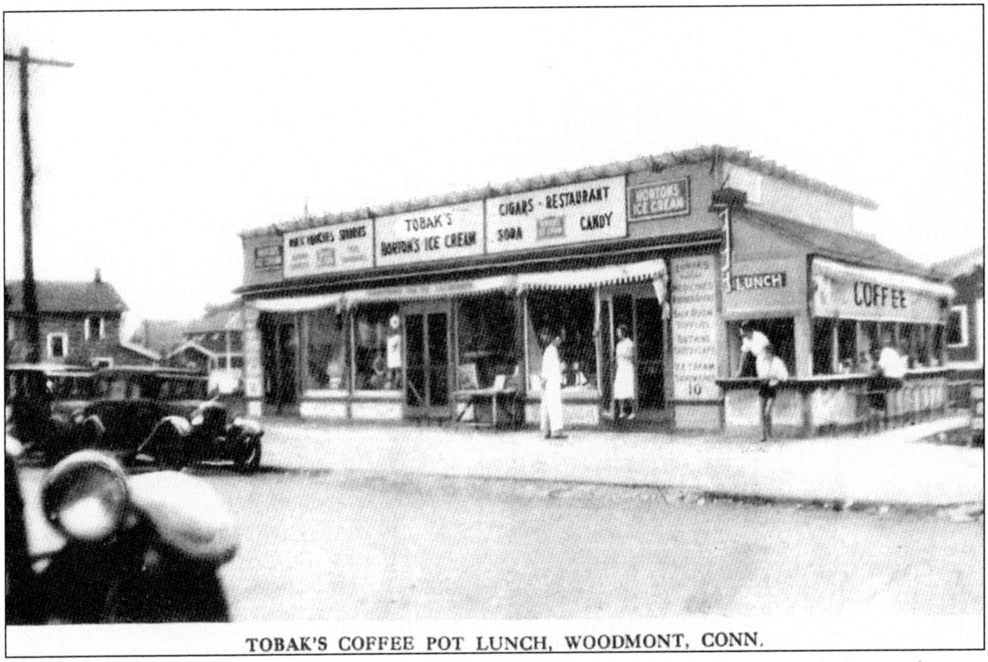

Tobak's Coffee Pot Lunch. Tobak's, a luncheonette owned by M. and V. Tobak, was famous for its hamburgers, french fries, steak sandwiches, and Raz-Lime sodas. It was located on the corner of Cherry Street (now Village Road) and New Haven Avenue (now Kings Highway), and today is a small park. (Courtesy of Joseph Cullen.)

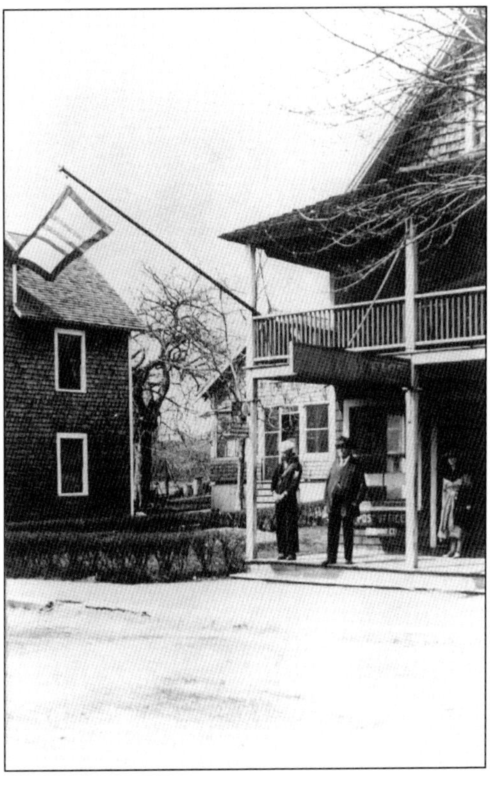

The Woodmont Post Office. This was the original location of the Woodmont Post Office, on the east side of Cherry Street (now Village Road). On March 8, 1918, the borough warden and burgesses held a special meeting to vote for authorization to pay for an honor roll to be erected on Cherry Street, listing the names of borough residents serving in World War I. The vote to pay $347.85 to construct an honor roll was passed unanimously. (Courtesy of Photography by Joseph.)

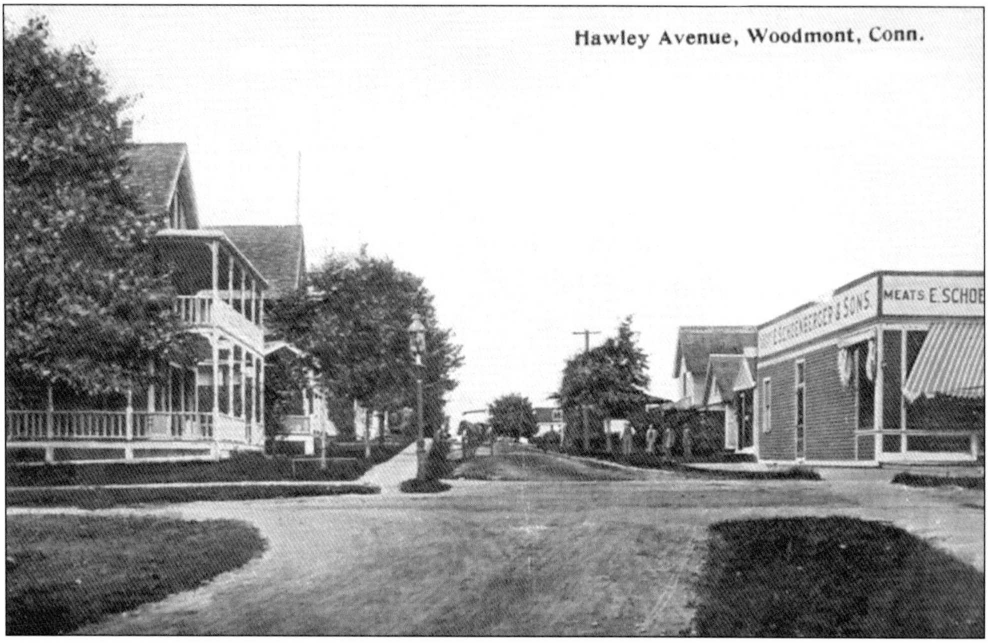

Schoenenberger and Sons, *c.* 1912. At the corner of Cherry Street and Hawley Avenue, another local meat store opened up to give Woodmont Grocery and Meat some competition, seen here around 1912. In the 1930s or 1940s, this building became the post office's second location on Cherry Street. Today a duplex house is on this site.

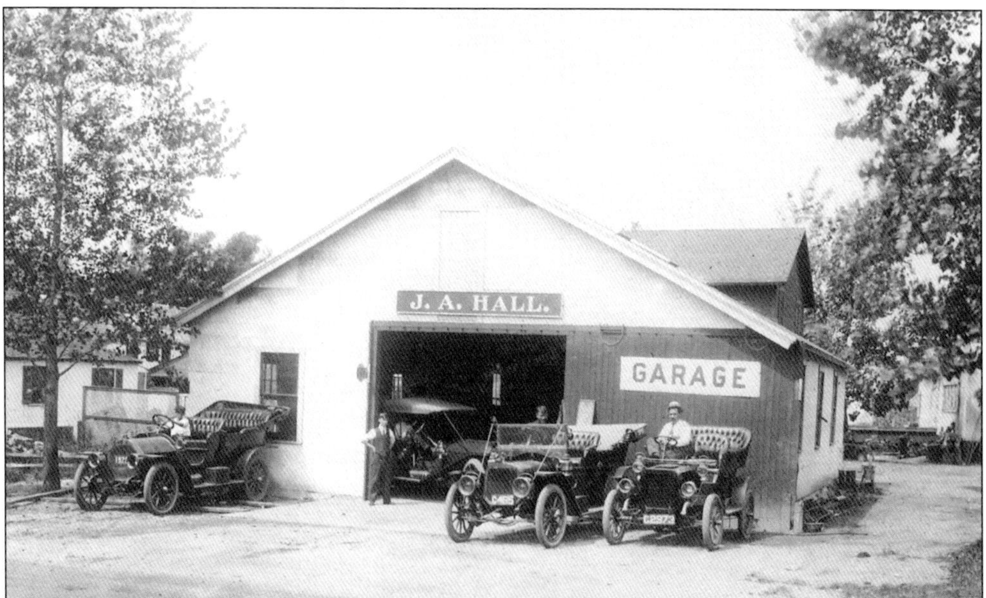

J. A. Hall Garage. From around the 1930s to the 1950s, the J. A. Hall Garage was located on Hawley Avenue between Cherry Street and Beach Avenue. It is possible that was also the location for an earlier garage, the Woodmont Livery and Garage, whose proprietor, H. R. Kellogg, advertised, "Automobiles stored, gasoline, and oils supplied, house painting, repairs and jobs, care of lawns, general storage, boarding stables, expressing, and moving, and all trains met." (Courtesy of Photography by Joseph.)

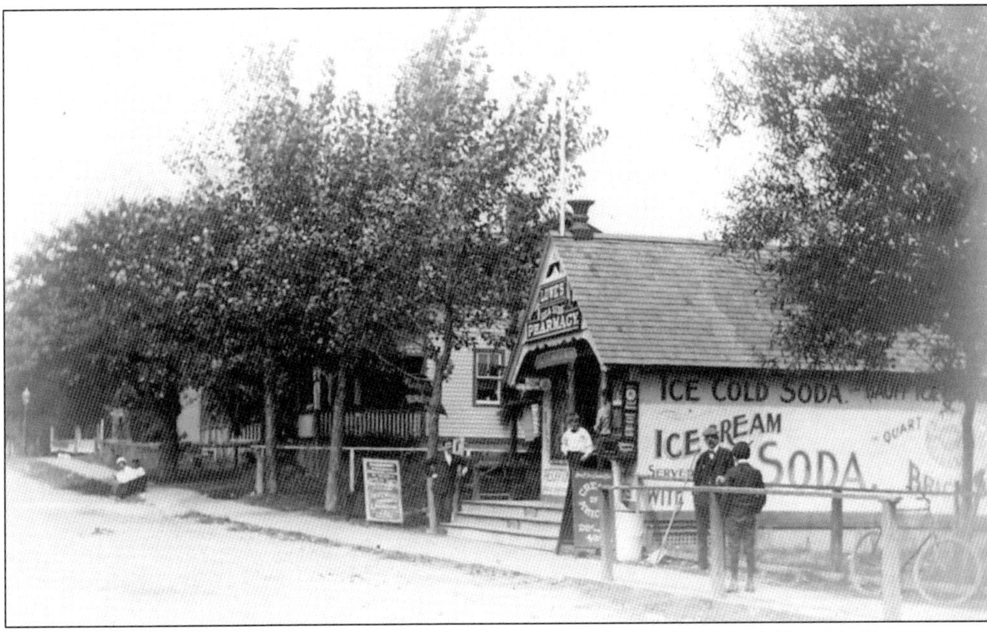

SOUVENIRS SOLD HERE. Around 1912, the advertising slogan for Lowe's Seaside Pharmacy on lower Cherry Street was "Lest You Forget," and they offered a large assortment of Woodmont souvenirs; Huyler's, Bell's, and Belle Mead sweet chocolates; and Seamon's ice cream (delivered anywhere at anytime). They also sold "everything in the drug line," and prescriptions were "carefully compounded." To the left of the pharmacy was the Woodmont Inn, now a private home.

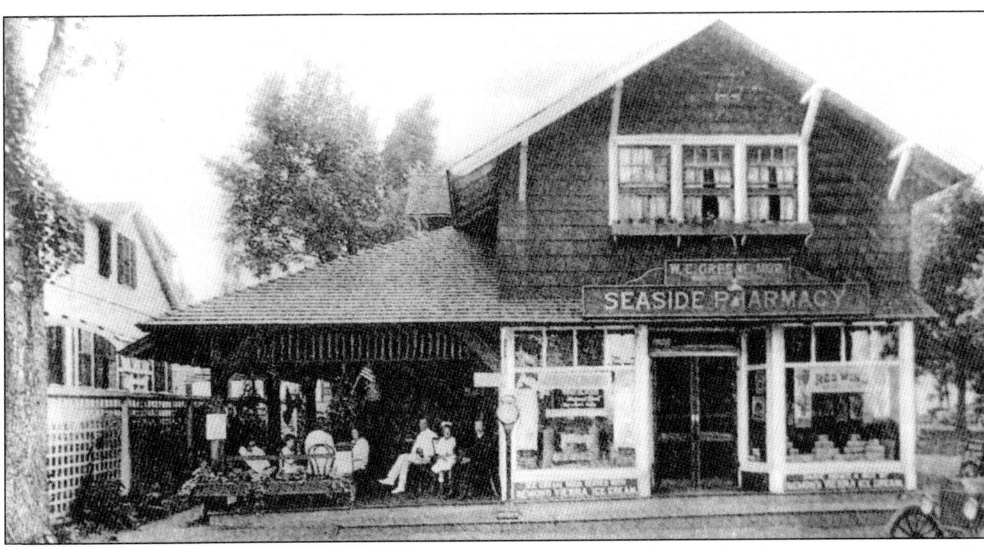

LOWE'S SEASIDE PHARMACY. Seen here in a later view, Lowe's Seaside Pharmacy was a popular for its soda fountain and sandwich shop, as well as prescription drugs, other common drugstore items, magazines, comic books, and beach paraphernalia. It was later known as Seaside Pharmacy and Woodmont Seaside Pharmacy. Said George Peacock, who grew up in Woodmont, "Doc Nolan, the pharmacist (and Woodmont warden) took care of a lot of minor illnesses; his soda fountain, display of comic books, and candy took care of whatever else was bothering a kid."

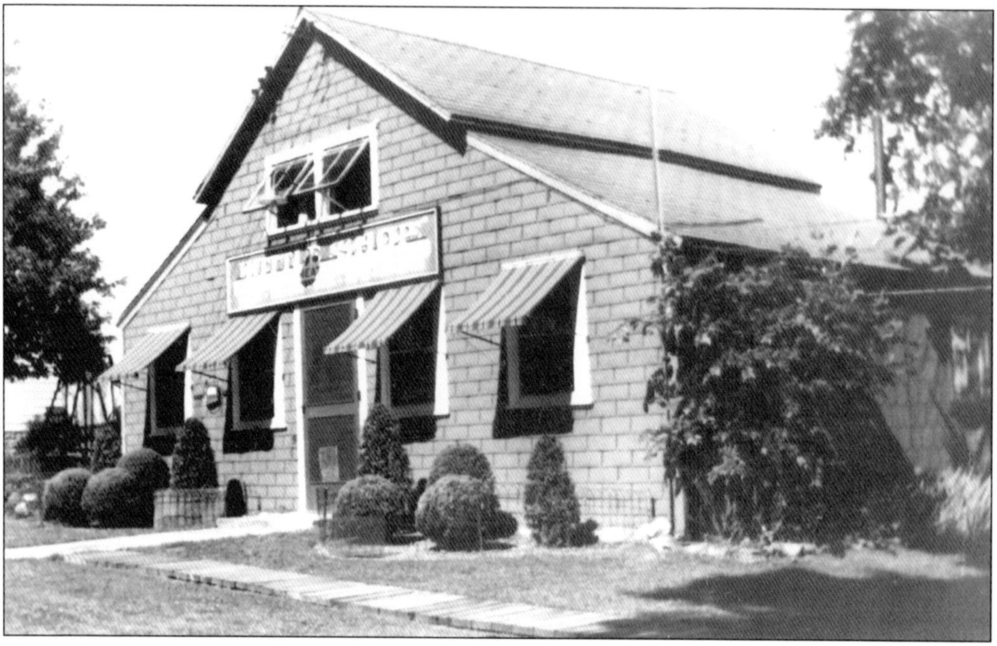

THE KITTLE SHOP. One of Woodmont's early convenience stores was the Kittle Shop, at the corner of Anderson and Hawley Avenues, run by Ernestine and George Kittle, from about the 1920s to the early 1960s. It sold milk, juice, soda, baby food, cold cuts, newspapers, and daily necessities, as well as candy, toys, and baseball cards. Before it became a mini grocery store, the Kittle Shop had been a tearoom, serving lunch and light refreshments to summer visitors. (Courtesy of Photography by Joseph.)

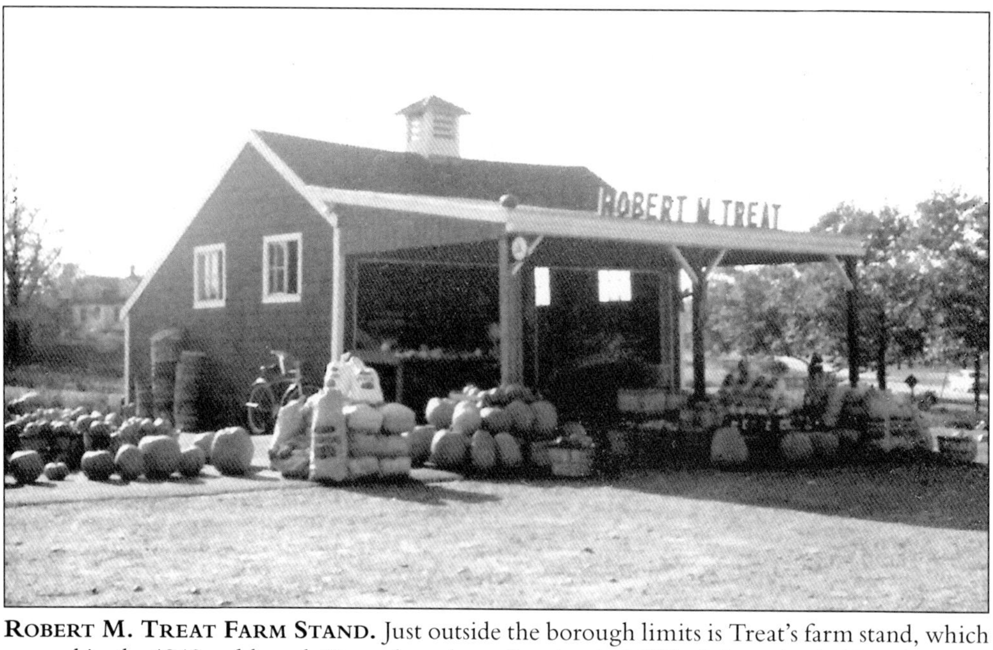

ROBERT M. TREAT FARM STAND. Just outside the borough limits is Treat's farm stand, which opened in the 1940s, although Treats have been farming in Milford since the 1600s. The stand was opened by Robert "Bear" M. Treat. The Treat family is still farming, and the stand has become a popular and well-respected garden center and produce market.

Seven

Street Scenes of Bygone Days

"Woodmont-on-the-Sound is known to everybody in Connecticut as a beautiful shore resort where hundreds of cottagers spend their summers and where leaders of society in Hartford, New Haven, Bridgeport, and other cities and towns of the state meet annually to enjoy the cooling breezes, the beautiful natural scenery, and a most delightful and somewhat exclusive society," read the *Saturday Chronicle* on August 22, 1903.

Progress came quickly. The first telephones were installed in Milford in 1881, and the Merwin Point House advertised in 1884 that "telephone connections will be completed early in the season." Woodmont had gas piped in from New Haven in 1901 to light its streets and homes.

A 1906 *Saturday Chronicle* stated that "Woodmont enjoys many of the modern privileges. Public water was introduced several years ago by the Milford Water Company and hydrants were put in by the company. It was between four and five years ago that the New Haven Gas Company ran pipes to Woodmont. It is used extensively for cooking as well as lighting. There are seventy gas lights on the streets—twelve of which are used all the year round, as between fifteen and twenty families now have their permanent homes there."

In September 1922, Woodmont's warden and burgesses voted "to install electric street lights in the Borough, to begin January 1, 1923 for five years in accordance with a contract submitted by the United Illuminating Co." And a year later, they voted "to approve the agreement made by the former Warden and the New Haven Gas Light Company, the Gas Light Company to take up all lamp posts and cart them away for the price of $3 each."

In many ways, however, Woodmont—perhaps because of its seasonal nature—was slower to adopt many of the modern conveniences. Most of the borough streets were not paved until after World War I. The horse barns and outhouses behind many of the cottages remained in use long after cars and indoor plumbing became common. The minutes of the borough meeting on November 8, 1904, stated that "the clerk was instructed to notify Mrs. E. Beach Clark that the outhouse between her cottage and that of her daughter is a nuisance and that the same must be removed on or before May 1, 1905."

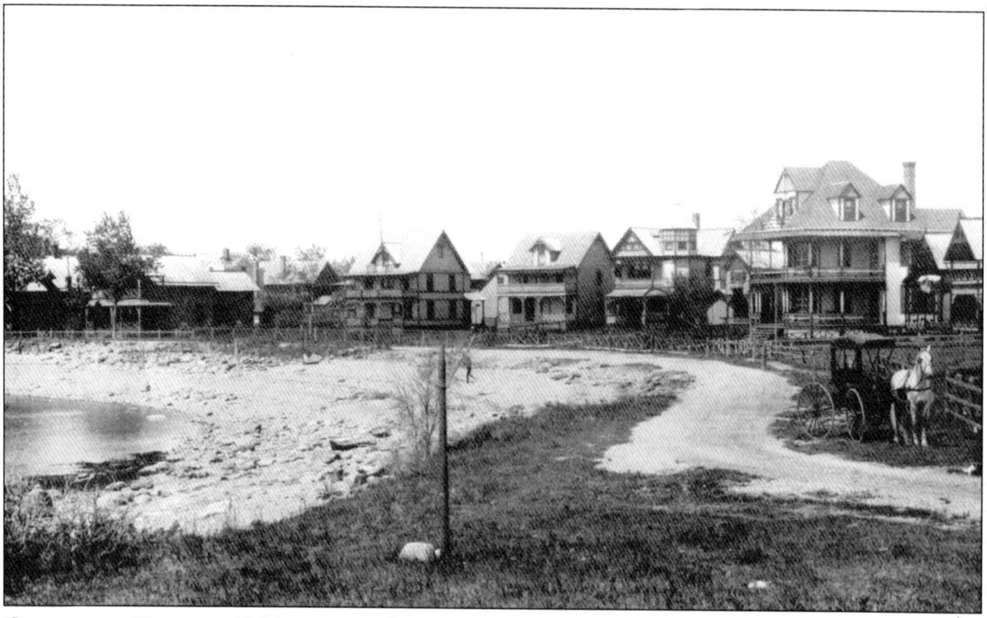

CRESCENT BEACH, 1890S. One of the earliest recorded views of cottages along Crescent Beach, this photograph shows Beach Avenue when it was just a dirt path for horses and carriages. (Courtesy of New Haven Museum and Historical Society.)

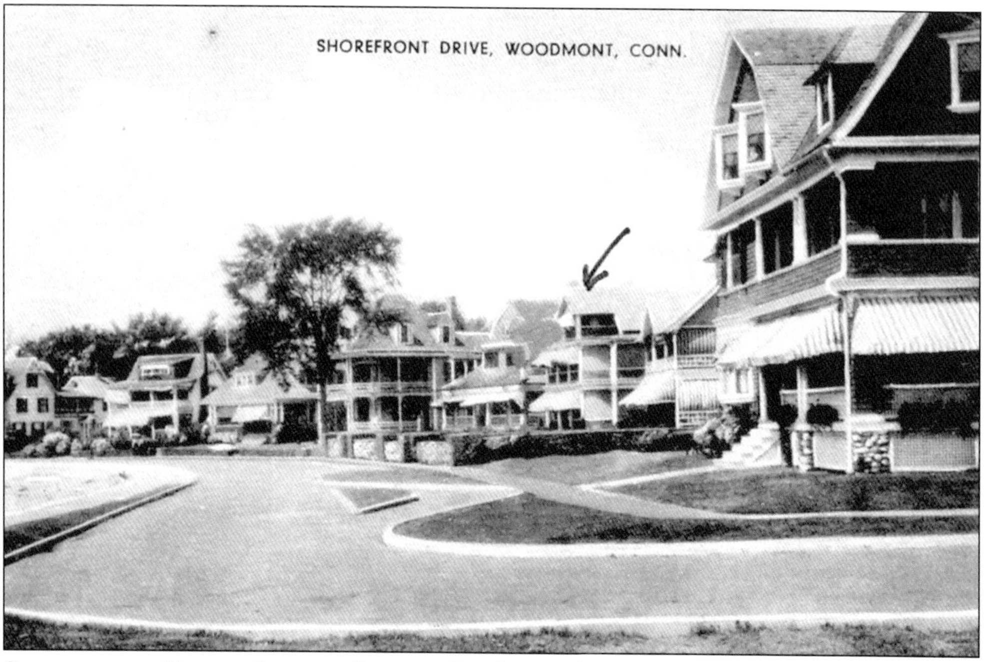

SHOREFRONT DRIVE. Just past Crescent Beach, Beach Avenue curves around the Blakeslee House. This postcard, mailed in 1944, is a similar view of the photograph above, and it shows the remarkable development that took place in the ensuing 50 years. Mailed to Miss Grant of New York City, the short message said, "Greetings from the politician." As it was unsigned, presumably Grant knew the identity of the sender.

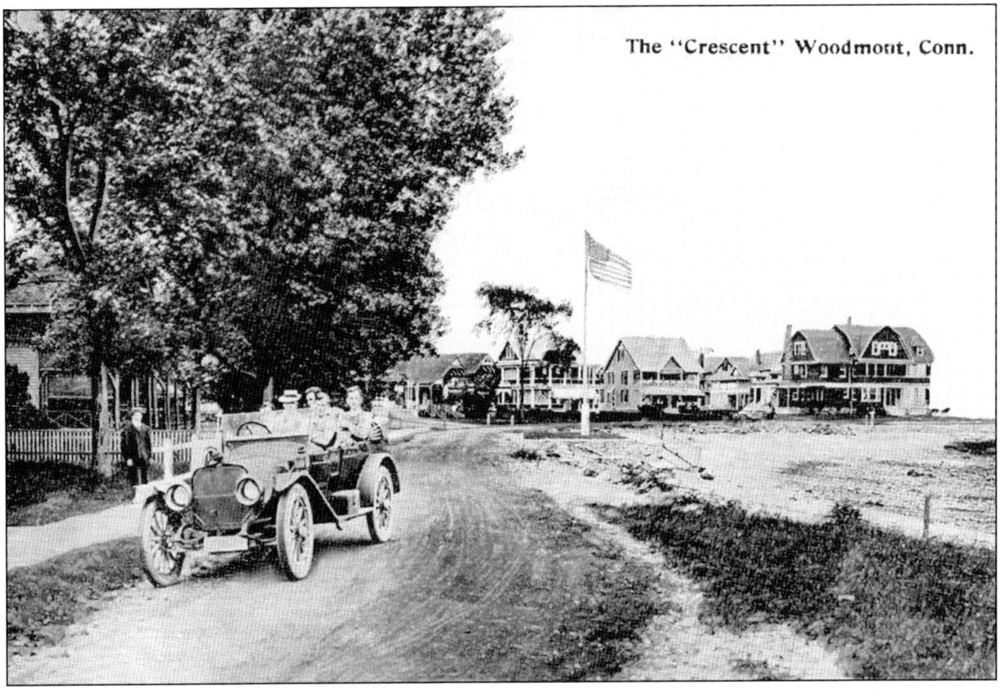

CONVERTIBLE ON THE CRESCENT, *c.* 1915. Early cars were exciting to some and a nuisance to others. Around 1905 or 1906, the first automobiles began to been seen in Woodmont, "raising enough dust and creating enough noise to scare the horses and citizens for blocks around." On July 28, 1910, the borough board "voted to oil Beach Avenue (the Crescent)" to keep the dust down." (Courtesy of George Peacock.)

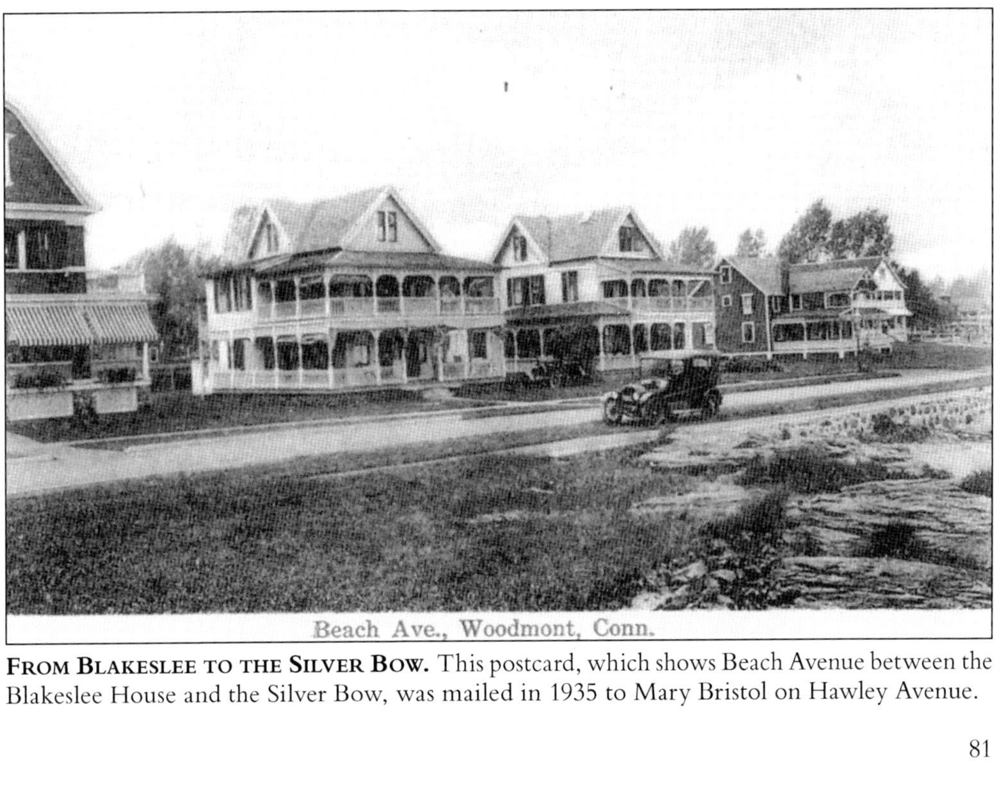

FROM BLAKESLEE TO THE SILVER BOW. This postcard, which shows Beach Avenue between the Blakeslee House and the Silver Bow, was mailed in 1935 to Mary Bristol on Hawley Avenue.

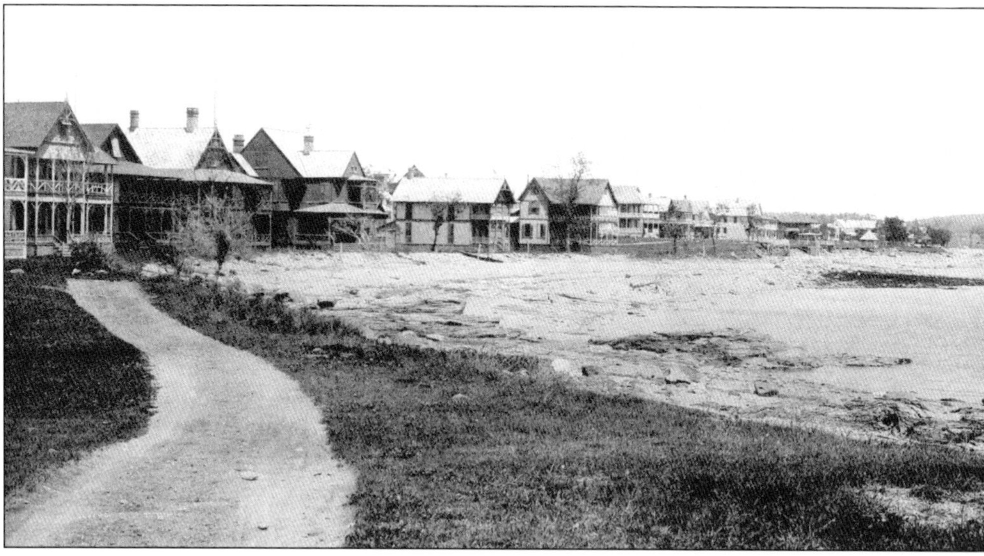

VIEWS OF COTTAGES AT WOODMONT. This photograph, taken in the 1890s, shows the cottages on the water between Chapel Street and Clinton Street. This area was subject to erosion from storms, and on September 8, 1905, the borough officials voted "that the Warden obtain from Civil Engineer H. J. Kellogg estimates for a sea-wall and walk extending along the shore from a point near the foot of Main Street [today Chapel Street] to a point near the foot of Clinton Street." (Courtesy of New Haven Museum and Historical Society.)

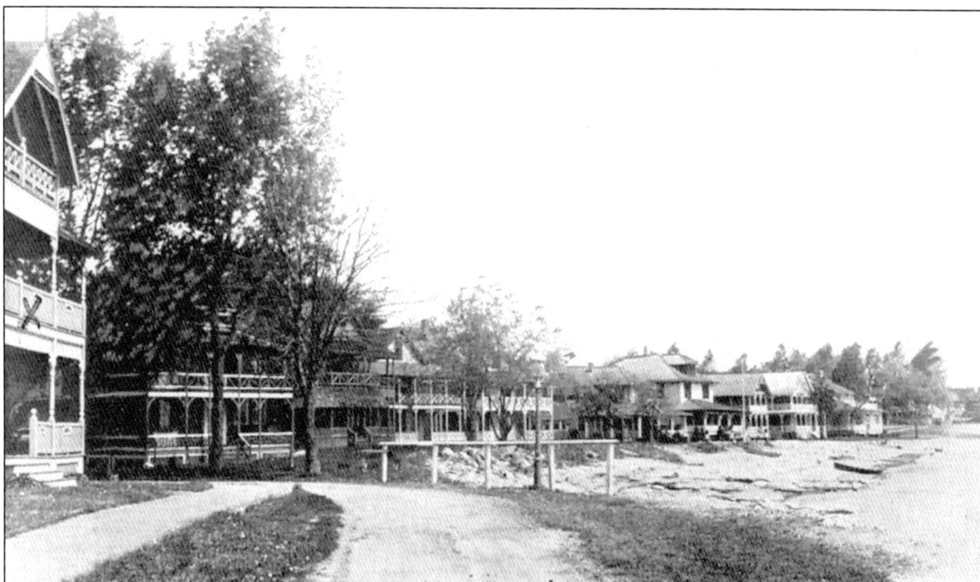

BEACH AVENUE, Woodmont, Conn.

TAKING THE TURN BY THE SILVER BOW. A later view of the photograph above shows part of the Silver Bow Hotel on the left, where Beach Avenue takes a sharp left turn and continues for two blocks behind the waterfront houses between Chapel and Clinton Streets. The borough was still getting estimates. On September 12, 1910, the borough "voted that a survey be made for a proposed Sea Wall from Clinton Avenue to Chapel Street and an approximate cost be obtained."

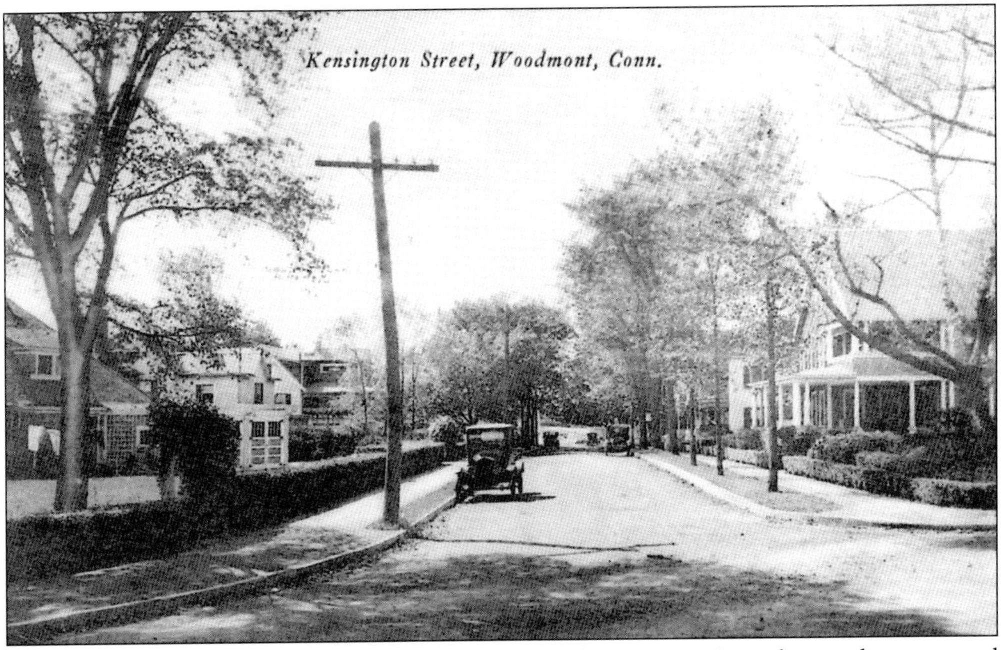

Kensington Street. This street was originally part of Kensington Street but was later renamed Blackall Road after a well-known family that lived on Beach Avenue for many years, with the back of their house on Blackall Road. Today there are about 820 houses or apartments in the borough, and only about 30 of them are still considered seasonal or recreational. (Courtesy of George Peacock.)

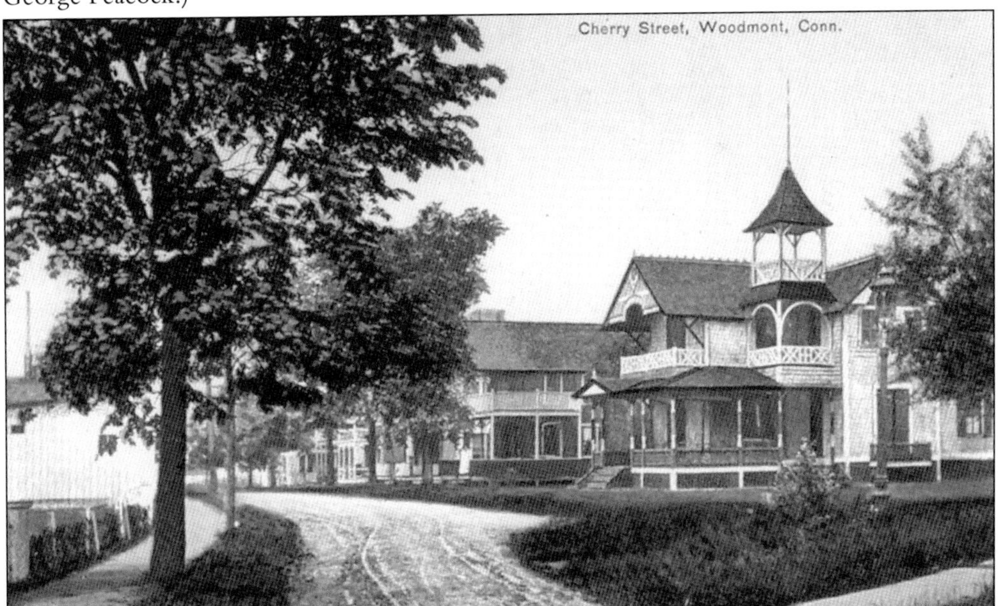

Cherry Street. As more and more cottages were constructed, the borough needed to take responsibility for safety and sanitation. Early in January 1904, when the borough was less than a year old, its governing board—a warden and board of burgesses—voted "that a committee be appointed by the Warden to make a contract for the collection of night soil, garbage, ashes, and lighting and care of the lamps."

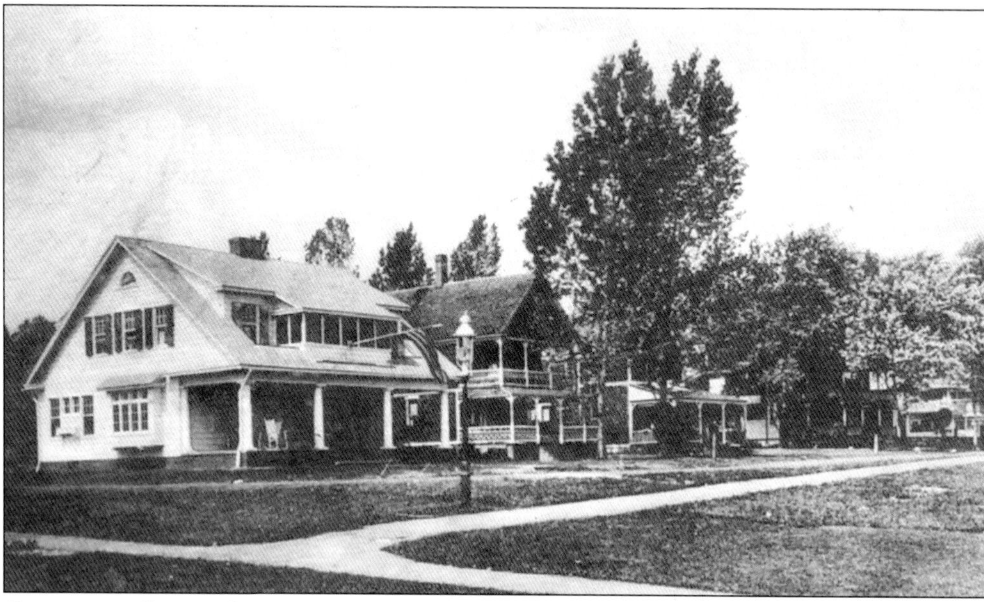

CORNER OF BEACH AVENUE AND CLINTON STREET. Beach Avenue makes a sharp left curve at the foot of Clinton Street This house later belonged to Milford judge Abraham Markle and has been in the family for nearly 60 years. It is now owned by his daughter.

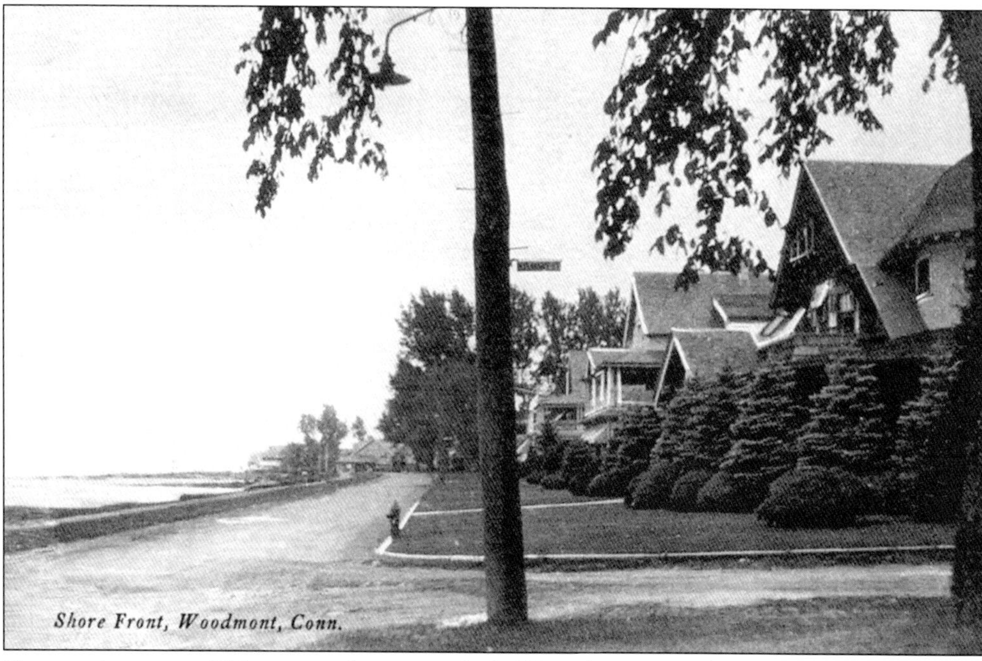

BEACH AVENUE. This postcard, postmarked 1934, shows Beach Avenue looking toward Milford. This narrow parcel of land was appropriated by the borough long before it was paved and populated with houses. According to the borough minutes of November 19, 1903, "The clerk reported that he had seen Mr. Usher and Mr. Devol with regard to strip of land between Beach Avenue and the Sound and they had agreed to give the land as part of the road."

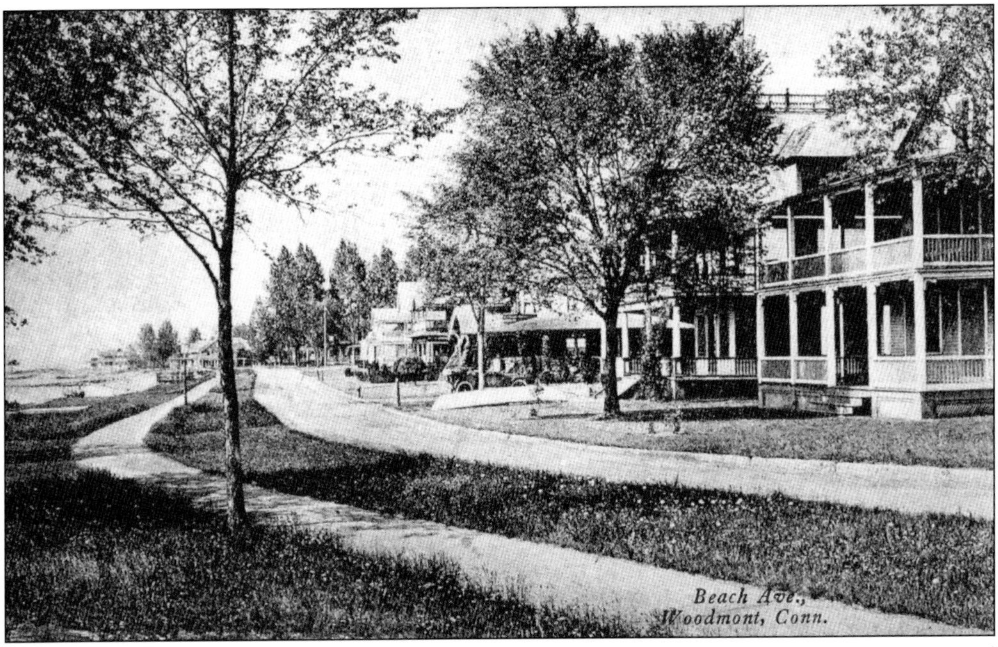

Looking West on Beach Avenue. The cottage at the right of this photograph was named I Love View. The photograph shows Beach Avenue, with the stone house in view just beyond the overturned boat and the car parked on Belmont Street, in the center of the picture. The Umbrella Tree is barely visible in the far distance on the left.

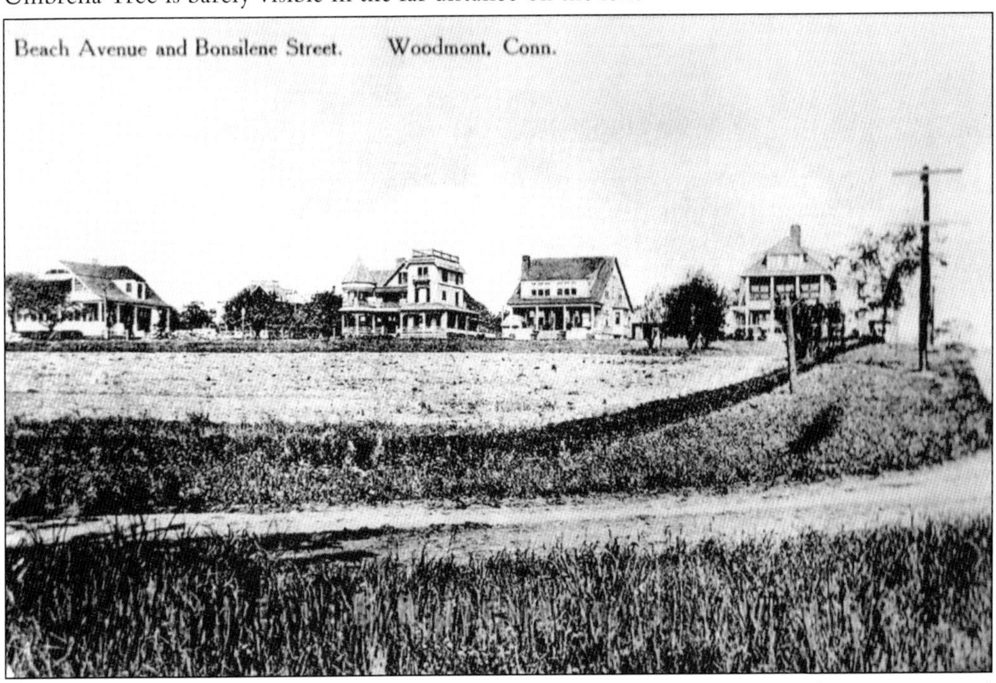

The Hawley Avenue Park. This block of land between Beach and Hawley Avenues, and between Clark Street (now Wall Street) and Bonsilene Street, has always been an open park and was once called Howard Park. In the 1970s, the park was renamed Trubee J. Doolittle Park in memory of the longtime borough secretary. (Courtesy of Photography by Joseph.)

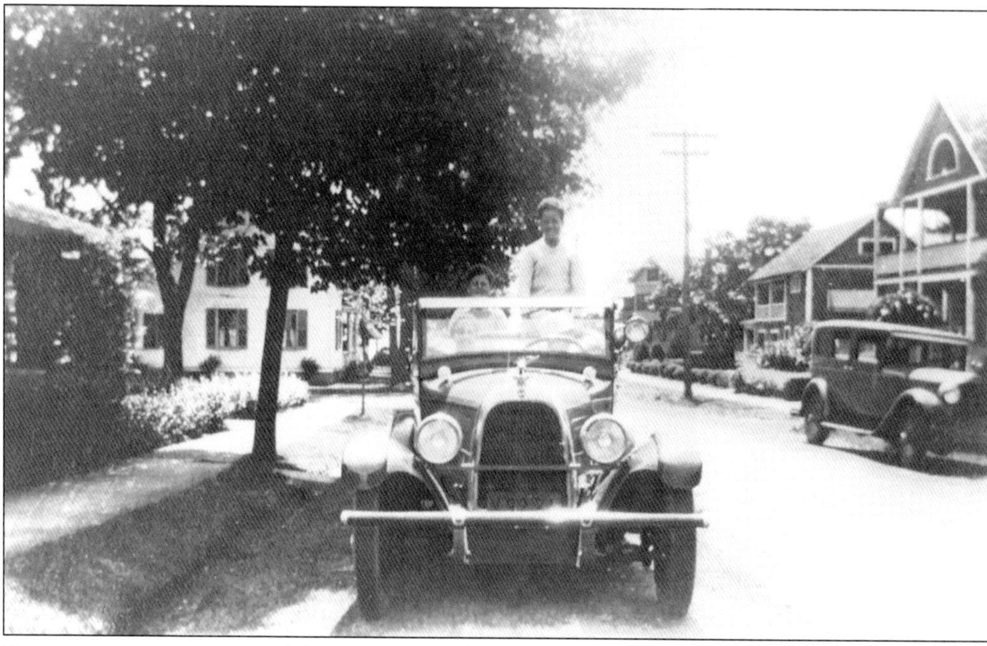

PARKING THE MACHINE. This car is parked in front of 8 Chapel Street. On June 17, 1918, the Woodmont board voted "to have the sheriff instructed to request all persons with automobiles standing more than five minutes on streets where no parking is allowed, to move on, and if they refuse to do so, take their number and their driver's license number." (Courtesy of Photography by Joseph.)

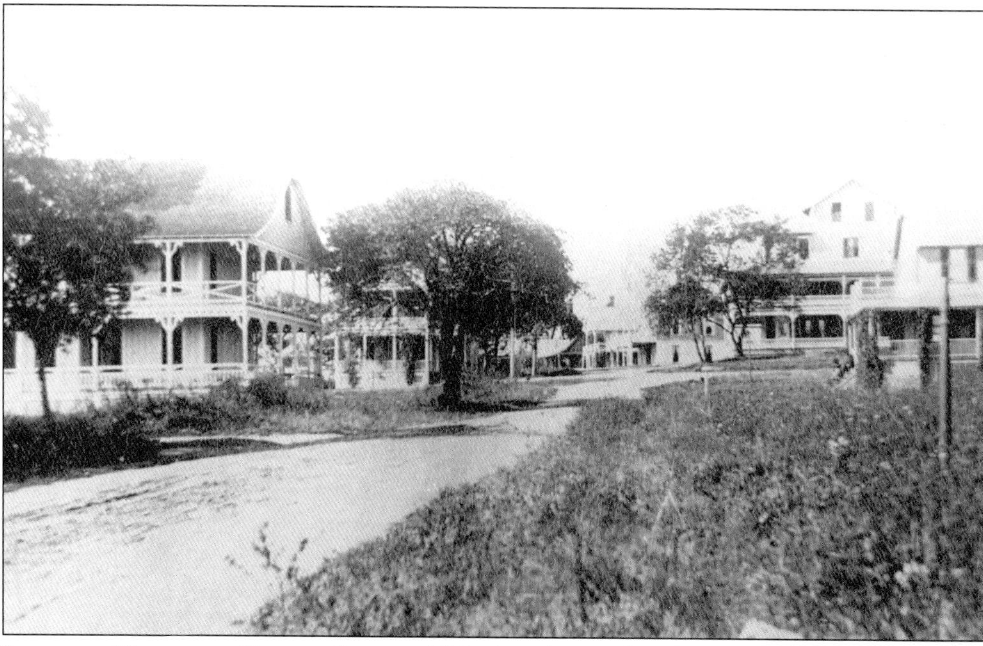

LOOKING NORTH ON CHAPEL STREET. This view shows Chapel Street where it intersects with Hawley Avenue. Chapel Street was the main road into West Haven and New Haven before the New Haven Avenue bypass was constructed around 1930. The Pembroke Hotel is on the right. (Courtesy of Joseph Cullen.)

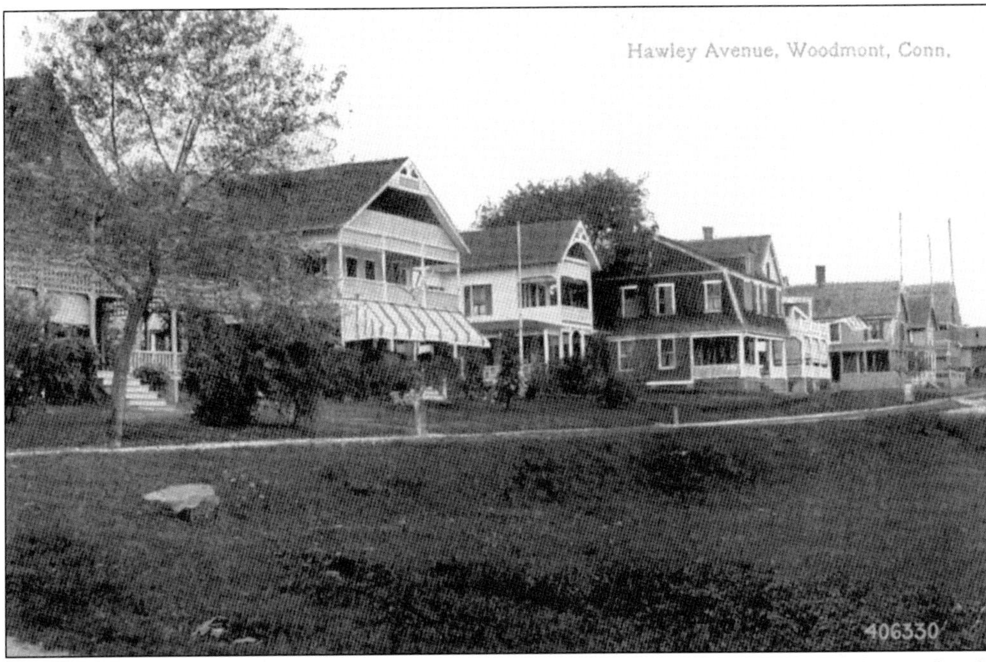

EARLY HAWLEY AVENUE. Early in the 20th century, houses were primarily on the north side of Hawley Avenue, with meadows between them and the water. In 1915, the borough voted "to arrange for house numbering in the limits of the Woodmont Association . . . the even numbers on the right hand side of the street and the odd numbers on the left hand side." This postcard is postmarked 1913.

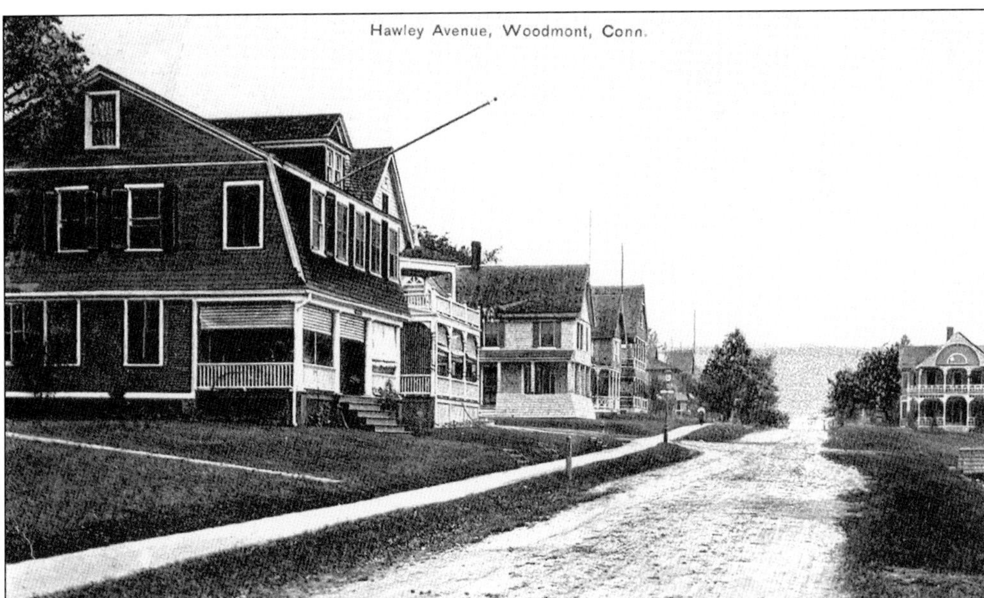

HAWLEY AVENUE. The illustrator who colorized this original postcard took some artistic license—he added Long Island Sound in the background. The only problem is that Long Island Sound is not at the end of Hawley Avenue, it was at the end of the cross streets! The gingerbread house on the right is also seen at the top of page 42.

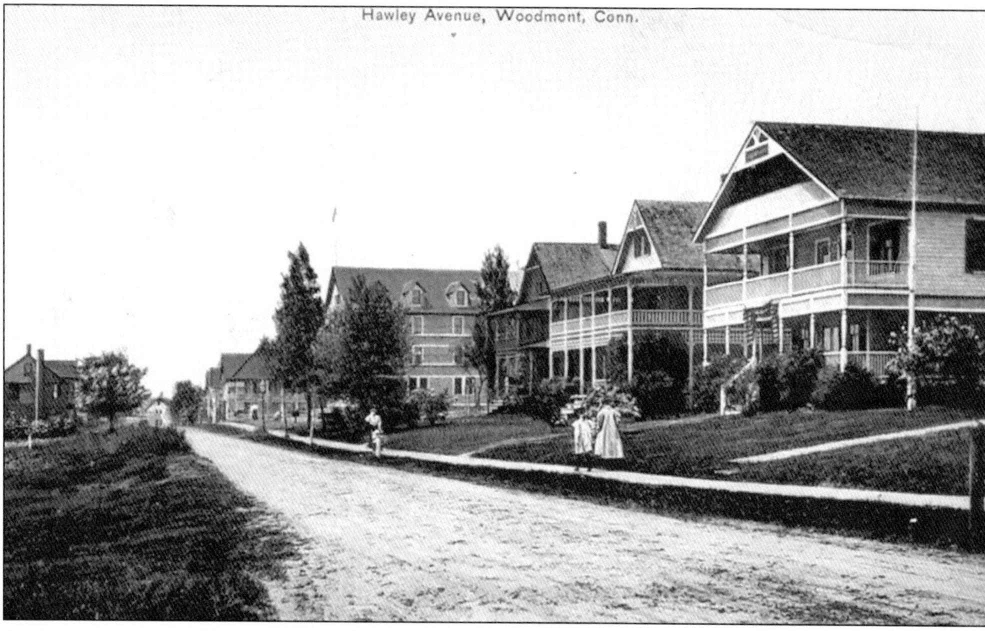

A View of the Pembroke. Looking down Hawley Avenue toward Anchor Beach, the Pembroke Hotel is visible in the center of the photograph. Again, there are very few homes on the south side of Hawley Avenue. This may have been shortly after Vue de L'eau Avenue was renamed Hawley Avenue.

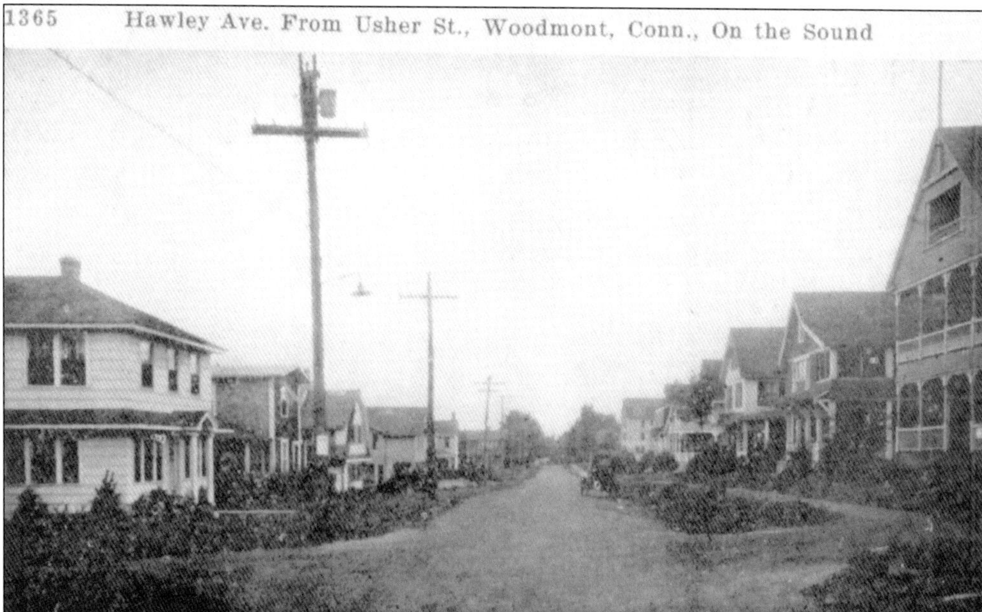

Hawley and Usher. This cottage at the corner of Hawley Avenue and Usher Street was built in the 1920s and was converted to year-round use after World War II. The view, looking down Hawley Avenue to the west, shows many more cottages on the south side of Hawley Avenue. In 1923, the borough voted "to give the Southern New England Telephone Company permission to set poles on Hawley Avenue, provided they get consent from the adjoining property owners." (Courtesy of Cable Postcard Collection, Antiquarian and Landmarks Society.)

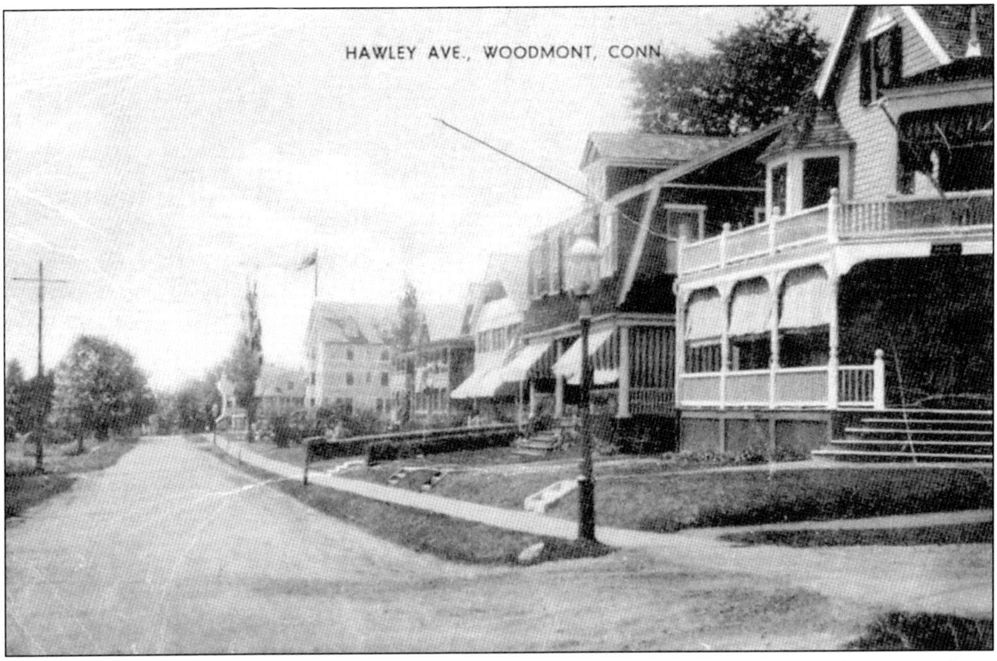

THE MAG COTTAGE AND THE PEMBROKE. This view of Hawley Avenue is looking west from Clinton Street. The house on the corner belonged to Meriden attorney I. Henry Mag. The cottage to its left was the Fitzsimons. In the distance, the Pembroke Hotel is visible. A close-up of the Mag cottage can be seen at the bottom of page 35.

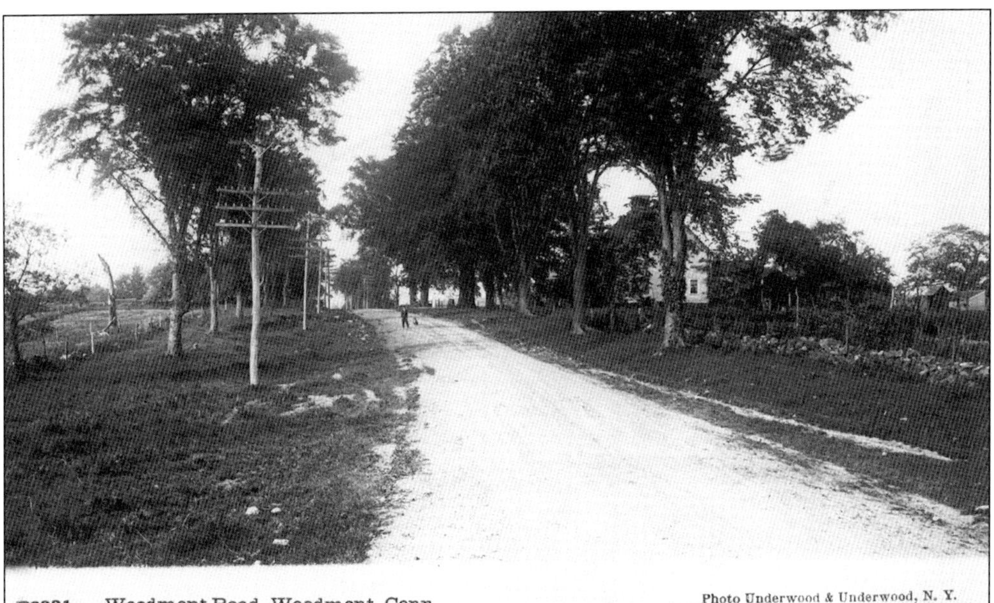

WOODMONT ROAD. This is a very early view of Woodmont Road, with acres of undeveloped land and an occasional house along tree-lined dirt roads. It might have been Chapel Street by the Treat farmhouse, heading into the borough, or it might have been what is now Depot Road, which led to the train station. (Courtesy of Cable Postcard Collection, Antiquarian and Landmarks Society.)

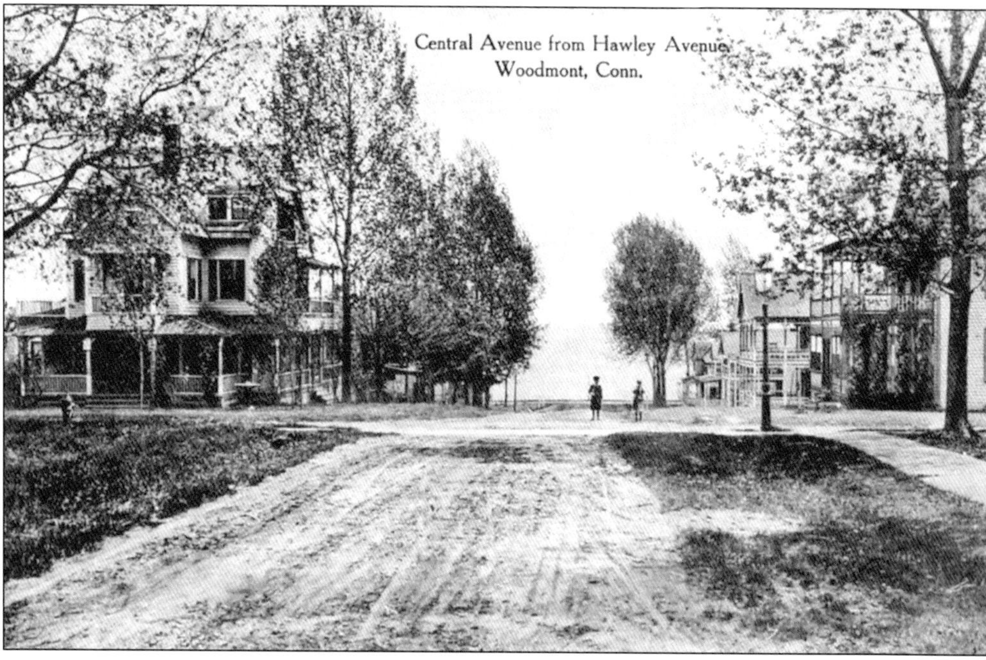

MAILED ON THE FOURTH OF JULY. This postcard, mailed on the Fourth of July, year unknown, shows Central Avenue (now Dunbar Road), where it intersects with Hawley Avenue. A close-up of the cottage on the left can be seen at the bottom of page 42. The streetlamps were still gas, as electric streetlights did not begin to be installed in the borough until 1923.

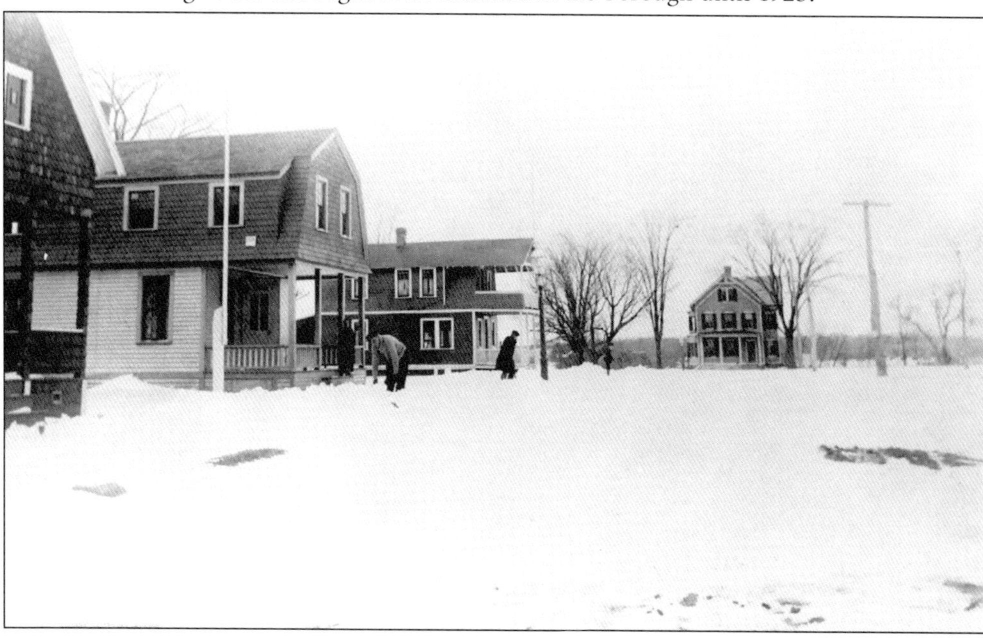

WINTER IN WOODMONT. This photograph of Central Avenue (Dunbar Road) was taken on Easter Sunday, April 4, 1915. The three houses (from left to right) are 13 and 17 Dunbar Road and 106 New Haven Avenue (now Kings Highway). The New Haven Avenue house (featured in the 1920 real estate advertisement in chapter 2) was built in 1868. (Courtesy of Photography by Joseph.)

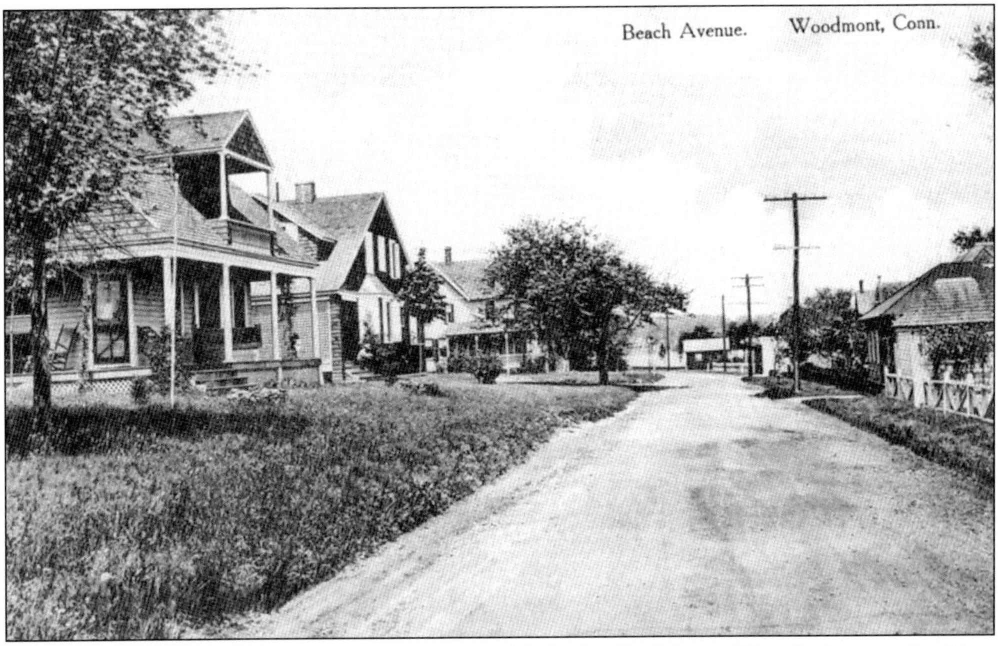

The Last Stretch of Beach Avenue. This is the final leg of Beach Avenue, looking east, as it winds its way from the Hawley Avenue Park past Green Street (now Swift Street) to its beginning at the foot of Spencer Street. This section of Beach Avenue runs behind the waterfront houses. This picture was taken around the 1930s.

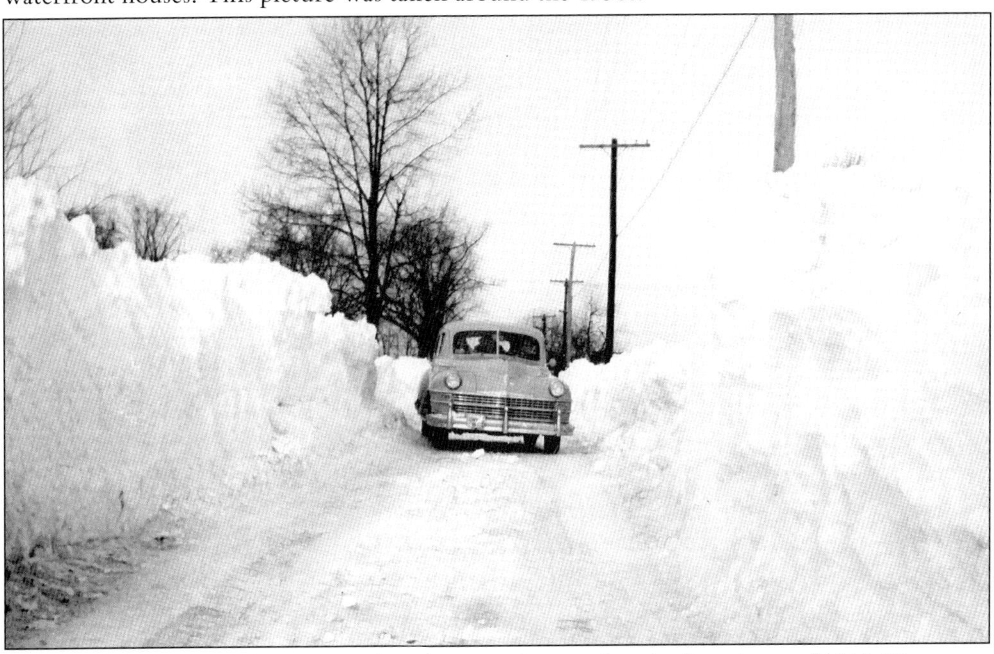

The Same Scene in Winter. This photograph was taken in the winter of 1946. Years ago, the borough would often close some of the streets—such as Central Avenue, Devol Street, and Belmont Street—so children could go sledding down the hills toward the beach. Being on the coast, Woodmont was sometimes spared from some of the large blizzards, but was clobbered, like the rest of Connecticut, during the great blizzard of 1978. (Courtesy of Kristina Sancher.)

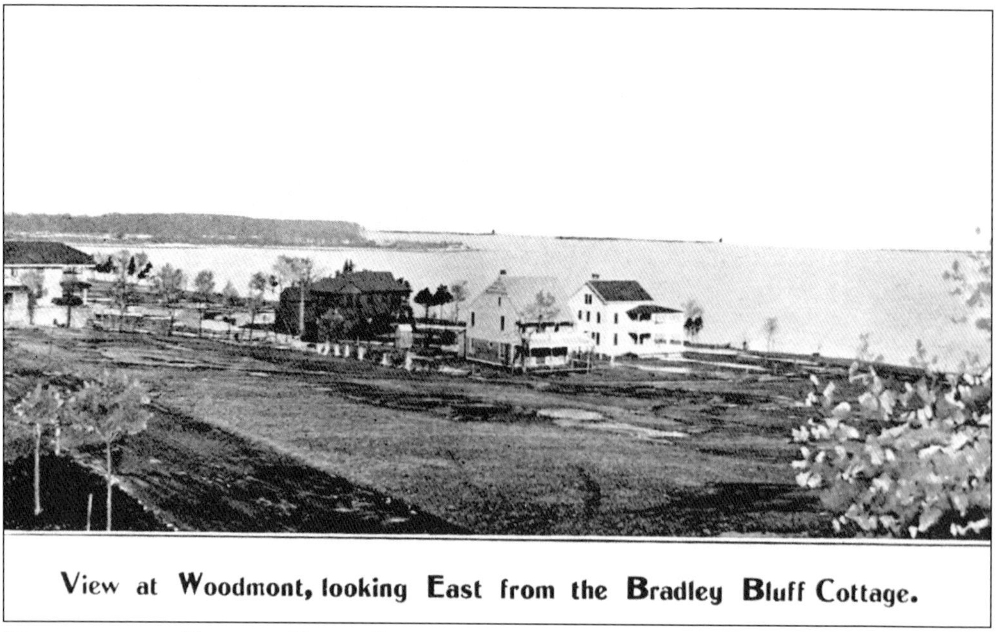

VIEW FROM THE BRADLEY BLUFF COTTAGE. A 1903 *Saturday Chronicle* advertisement described the Bradley Bluff Cottage as "overlooking the Sound at a delightful elevation." Proprietors E. M. Bradley and his brother claimed, "This resort is especially suited to the taste of those seeking rest and quiet. Perfect drainage. Cuisine under the supervision of the proprietor, who is bred to the business. Shore dinners a specialty, also meals a la carte. Bathing, boating and fishing. Golf, tennis, and other amusements." (Courtesy of Photography by Joseph.)

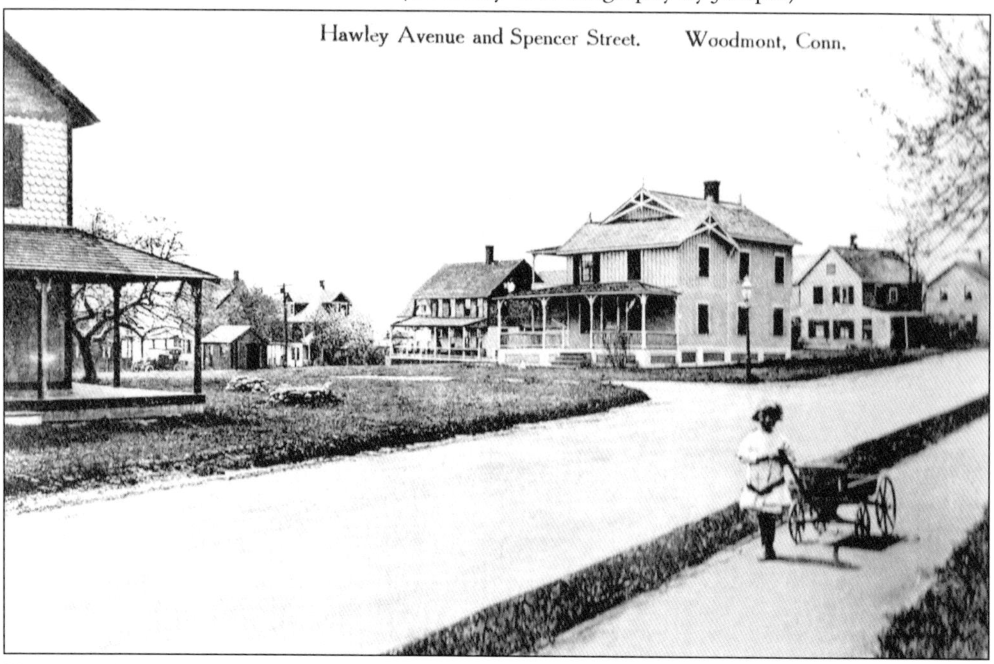

HAWLEY AVENUE AND SPENCER STREET. The young girl pulling her wagon is on Hawley Avenue just past the intersection with Spencer Street. This photograph was taken from the Kittle Shop. (Courtesy of Photography by Joseph.)

Eight

AT THE WATERFRONT

In Woodmont, local American Indians had been enjoying fish, oysters, clams, and lobsters long before recorded history. When the settlers of the new world first came from Europe, they too were attracted to the water's edge—for food, bathing, and recreation. Swimming, fishing, boating, and sunbathing have brought vacationers to Woodmont since the late 1800s.

The residents of the borough loved to celebrate Woodmont and its scenic attractions with an annual water carnival or Woodmont Day. The early water carnivals were held in late August by Anchor and Crescent Beaches. Sometime between World War I and World War II, the annual celebration was discontinued. It was revived in 1962, with the "modern" Woodmont Day, which has been held at the Hawley Avenue playground between Wall and Bonsilene Streets for close to half a century.

One of the major problems with Woodmont has always been its rocky shoreline. For many years, the summer residents would gather together to move the rocks and clear a path to the water at the foot of each street. Later this was formalized and the borough of Woodmont hired a contractor to perform this task each year at the beginning of each swimming season.

The beach erosion from Hurricane Carol in 1954 was so severe that a group of Woodmont residents gathered at the home of Herb Borman early in 1955 to discuss the problem and the possibility of corrective action to slow down the sound's march into homes, roads, and the beaches. Interestingly, Borman lived in the former home of Rev. Joseph Anderson, Woodmont's very first cottage.

In 1957, as part of a beach restoration project, five large granite groins were constructed by the Army Corps of Engineers to slow the erosion. A large dredge was anchored about 200 yards from the rock formations off Blakeslee Point. The dredge pumped offshore sand onto the shore where sand had never been seen before. The dredging took place from Crescent Beach to Anderson Avenue Beach at the eastern end of the borough. Over the years, there have been several replenishment projects since erosion keeps trying to return Woodmont's coastline to its natural rocky state.

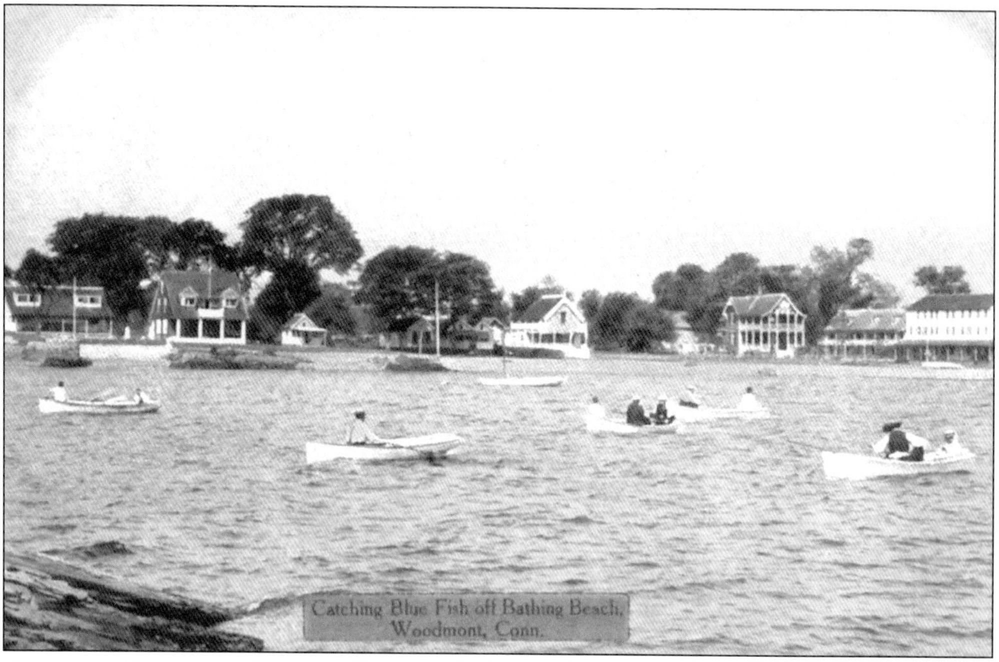

CATCHING BLUES OFF ANCHOR BEACH. Fishing has been a popular activity in Woodmont for more than 100 years, especially for bluefish and mackerel. This postcard is postmarked 1909.

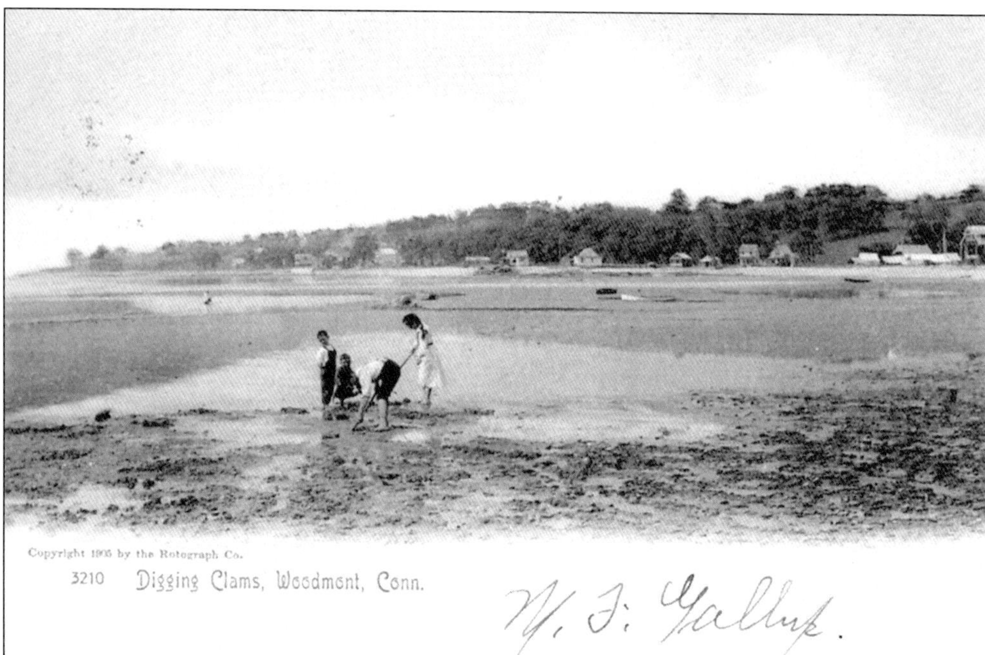

CLAMMING IN WOODMONT. Until modern times, when pollution of Long Island Sound has been a problem, clamming for steamers, littlenecks, and quahogs was common along the shore in Woodmont.

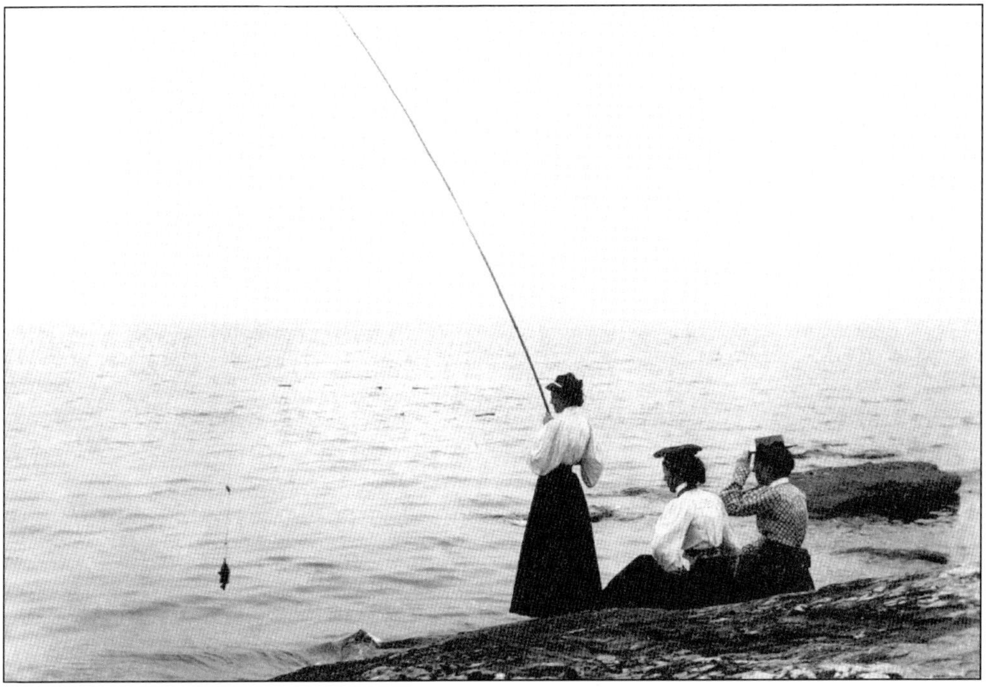

FISHING FROM THE ROCKS. These ladies, although careful to cover their heads, enjoyed the day fishing for blues off the rocks near Merwin's Point. The photograph was taken around 1900.

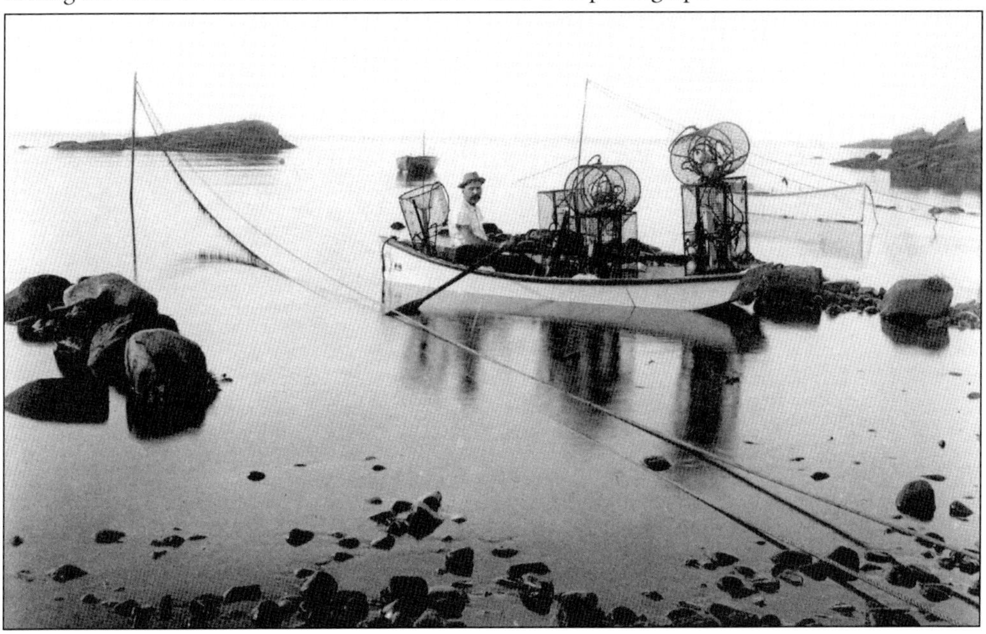

SHELLFISH FISHING, *c.* 1900. Clams, mussels, oysters, and lobsters were plentiful along the Woodmont shore. The earliest settlers were introduced to shellfish fishing by the Paugussets. Oystering was a major business in Milford's early years, peaking around the beginning of the 20th century. But pollution during the 1920s and 1930s, and the hurricane of 1938, devastated the oyster beds. Environmental efforts in the early 1970s led to the reopening of shellfish beds in the 1980s.

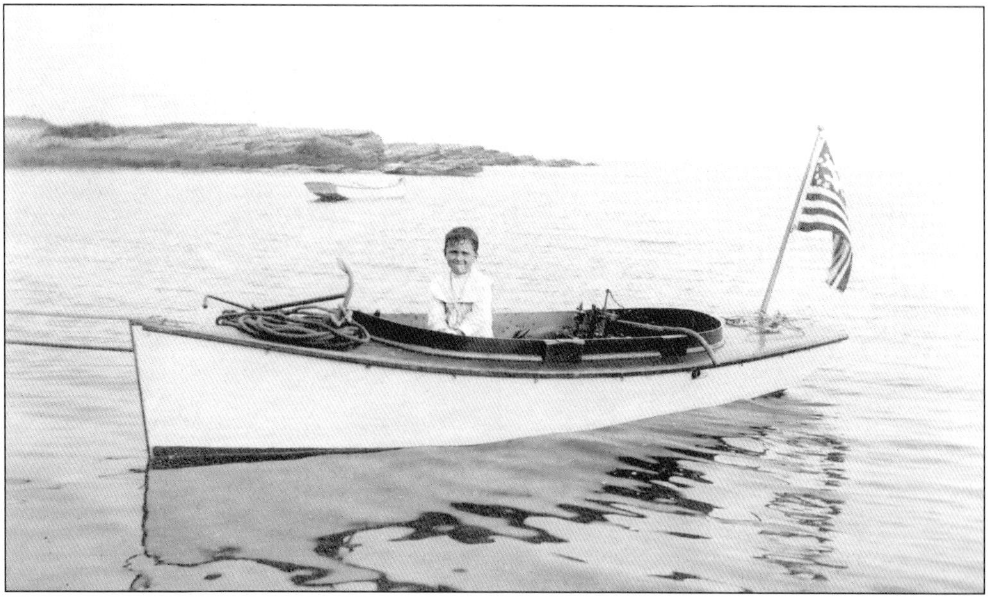

BOY IN A BOAT. Apparently this youngster was placed in the boat to have a photograph taken, as the boat seems to be securely moored at Crescent Beach. This photograph was taken around 1900.

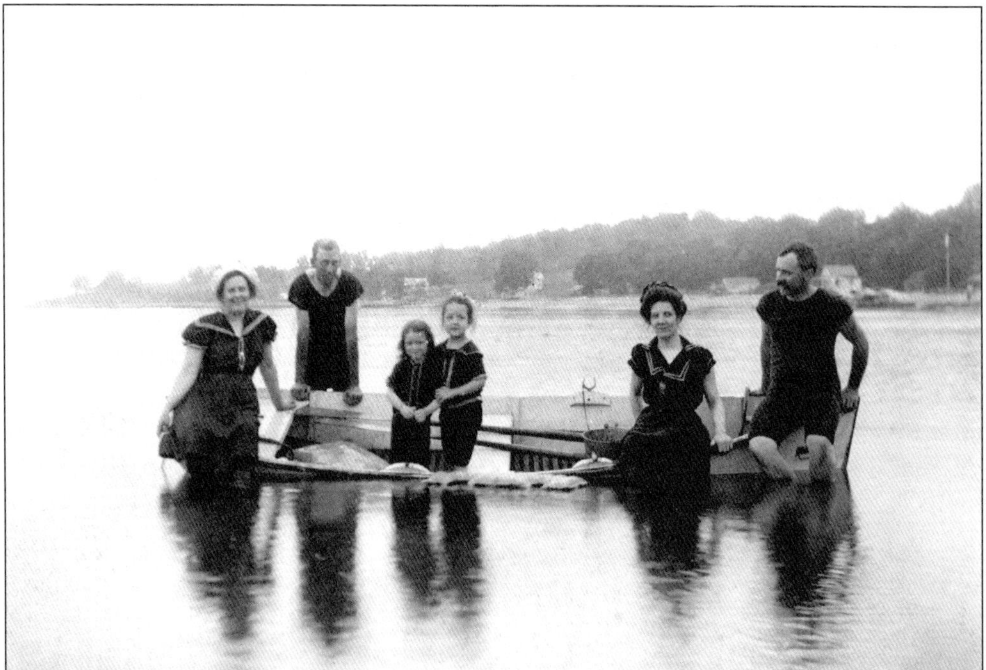

ON THE EDGE OF THE DINGHY, *c.* 1900. A family enjoys a day at the beach, with their boat in shallow water. The borough passed ordinances to keep the beaches clean and safe, including this bylaw from 1927: "No person shall store boats, pitch a tent, or locate a counter for the sale of confectionary lemonade or other merchandise on any street, park, or public land."

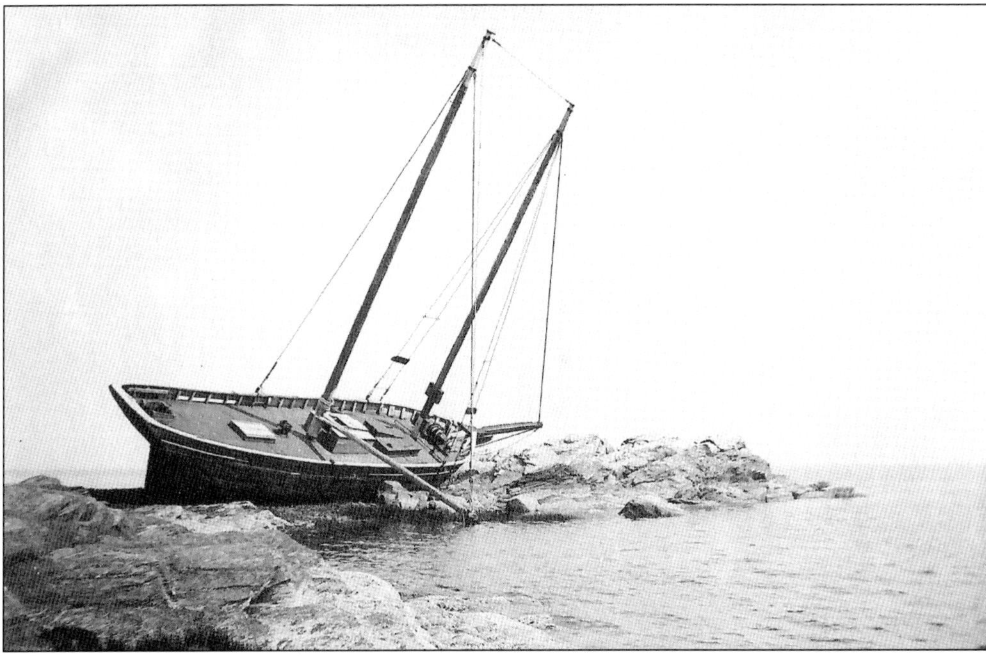

Shipwreck in Woodmont. The rocky coast claimed many boats over the years, including this wooden sailing vessel around 1900. Boats were often casualties in hurricanes. Some of the more memorable storms in Woodmont included the great hurricane of 1938 and another huge hurricane in 1944. Hurricanes Carol in 1954, Belle in 1976, and Gloria in 1985 caused serious beach erosion, and downed trees and power lines.

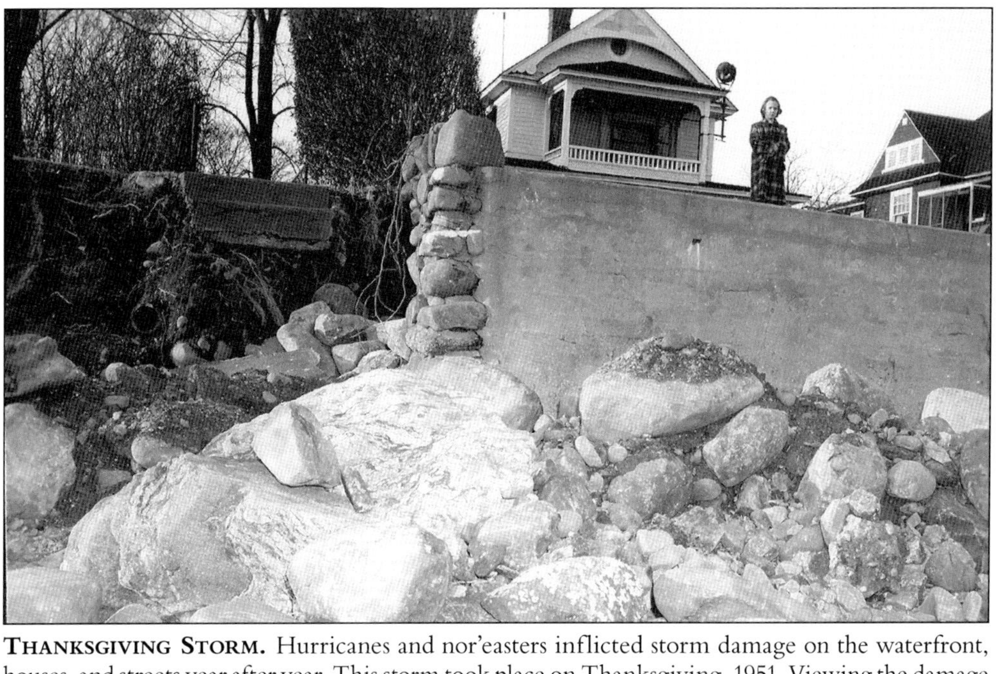

Thanksgiving Storm. Hurricanes and nor'easters inflicted storm damage on the waterfront, houses, and streets year after year. This storm took place on Thanksgiving, 1951. Viewing the damage is Sara Fugal in front of her parents' home on Beach Avenue. (Courtesy of Kristina Sancher.)

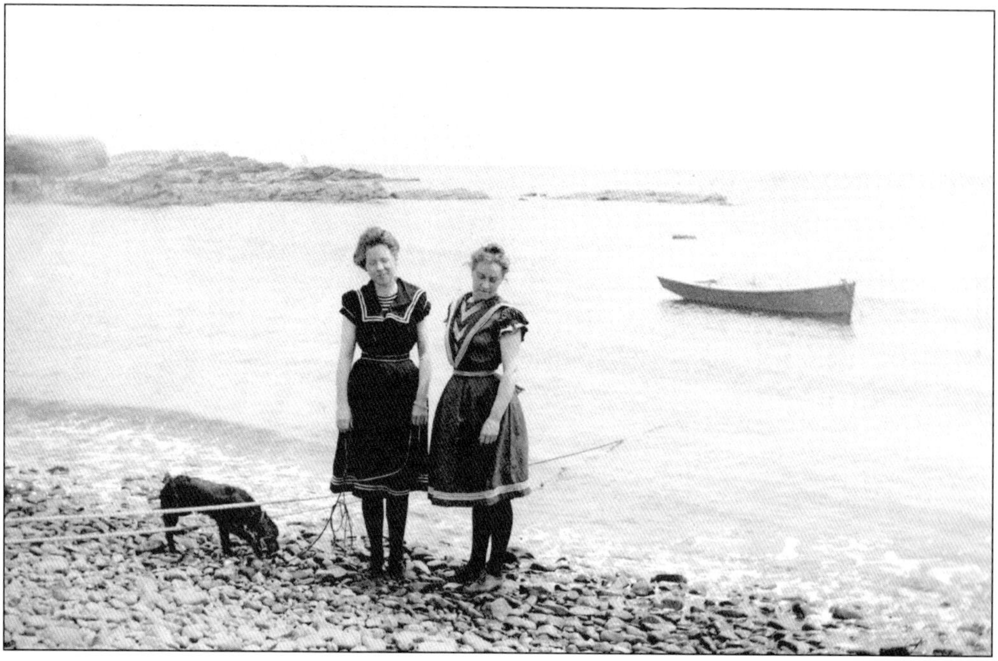

TWO LADIES AND A DOG. Pets in the borough, particularly at the beach, have always been a matter of serious debate. These women who took their dog for a walk along the beach around 1900 would not have been allowed to do so 100 years later. But at least they had the dog on a leash!

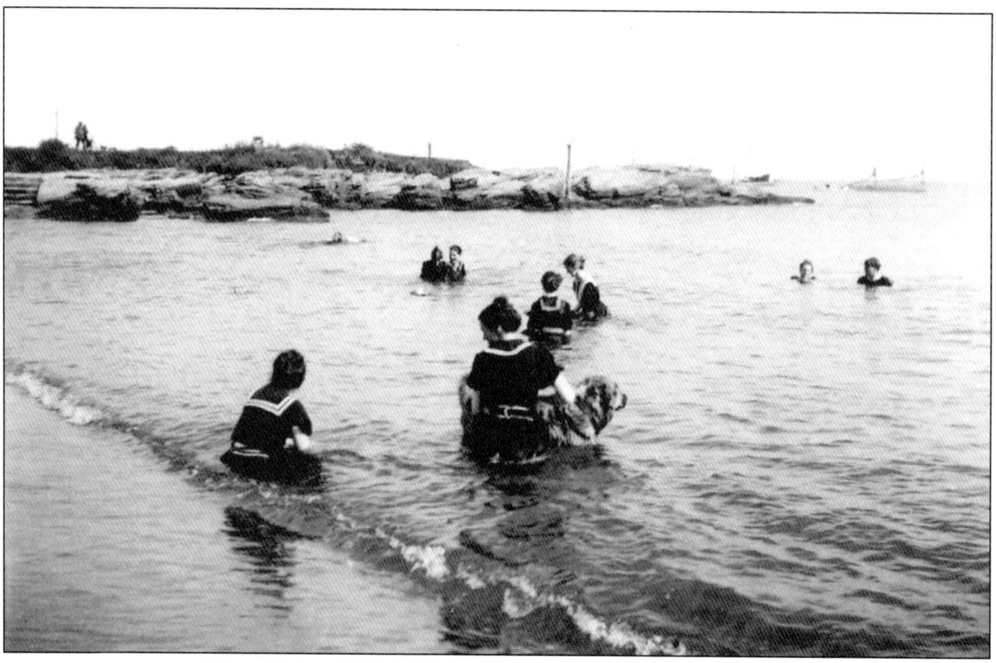

DOG-PADDLING, C. 1900. This furry dog is either getting a bath or a swimming lesson. Animals sharing spaces with humans can often lead to friction. On June 2, 1915, the borough board actually "voted to have the clerk write to W. H. Bradley in reference to the bleating of his calf and the barking of his dog, and have the noise stopped immediately."

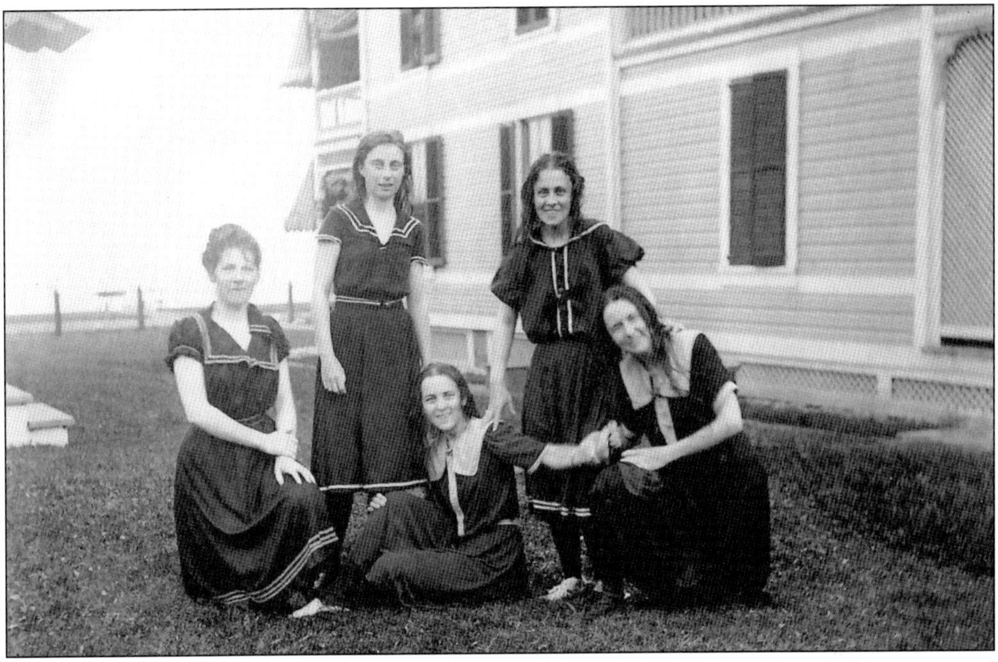

Party Girls. Even as far back as 1900, Woodmont has attracted young people for parties and fun. In 1917, the borough voted "to answer Mrs. W. H. Bradley's complaint about the house party of girls making so much noise near her property, saying that the disturbance will be taken care of at once, and it is not the Warden and Burgesses idea to have anyone coming to Woodmont to spend a quiet summer to be disturbed in any way."

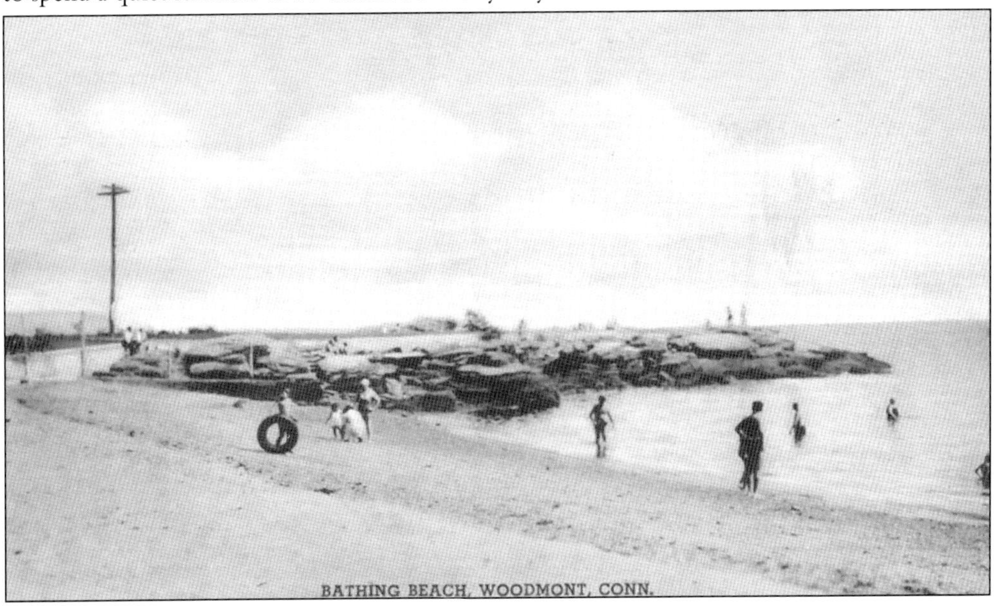

Tubing at Anchor Beach. At the June 2, 1915, borough meeting, the following ordinance was passed: "Indecent bathing suits will not be allowed to be worn in the Borough of Woodmont . . . with the same consequences as when the ordinance was passed the previous year [arrest and imprisonment or a fine of not less than $5 or both]." Inner tubes have not been seen in Woodmont for many years.

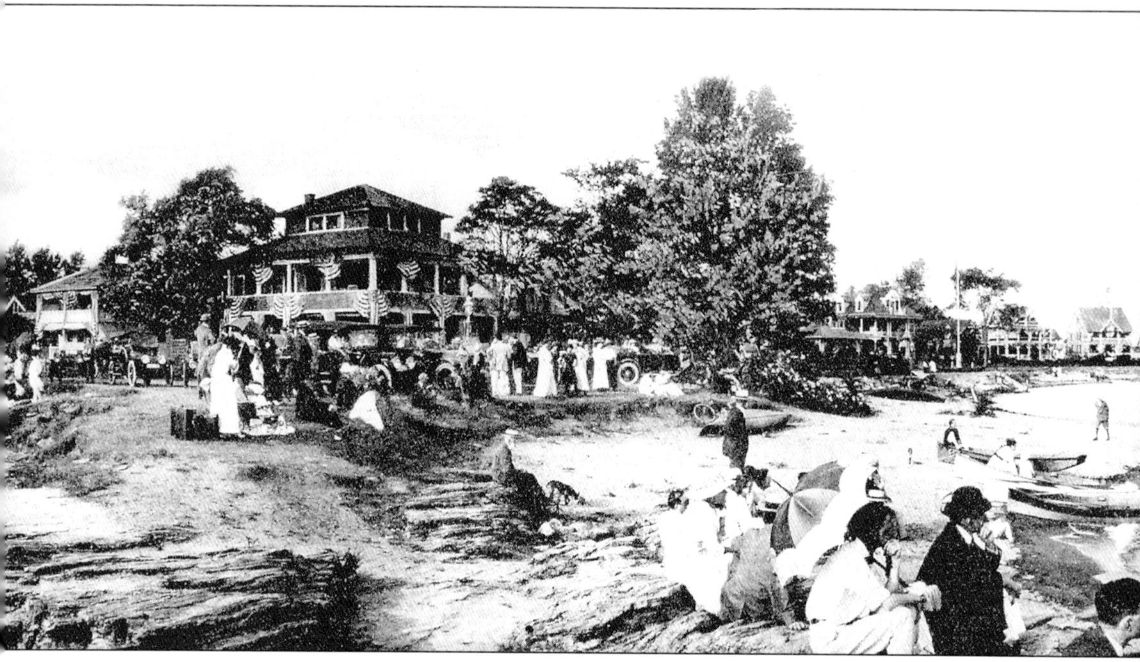

Fourth of July at Randall's Point, *c.* 1915. This gathering of Woodmonters on the rocks at Randall's Point and Crescent Beach shows onlookers enjoying the festivities, which include canoeing and swimmers diving off the board at the end of the Signal Rock pier. The Blakeslee house is visible in the distance. The borough had concerns about fireworks safety. On

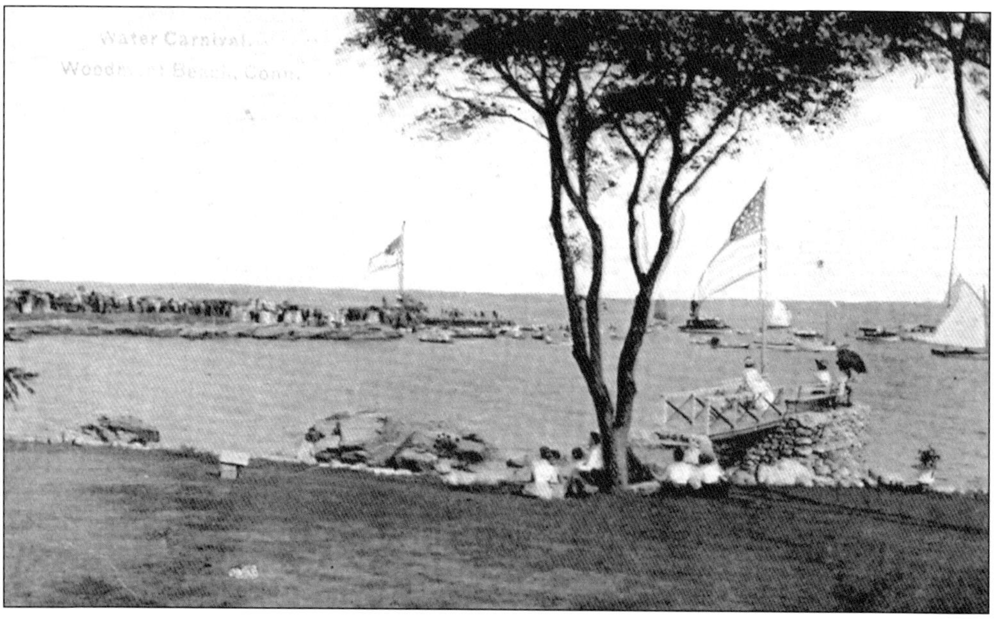

View of the Water Carnival from Merwin's Point. This card was mailed from Ansonia, Connecticut, to Mary Bristol in Woodmont on August 30, 1911. The news was not good. Said H. E. M. L., "Am flat on my back again and Albert has to stay home as Mary has broken her leg on trolley car."

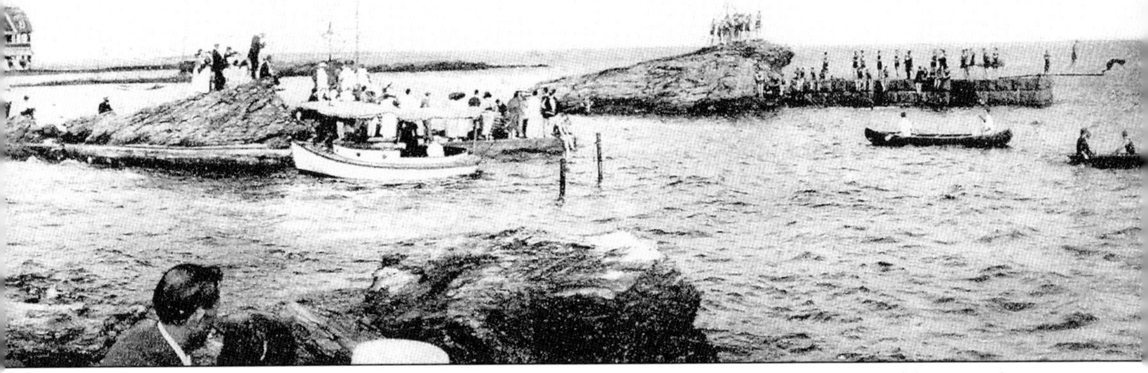

June 2, 1915, the board passed two ordinances—one prohibiting firearms to be sold, carried, or discharged in the borough without a special permit granted by the board; and "no explosives for purposes of celebration shall be sold or used except on July 3 or 4 or, when the 4th falls on a Sunday, July 5th."

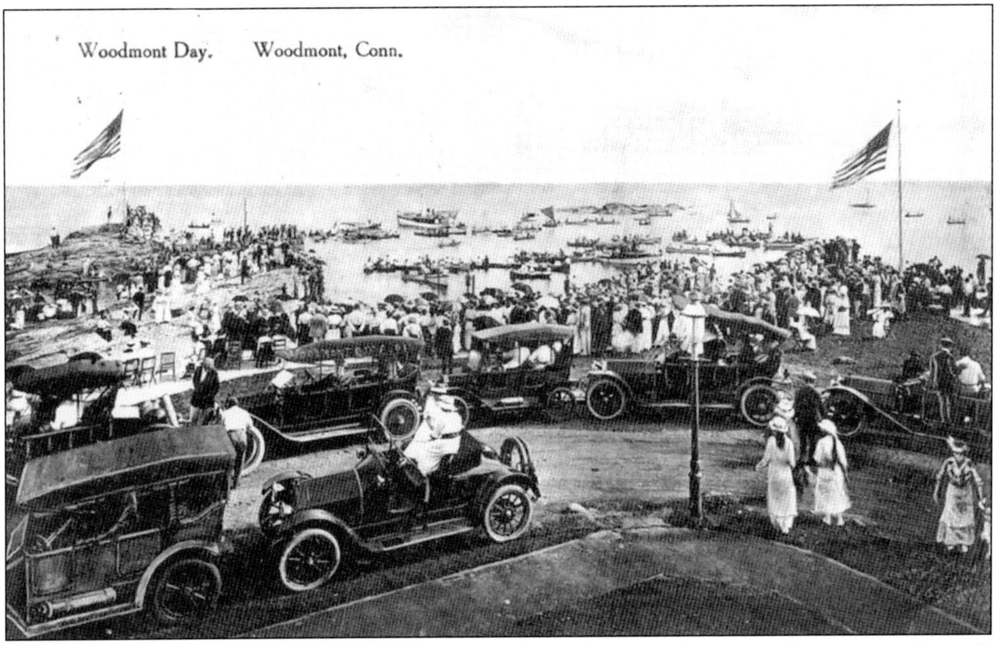

WOODMONT DAY. The annual water carnival festival attracted more and more people each year, and by 1917, when this postcard was mailed, many of them came by automobile. The cars are taking the turn by Randall's Point.

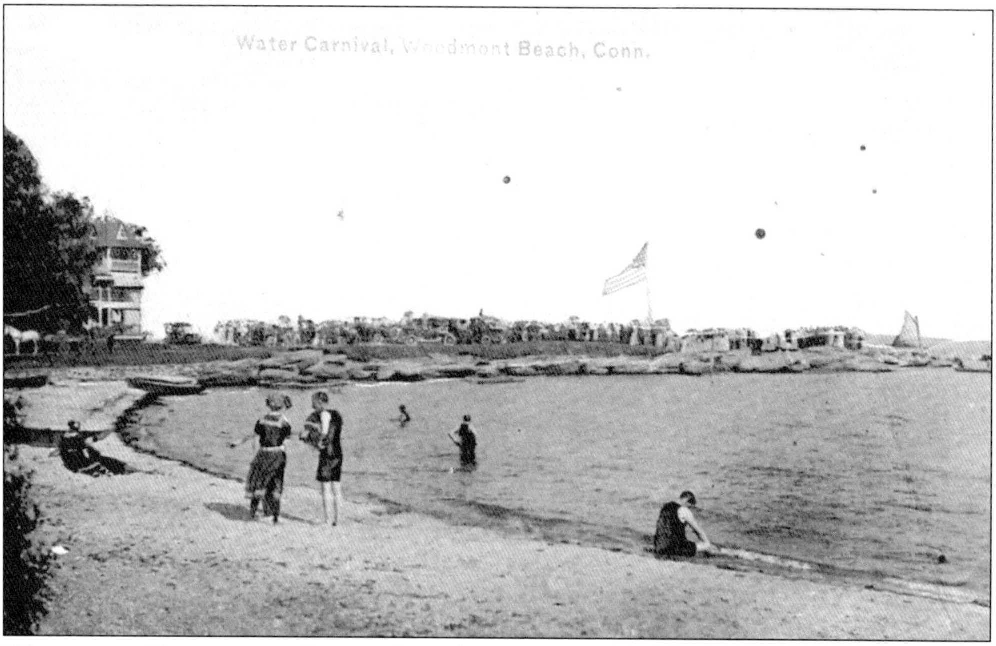

Woodmont Day at the Point. According to the note on the back of this postcard, Will rode to Woodmont on his motorcycle in August 1914. After making the 80-mile trip, he was "spending a couple of weeks at this place. Am having a great time fishing, swimming, and riding my motor cycle."

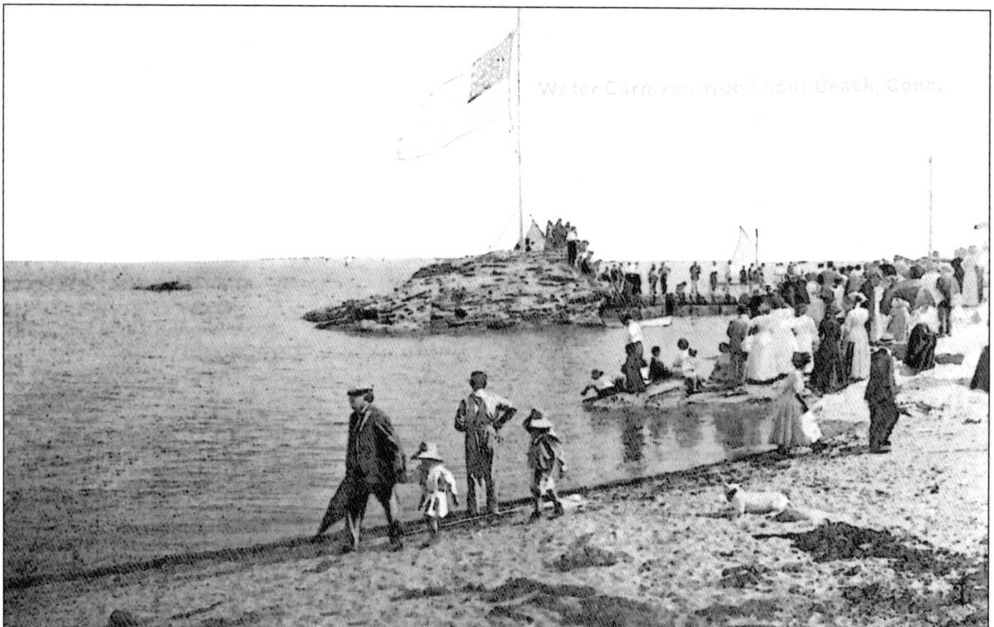

Water Carnival. On August 7, 1922, the borough board voted "to give the Warden power to have Abigail Street closed between Merwin Avenue and Mark Street August 15 and 16 during Mrs. Poli's carnival, also the same power to close the Crescent during the water carnival." Today Woodmont Day, which marks mid-summer, is held at the Hawley Avenue playground and beach on the last Saturday in July. (Courtesy of George Peacock.)

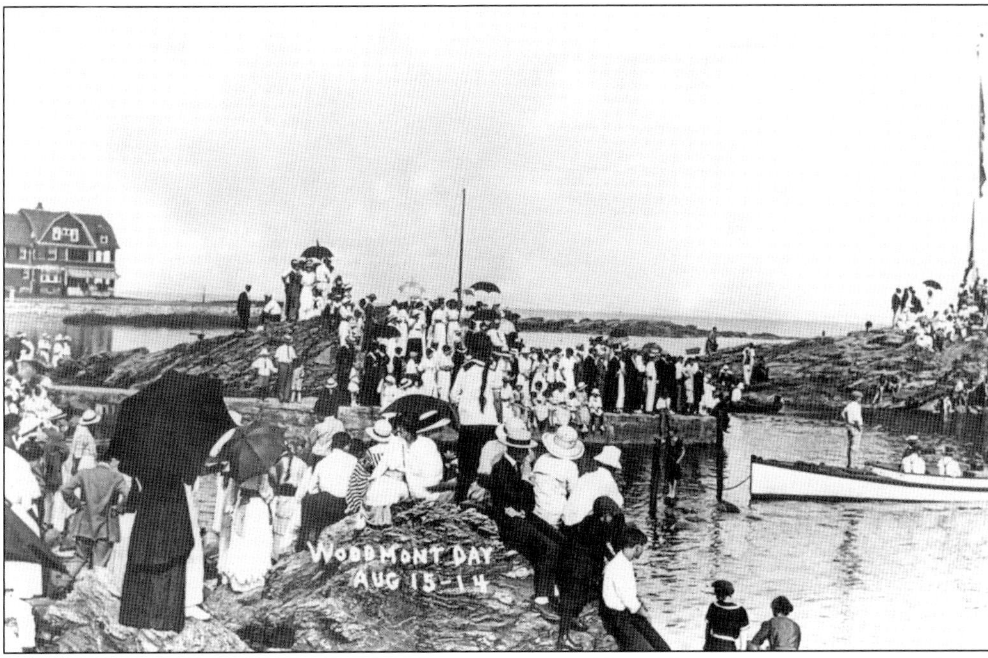

WOODMONT DAY, AUGUST 15, 1914. With the annual beachfront festivities attracting larger crowds, the borough started to take its public safety role more seriously than ever. On September 12, 1914, the board "voted to have the clerk buy a pair of handcuffs and a black jack for the sheriff." (Courtesy of Photography by Joseph.)

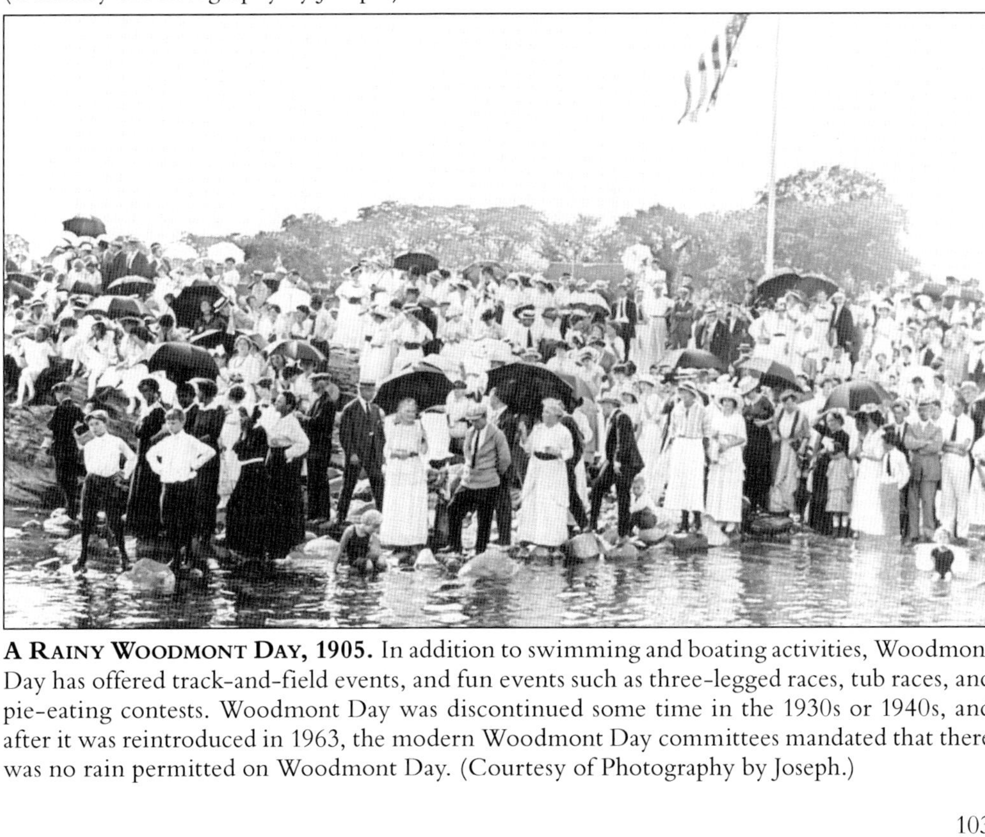

A RAINY WOODMONT DAY, 1905. In addition to swimming and boating activities, Woodmont Day has offered track-and-field events, and fun events such as three-legged races, tub races, and pie-eating contests. Woodmont Day was discontinued some time in the 1930s or 1940s, and after it was reintroduced in 1963, the modern Woodmont Day committees mandated that there was no rain permitted on Woodmont Day. (Courtesy of Photography by Joseph.)

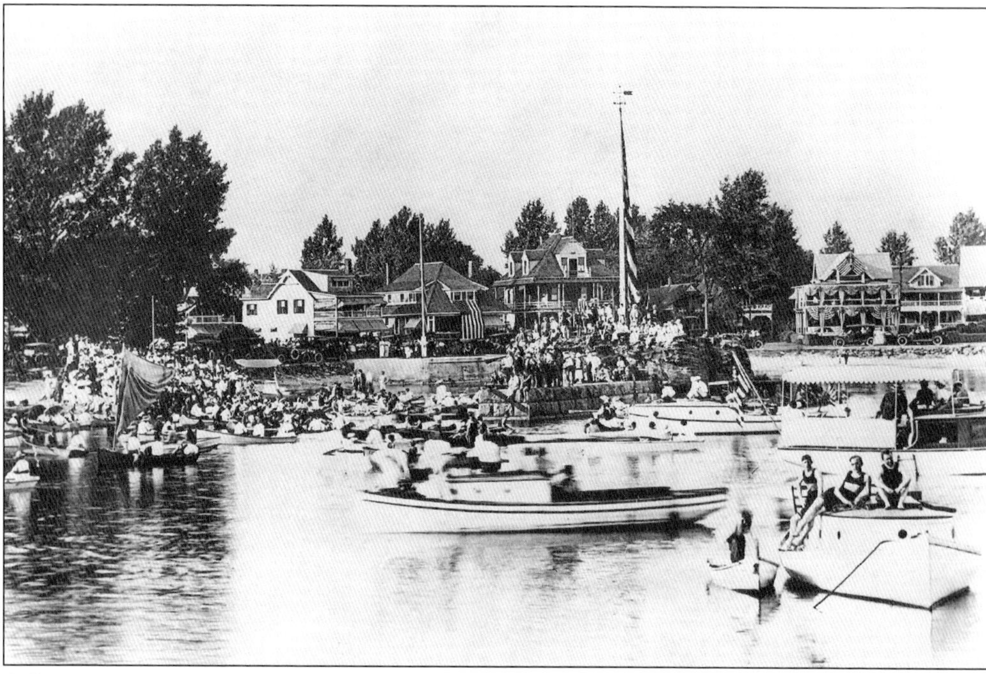

A Boating Celebration. Boaters for miles around flocked to Woodmont Day. "The little shore town of Woodmont-on-the-Sound has its annual water carnival today. It is the biggest day of the year for the summer colony. Besides those who come down by trolley or automobile, there are always many who sail over. There is sure to be a fine fleet of boats in the harbor this afternoon," read the August 19, 1911, edition of the *Saturday Chronicle*. (Courtesy of Photography by Joseph.)

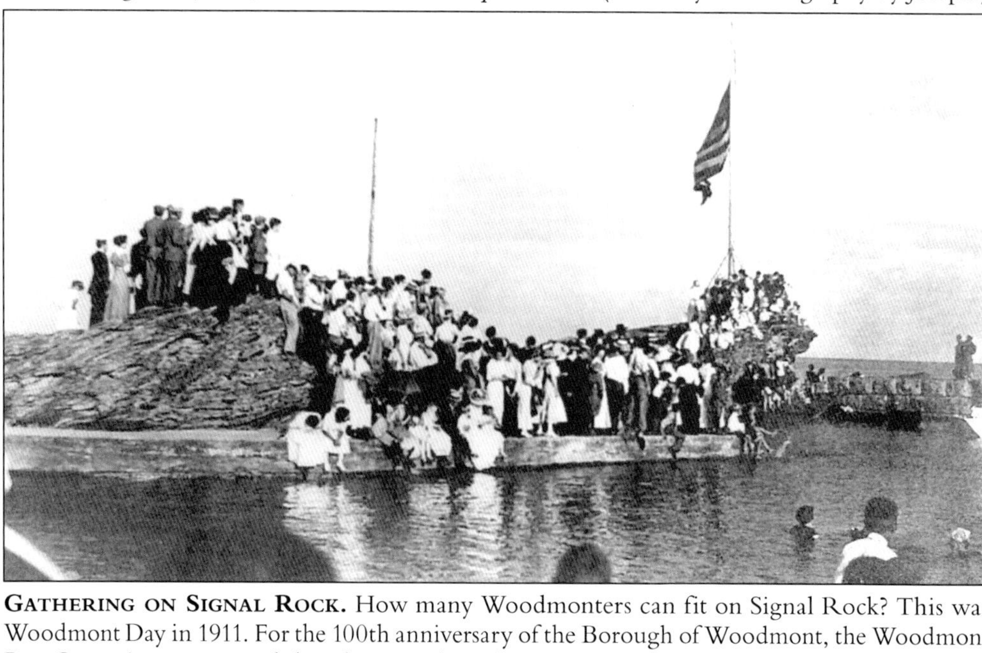

Gathering on Signal Rock. How many Woodmonters can fit on Signal Rock? This was Woodmont Day in 1911. For the 100th anniversary of the Borough of Woodmont, the Woodmont Day Committee reenacted this photograph with dozens of residents gathering on Signal Rock at low tide. Today there are about 810 families in Woodmont, and the current population is approximately 1,770. (Courtesy of Photography by Joseph.)

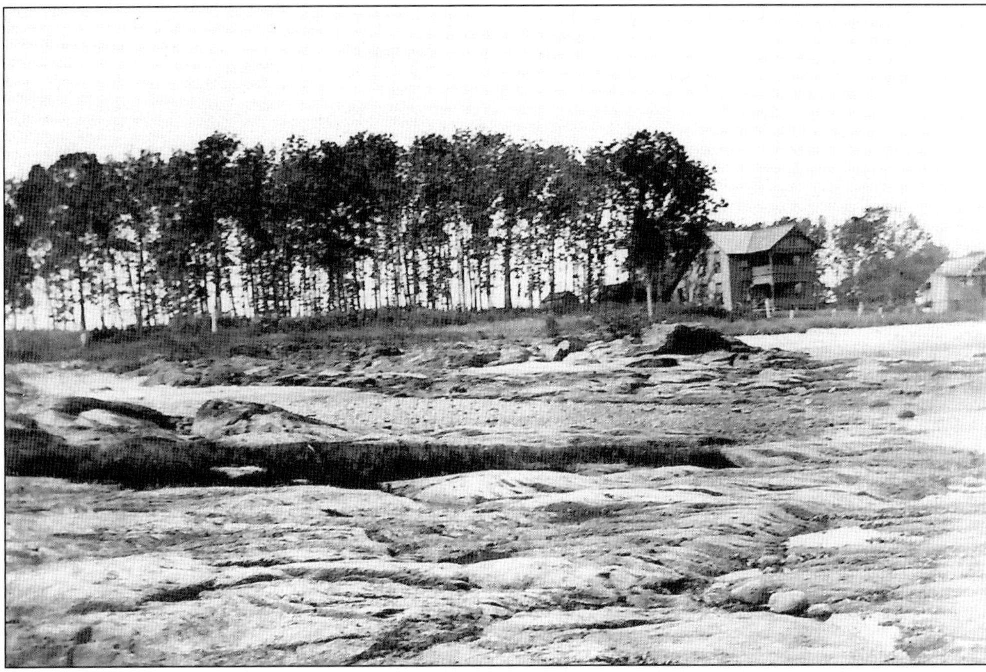

WOODMONT SHORE, C. 1892. Woodmont's coast was mostly rocky shale, which made swimming and boating difficult in most areas. Said lifetime resident Michael Krauss, "I never swam on a sandy beach until I was 12 years old and sand was pumped in from offshore. We all wore our U.S. Keds from the previous summer while in the water to minimize the scrapes and cuts from barnacles and sharp rock formations." (Courtesy of Milford Historical Society.)

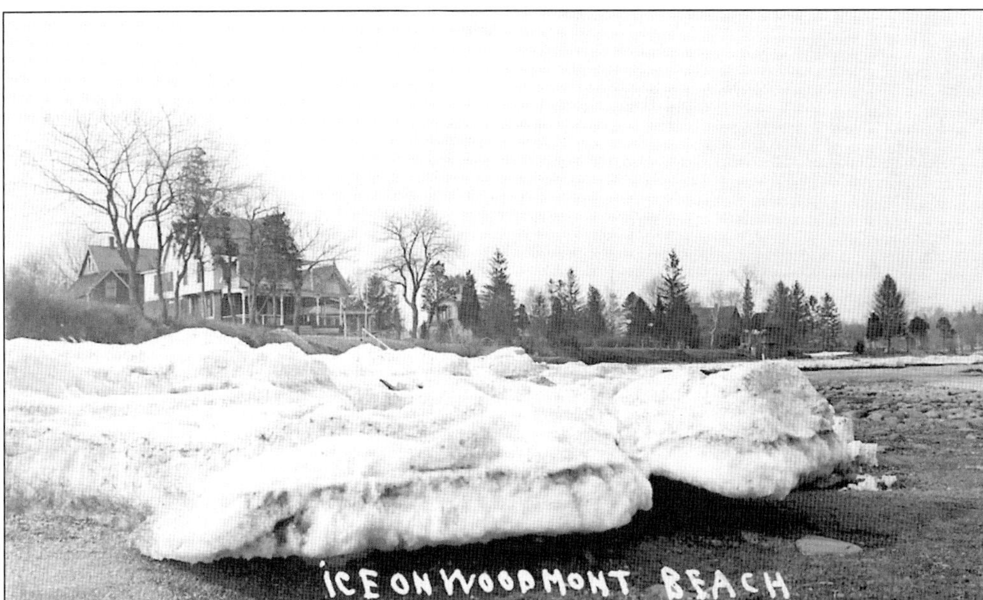

ICE ON WOODMONT BEACH. This photograph was taken during a long cold snap in the winter of 1907. The view is of Anderson Avenue Beach; the house to the far right, with a small shed in front of it, appears to be Rev. Joseph Anderson's cottage. (Courtesy of George Peacock.)

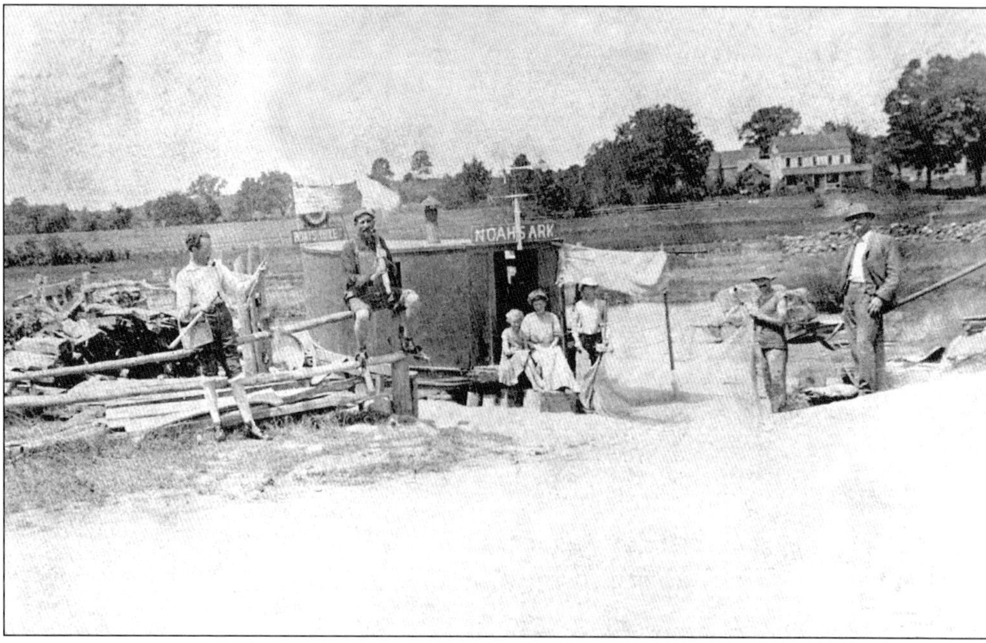

NOAH'S ARK. No one seems to know the story of Noah except that he was a local character who lived with his family in a shanty on the beach near Oyster River many years ago. Woodmont has had its share of colorful characters, and even today is a multiethnic, socioeconomically diverse neighborhood. (Courtesy of Photography by Joseph.)

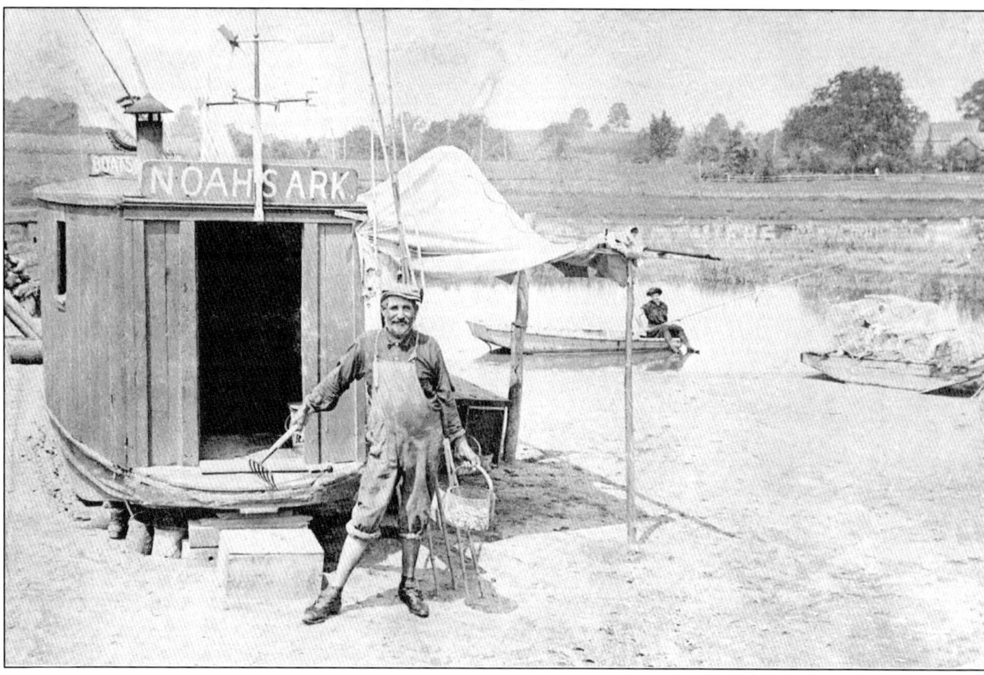

NOAH. Noah was a fisherman and a clammer, perhaps an immigrant. For the past century, Woodmont has been a haven for immigrants, predominantly European, a tradition that still continues, although to a lesser extent. Even today, almost seven percent of the Woodmont population was born in another country or continent. (Courtesy of Photography by Joseph.)

Nine

The Anchor and the Crescent

The beaches in Woodmont stretched from the Lazy Rock, just west of Merwin's Point, to Oyster River on the eastern end of the borough. The beaches included Merwin's Beach, Anchor Beach, Crescent Beach, Long Beach (between Clinton Street and Bonsilene Street), and Anderson Avenue Beach. But of the mile and a half of waterfront, by far the most popular beaches were the Anchor and the Crescent.

"The Woodmont beaches were a huge mass of moss, seaweed, and barnacle-covered stones—a dangerous place to enter the water. If one really wanted to go swimming, it was necessary to go down to the Anchor," explained the late Lou Carroll, longtime Woodmont resident and borough magician. Anchor Beach is a triangular, naturally sandy beach, strategically located across the street from the former Sanford House, one of Woodmont's largest hotels.

In its earliest years, it was called Sandy Beach. Anchor Beach was a natural cove, a protected stretch between Merwin's Point and Randall's Point, and for over a century the most popular bathing beach in Woodmont.

At the September 10, 1903, borough meeting, "a petition was read from Mr. A. H. Smith and others asking for a walkway from the fish market to and across the corner near the Sanford House and down on the opposite side to Sandy Beach." Sandy, or Anchor Beach, was calm enough for amateur swimmers, canoes, rowboats, and in later years, kayaks and inflatable boats.

Adjacent to the Anchor was Crescent Beach, a crescent-shaped beach lined with some of Woodmont's most impressive cottages. The Crescent was between Randall's Point and Blakeslee's Point. Unlike the Anchor, the Crescent was pebbly and rocky, used less for bathing and more for mooring small rowboats and dinghies for fishing and sightseeing. The boats were left in the water, moored to a wooden stake just offshore and attached with a pulley to reel the boat onto shore. Just off Crescent Beach is Woodmont's most famous landmark, Signal Rock, a large natural rock formation that has had a flagpole on it for over 100 years.

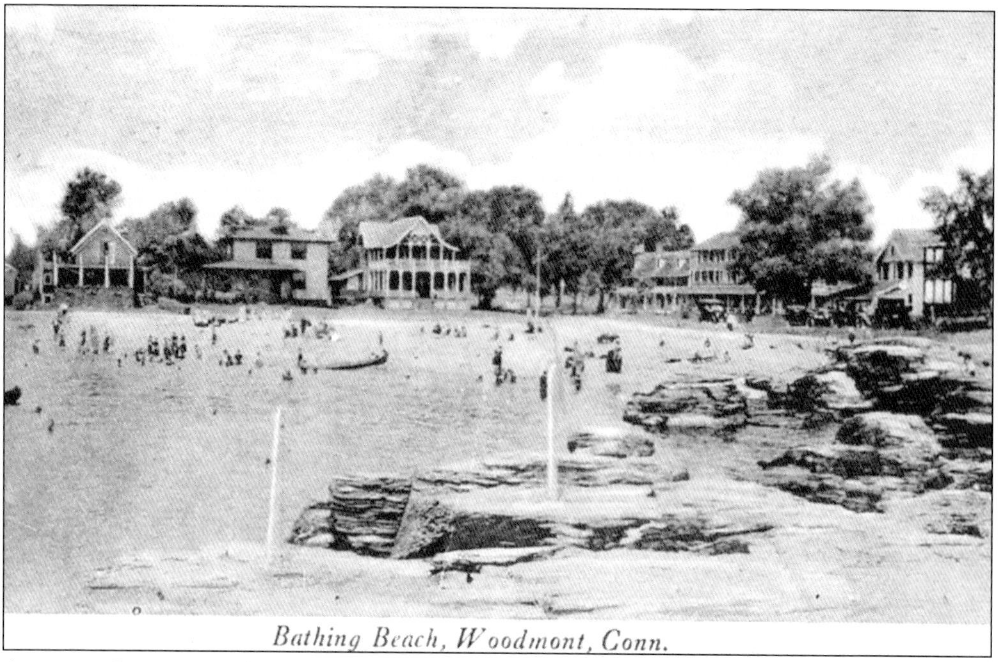

ANCHOR BEACH. Anchor Beach is the only naturally sandy beach in Woodmont's mile and a half of shoreline. Natural rock formations framed both sides of the triangular beach, which was the most popular swimming beach in the years before sand was dredged in. It was on Beach Avenue across from Woodmont's famous hotel, the Sanford House.

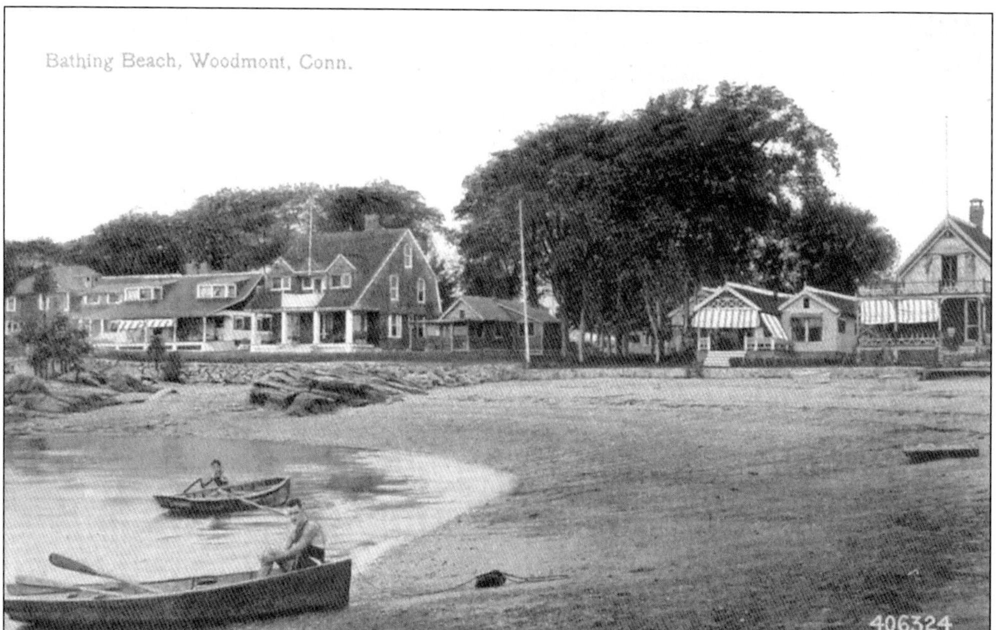

SANDY ANCHOR BEACH, *c.* 1913. The original name of Anchor Beach was Sandy Beach because it was the only area along the Woodmont shore, except near Oyster River, where there was a naturally sandy beach. The named changed to Anchor Beach in the early 20th century.

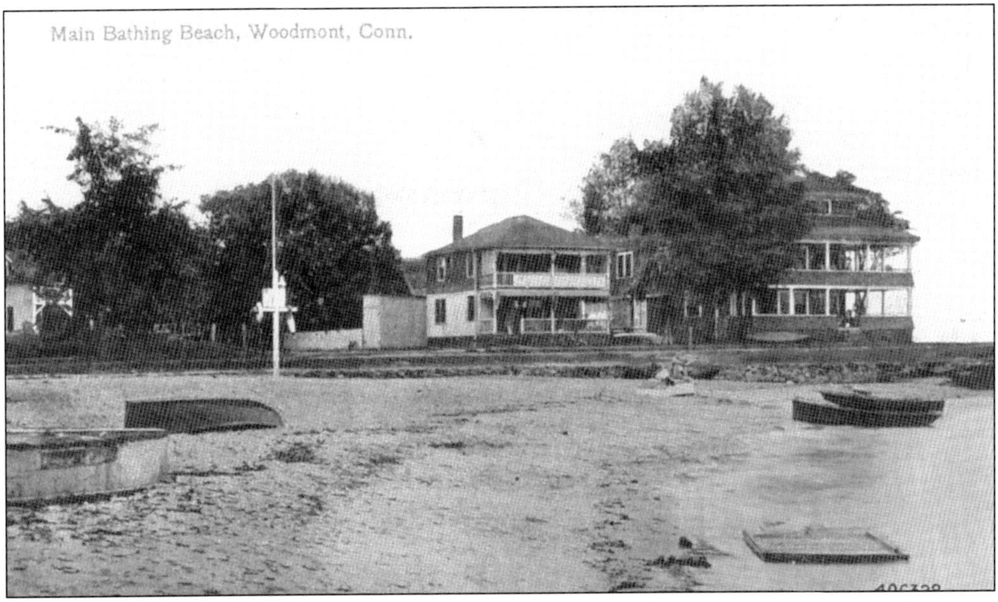

RANDALL'S POINT, ANCHOR BEACH, *c.* 1913. According to the borough minutes, on August 1, 1914, "A special meeting was held at [Burgess] Walter Randall's cottage. Mr. S. Z Poli was present at the meeting and the closing up of Division Street and Mark Street was discussed, after which it was voted to have Mr. Poli present a plan which would meet with the approval of the Warden and Burgesses." Notice how much this cottage has changed since 1900 (see top of page 40).

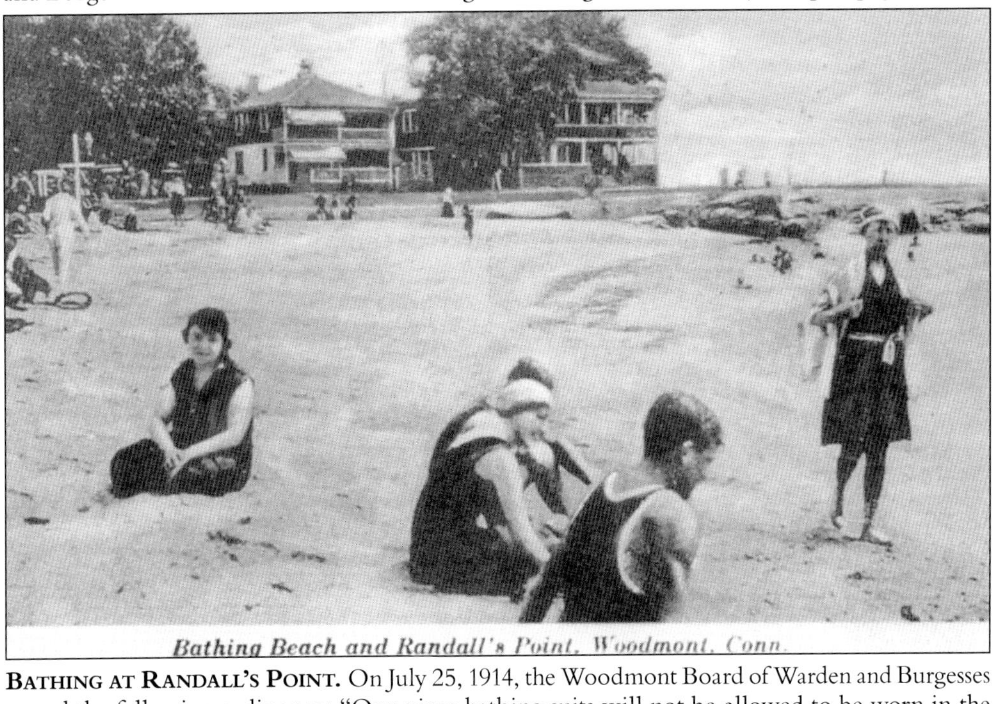

BATHING AT RANDALL'S POINT. On July 25, 1914, the Woodmont Board of Warden and Burgesses passed the following ordinance: "One piece bathing suits will not be allowed to be worn in the Borough of Woodmont. Any person violating this ordinance will be liable to arrest and imprisonment or a fine of not less than $5 or both. Dogs must be kept off all bathing beaches." By the time this postcard was mailed in 1923, one-piece bathing suits were apparently permissible.

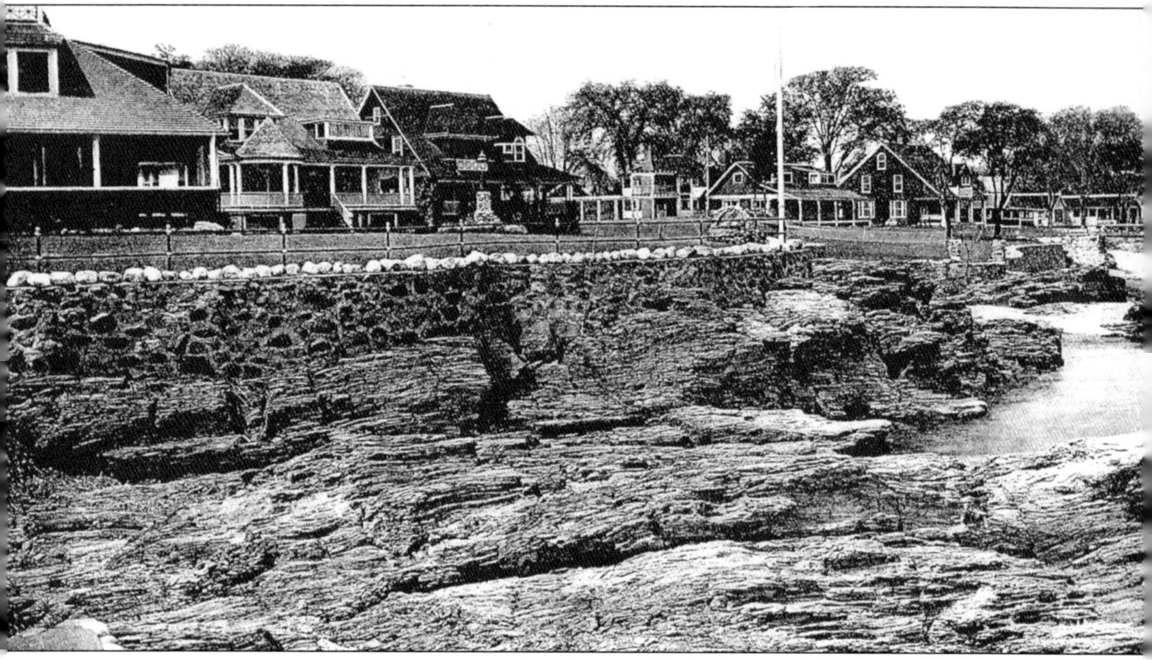

Panorama of Anchor and Crescent Beaches. Between 1890 and 1920, Woodmont was a summer playground for high society from Connecticut and other states. It was featured regularly in the *Saturday Chronicle*, a society paper published between 1903 and 1916. For example, a 1904 entry read, "A birthday surprise party was given by Mr. G. W. Goodsell Wednesday evening at his cottage on the Point. All of the families on the Point were represented and the company

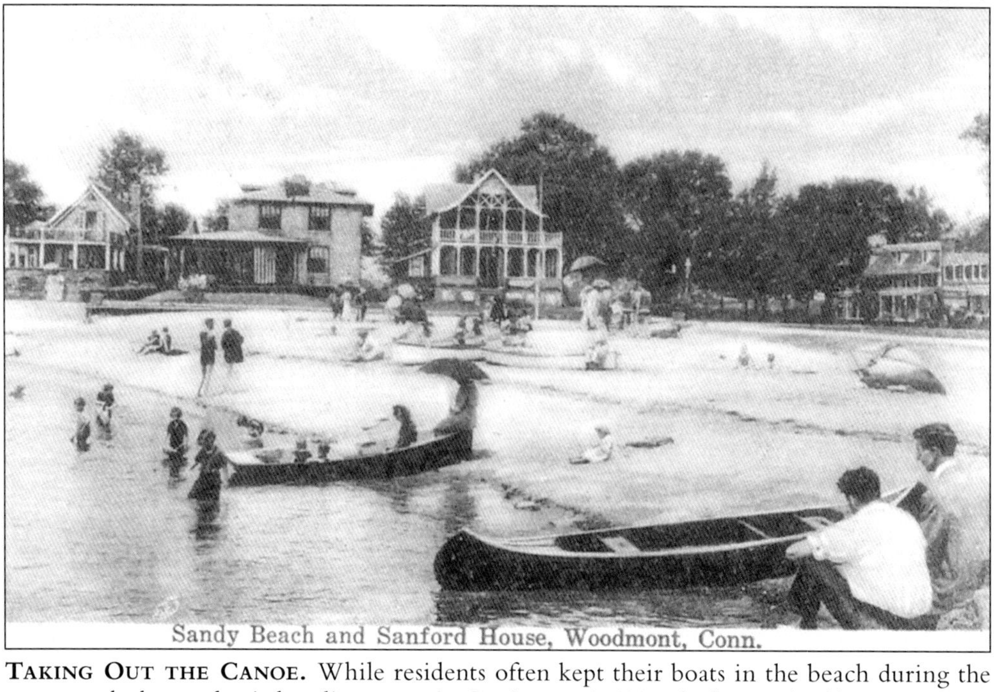

Sandy Beach and Sanford House, Woodmont, Conn.

Taking Out the Canoe. While residents often kept their boats in the beach during the summer, the borough tried to discourage it. On August 1, 1914, the borough officers voted "to have the canoe shed recently erected on the bathing beach removed at once."

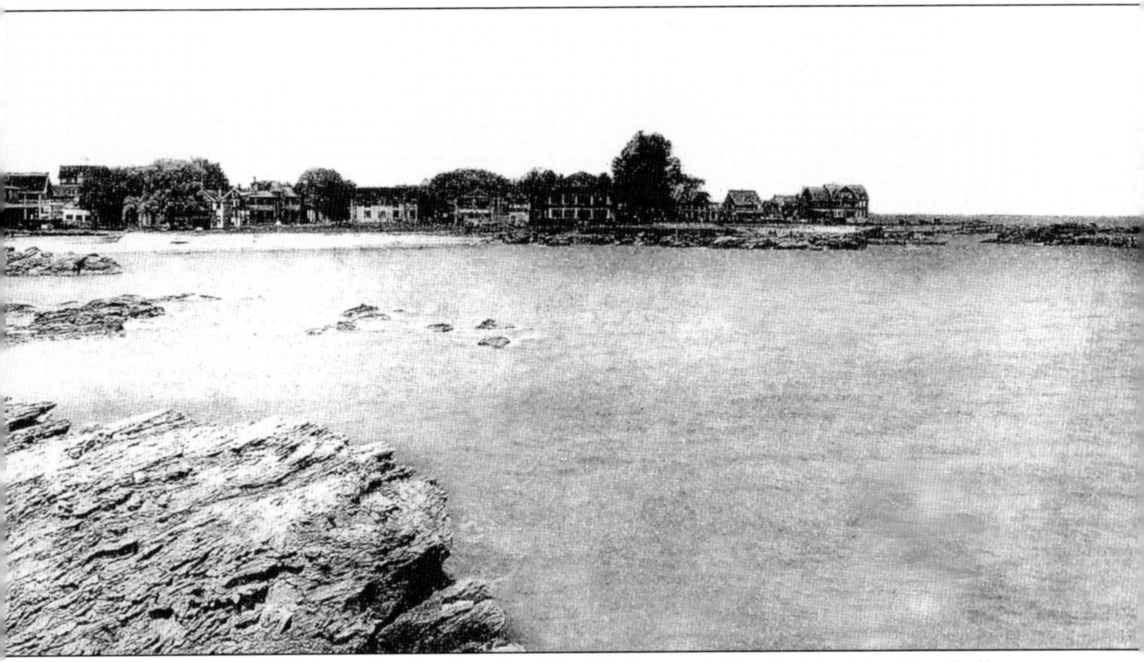

was entertained by phonograph selections by Mr. Walker and Mr. Smith. Mr. Goodsell was presented with a very handsome cut-glass loving cup with an engraved silver top. A tournament for the men will be held on the golf ground today, beginning at ten o'clock. It will be a match play tournament and only those holding season tickets will be entered. The trophy, a silver cup, has been offered by Mr. W. W. Walker."

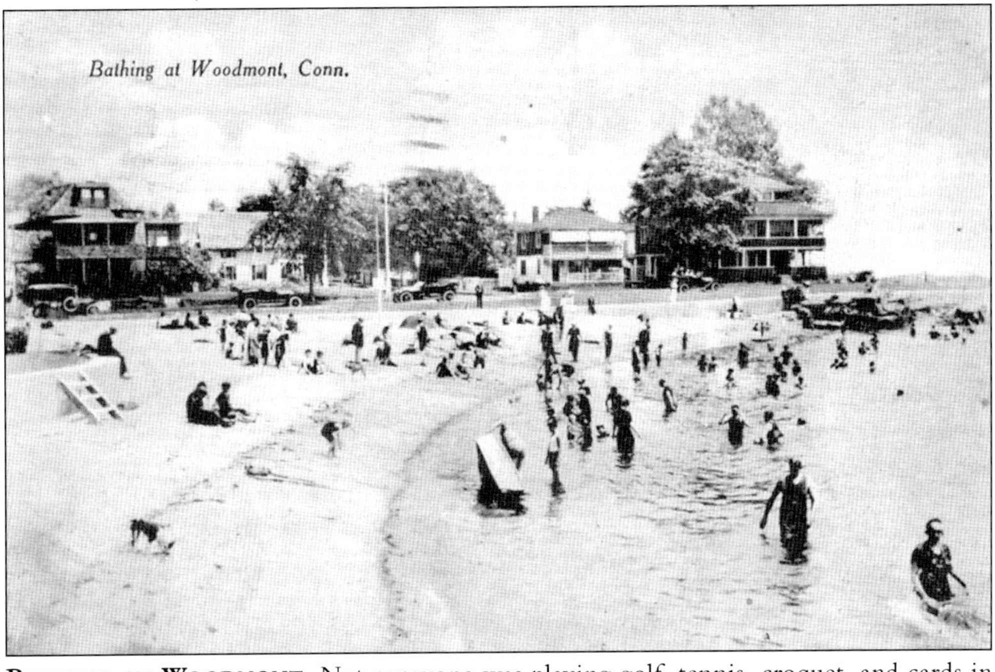

BATHING AT WOODMONT. Not everyone was playing golf, tennis, croquet, and cards in Woodmont. Sunning and swimming was as popular at the end of the 19th century as it is at the beginning of the 21st. This postcard is postmarked July 1921.

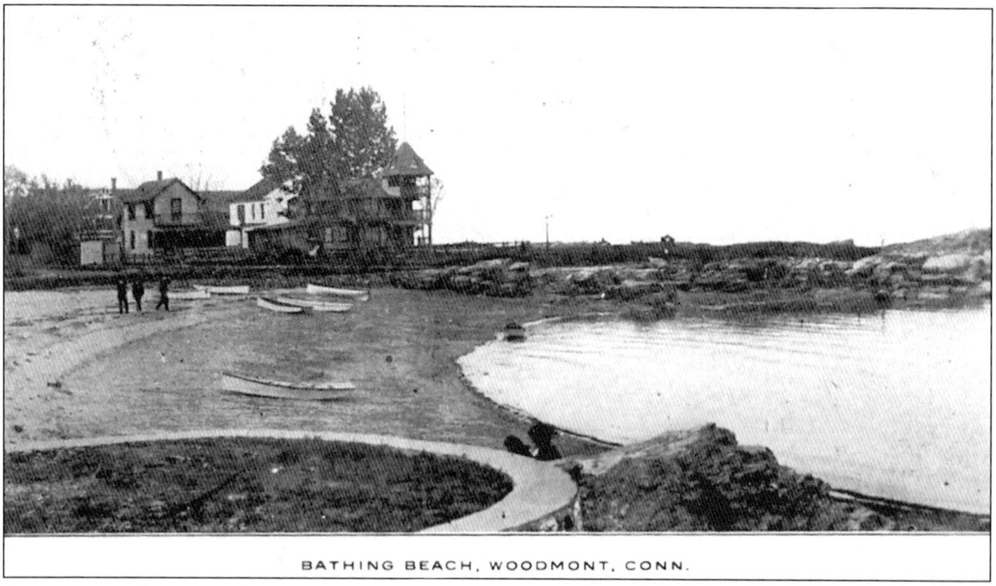

AN EARLY VIEW OF ANCHOR BEACH. Boats are pulled up on the beach, and the few people on the beach are warmly dressed, suggesting that this photograph was taken in autumn. This postcard is postmarked 1907.

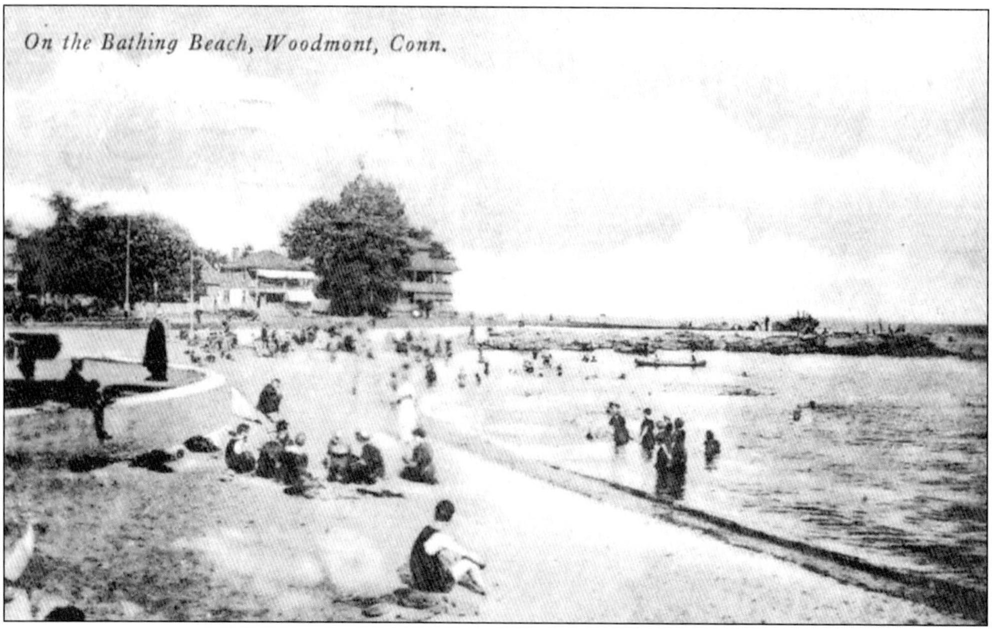

ANCHOR BEACH, 1920S. The borough board voted on July 16, 1928, "to have the clerk write to J. A. Hall calling his attention to people changing their clothes in automobiles on his property and send a copy of the letter to the police commissioner of Milford." This postcard is postmarked 1921.

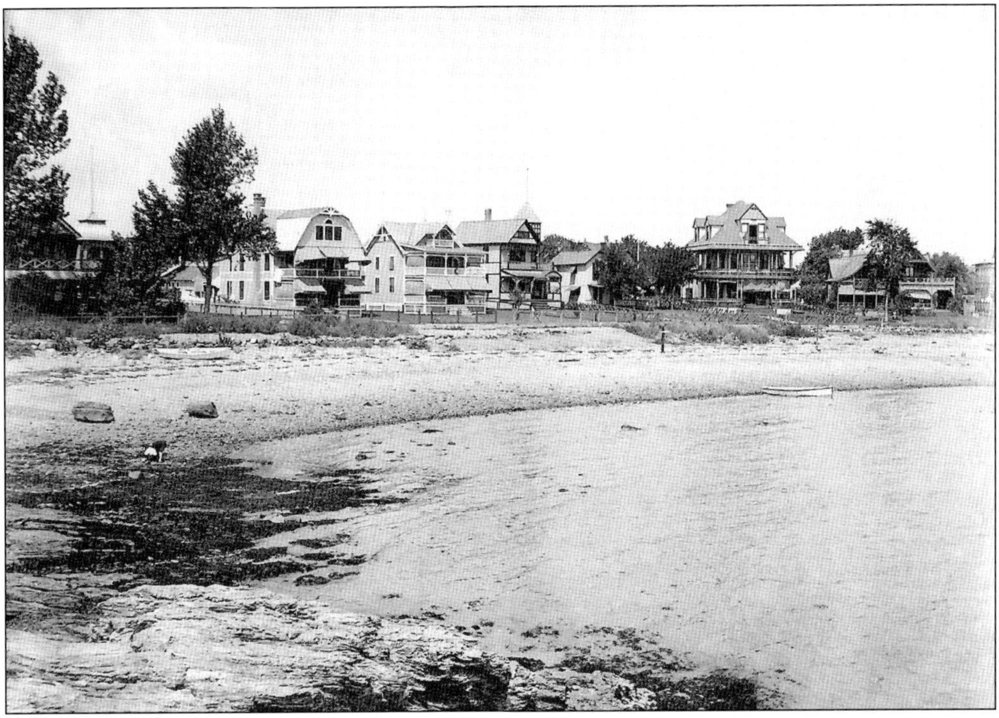

COTTAGES ON THE CRESCENT, C. 1900. According to the *Saturday Chronicle* of July 2, 1904, "There are a great many cottages at Woodmont that are occupied each year by their owners, but many, on the other hand, are rented. Some, of course, after spending a few years at one place, become tired of the surroundings and go to an inland resort."The Crescent Cottages were among the finest in Woodmont.

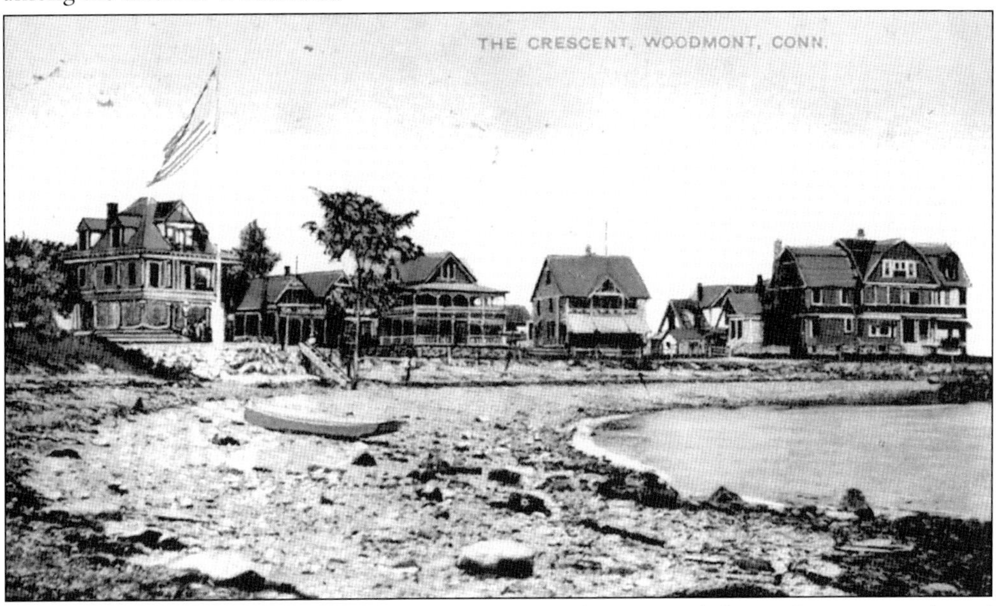

CRESCENT BEACH AND BLAKESLEE'S COTTAGE. This postcard shows the crescent-shaped beach and the cottages along the Crescent, including Blakeslee's at the far right. It was mailed in 1908 to D. W. Blakeslee in North Haven, Connecticut.

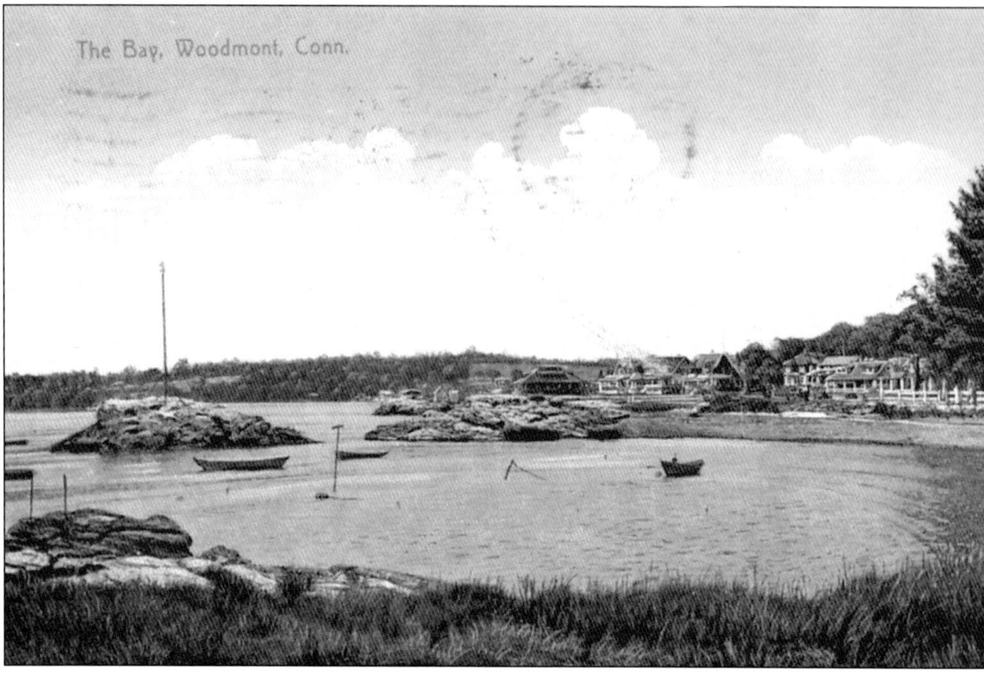

CRESCENT BEACH. High tide left a line of seaweed on every beach twice a day. Section 7 of the borough bylaws of 1927 read, "Any person collecting sea-weed and gathering it into heaps upon the beach or highways shall remove said sea-weed within 48 hours of the time of gathering it." This postcard is postmarked 1912.

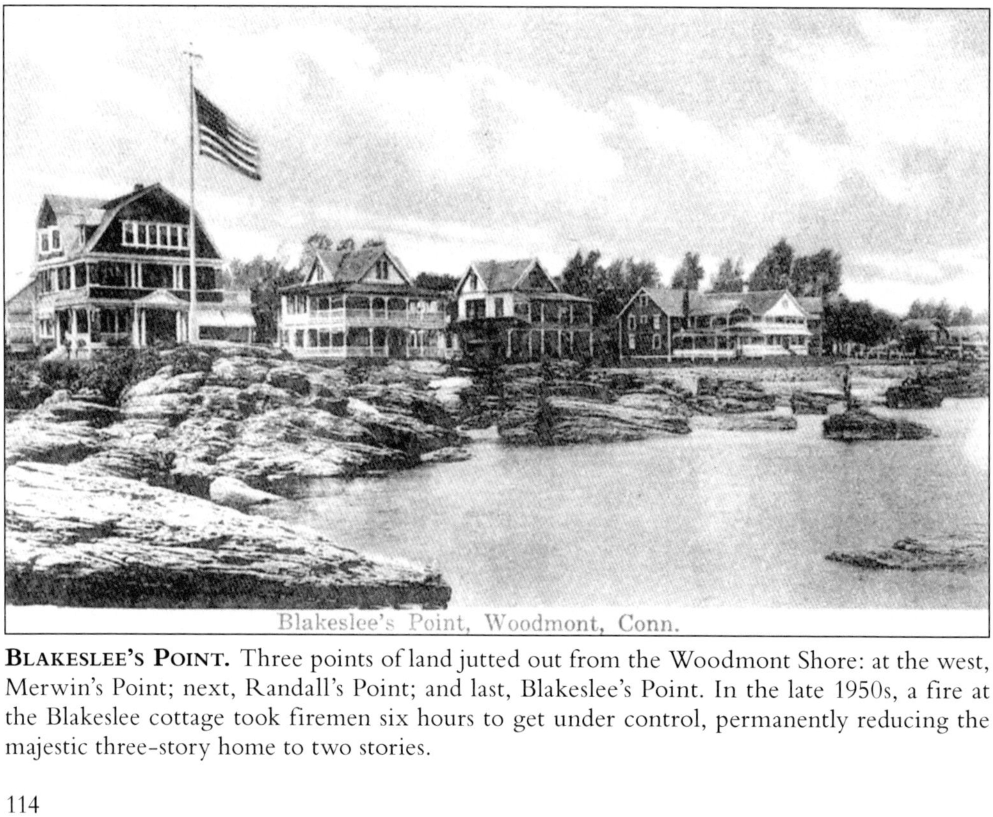

BLAKESLEE'S POINT. Three points of land jutted out from the Woodmont Shore: at the west, Merwin's Point; next, Randall's Point; and last, Blakeslee's Point. In the late 1950s, a fire at the Blakeslee cottage took firemen six hours to get under control, permanently reducing the majestic three-story home to two stories.

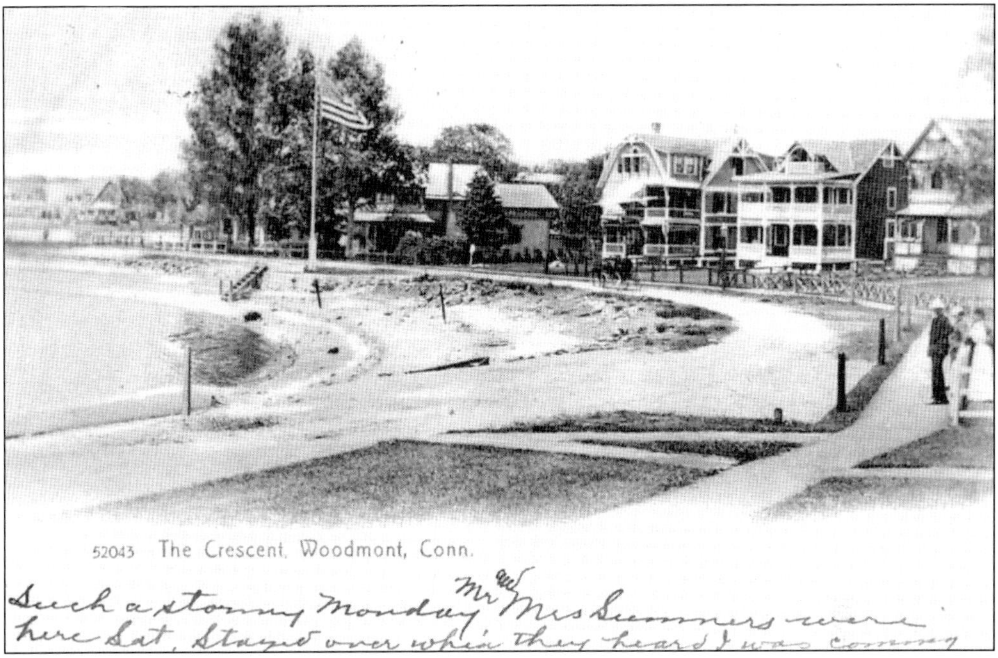

CRESCENT BEACH, C. 1906. In addition to its nautical pleasures, Woodmont offered landlubbers plenty of recreation, including a country club and golf and tennis. On August 1, 1906, the borough board voted "to accept the report of the committee on securing golf grounds and to instruct the committee to secure our option for at least six months." However, the purchase of the Fulton property for a municipal golf course was voted down at the borough's annual meeting three weeks later.

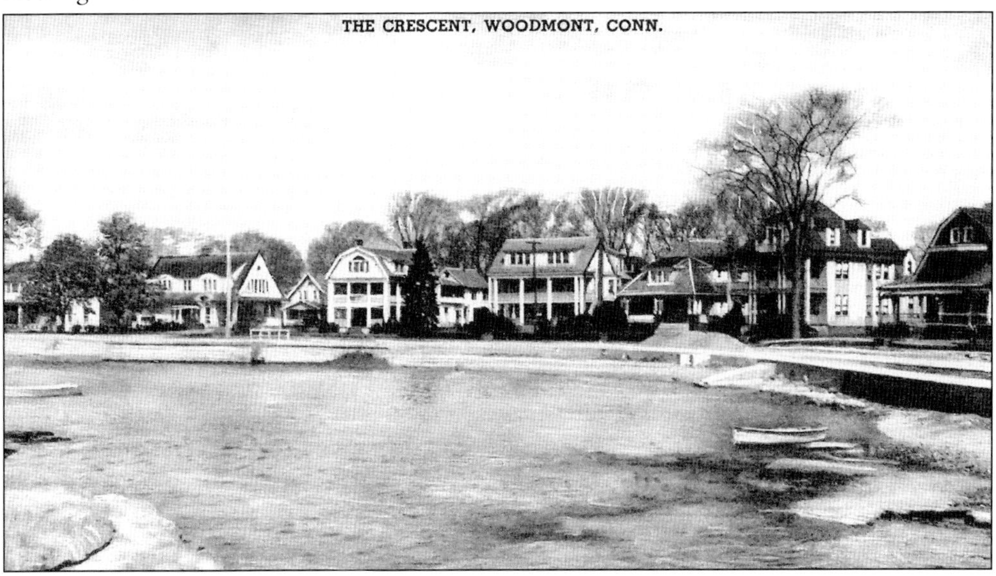

CRESCENT BEACH, C. 1940. Even as late as 1939, the borough bylaws included some quaint regulations, such as prohibiting "any person crying newspapers for sale on Sundays or offering for sale on the streets peanuts, pop-corn or other articles of merchandise, and any person making undue noises on Sunday, or conducting himself in such as manner as to disturb public worship, or the peace, quiet, and comfort of the inhabitants."

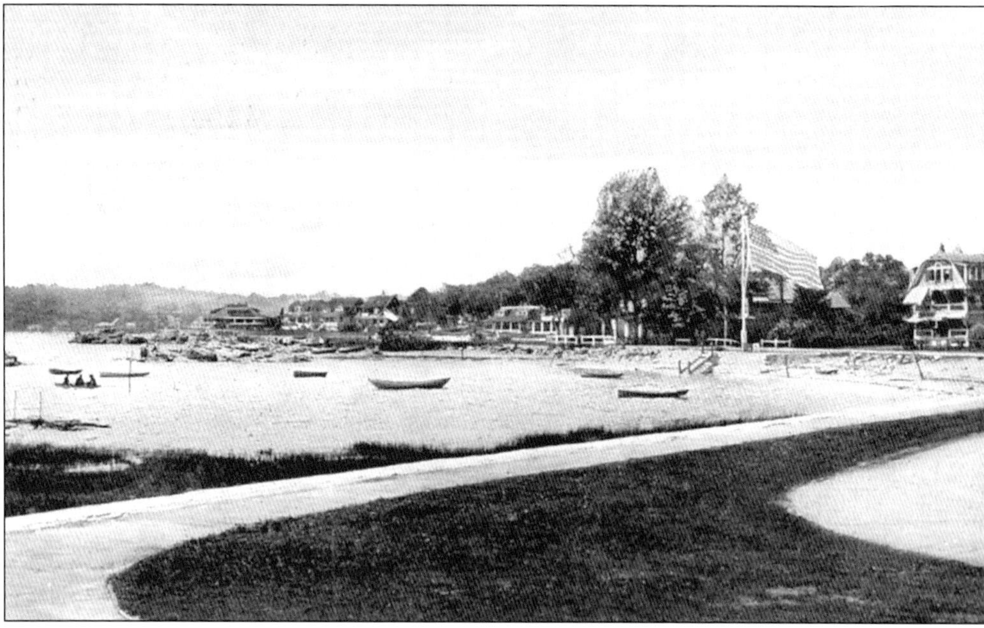

BOATS ON THE CRESCENT. Because Crescent Beach was quite rocky, it was used more for mooring and launching boats than for swimming. Local owners would rent their boats by the hour or the day. This postcard is postmarked 1912.

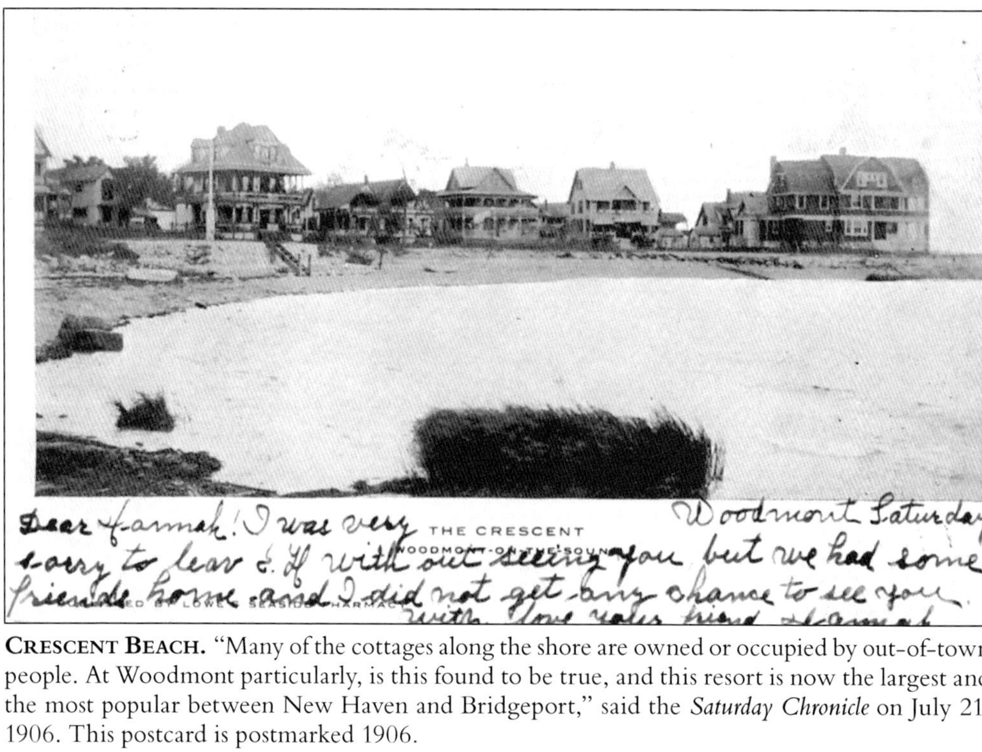

CRESCENT BEACH. "Many of the cottages along the shore are owned or occupied by out-of-town people. At Woodmont particularly, is this found to be true, and this resort is now the largest and the most popular between New Haven and Bridgeport," said the *Saturday Chronicle* on July 21, 1906. This postcard is postmarked 1906.

Ten

Landmarks

Generation after generation of Woodmont residents have passed down stories, traditions, family homes, and a fondness for landmarks such as Lazy Rock, Great Rock, Signal Rock, Potato Rock, the Umbrella Tree, and others.

Signal Rock is the single most identifiable image of Woodmont. A natural rock formation in the water off Crescent Beach, the rock has held a flagpole for more than 100 years, a favorite for locals, photography enthusiasts, swimmers, fishermen, and seagulls.

On the eastern corner of Crescent Beach is another famous landmark called Potato Rock. The russet-colored rock, not native to the area, is unique in its shape and color, completely different from all the other rock formations in the area, which are gray shale. The boulder was likely deposited by the glaciers, which created Long Island at the end of the Ice Age. Around Potato Rock, area residents can mark the seasons by the "eel grass," which starts to grow in the spring, becomes tall and green in mid-summer, and turns amber in the autumn, but waves with the tides through all three seasons.

A few hundred feet to the east of Potato Rock, the Umbrella Tree crouches over the rocks near Beach Avenue at the foot of Chapel Street. The original Umbrella Tree in Woodmont was a Cedar of Lebanon—a scruffy, hearty, flat-topped evergreen with a short trunk and spreading horizontal branches. It succumbed to a hurricane in the 1950s, most likely Hurricane Carol in 1954, and was replaced by longtime Woodmont resident Stubby Hall, who planted a Scotch pine. The new Umbrella Tree has lasted more than 50 years.

The landmarks have endured as they have been loved. Unlike them, Woodmont itself has changed with time.

Woodmont weathered Prohibition, the Great Depression, numerous hurricanes, and two world wars. Yet today its charm and simplicity are being threatened by the modern era—old cottages are being demolished and replaced with large modern houses, which clash with the quaint, charming, and timeless neighborhood of the last century. The question is, can what is left be preserved?

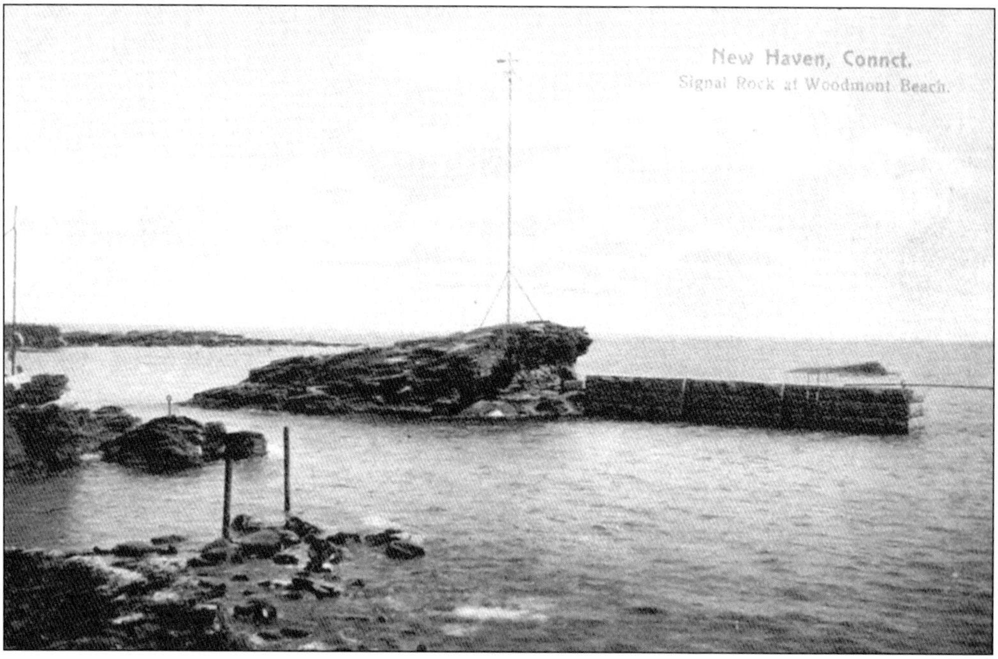

SIGNAL ROCK. Little is known about the exact origins of the flagpole at Signal Rock. It stands almost 50 feet tall and is made of cedar with a 12-inch diameter. It was probably originally about 80 feet tall and used as a mast atop a sailing ship with yardarm and cross rigging. It was refitted and mounted on Signal Rock in the 1890s.

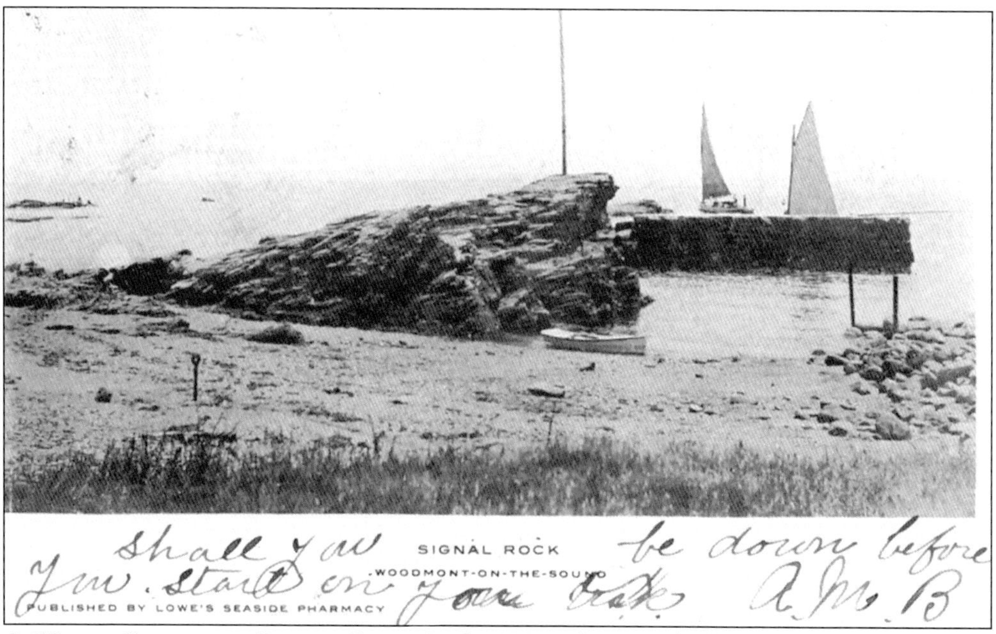

A "SIGNAL" FOR THE OYSTER BEDS. In the 1800s, the state shellfish commission published what was called a "signal book," listing the official signals or landmarks (such as flagpoles, water towers, and church steeples) that were designated to mark the boundaries of the oyster beds. Used as a horizontal sextant, oystermen found the coordinates of these signals to establish the corners of the oyster beds, so they would know where to fish.

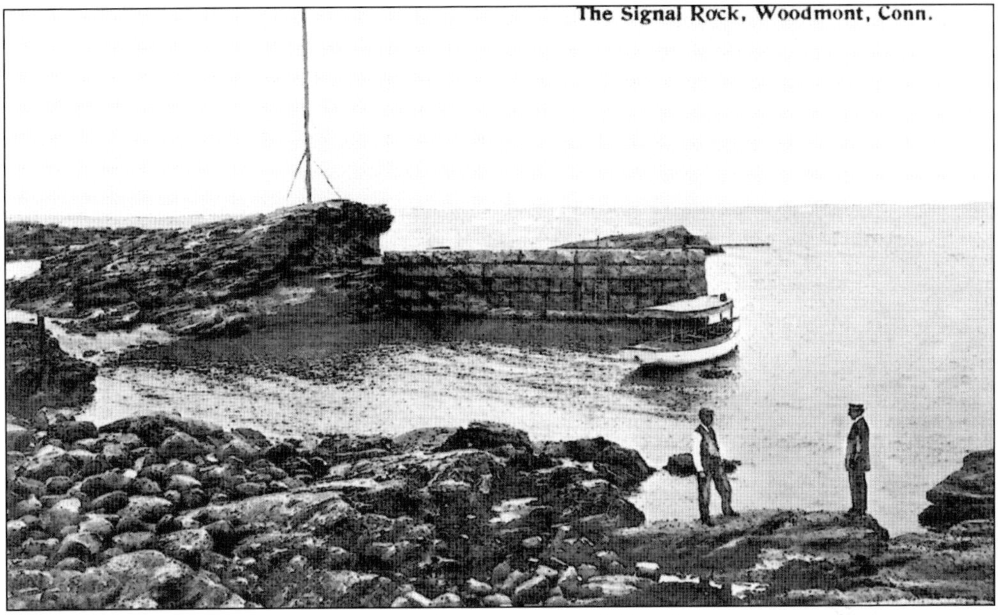

SIGNAL ROCK AND PIER, *C.* 1913. "The advantages of Woodmont as a summer resort need no amplification. It has been inhabited by cottagers for a longer period than most shore places and is now a little city by itself. The price of land there is prohibitive to a man with a lean pocketbook. The place is now under a borough government and is excellently governed. It is estimated that seventy families live there the year round," read the July 20, 1912, edition of the *Saturday Chronicle.* The piece of property in Woodmont is still prohibitive to a man with a lean pocketbook.

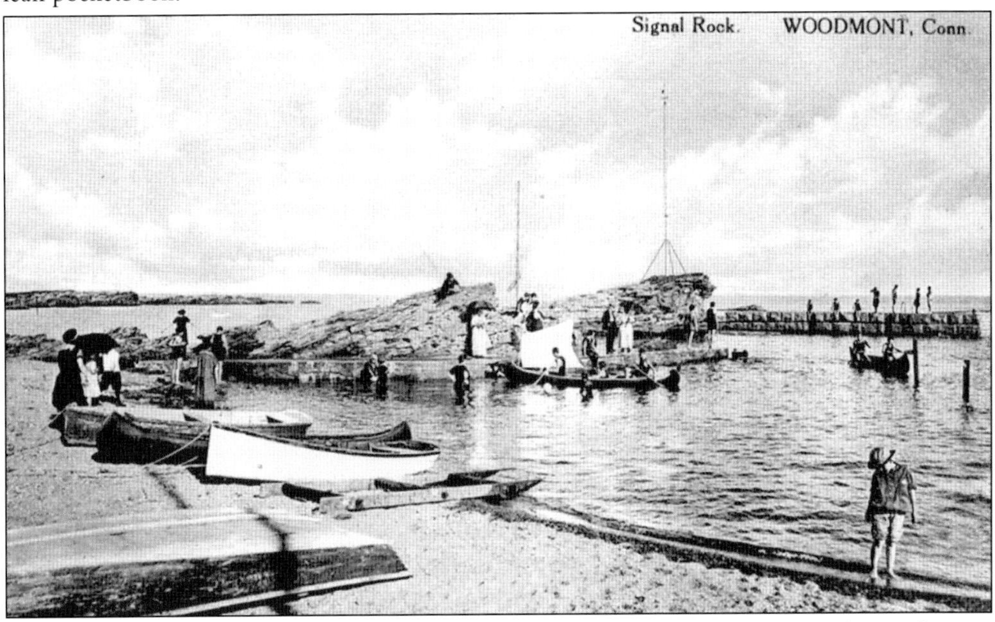

BOATING NEAR SIGNAL ROCK. Diving off Signal Rock at high tide has always been a favorite pastime for youngsters. In years past, when the granite pier was intact, there was much more boating activity, since people could moor their boats at the pier and swim (at high tide) or walk (at low tide) to the beach.

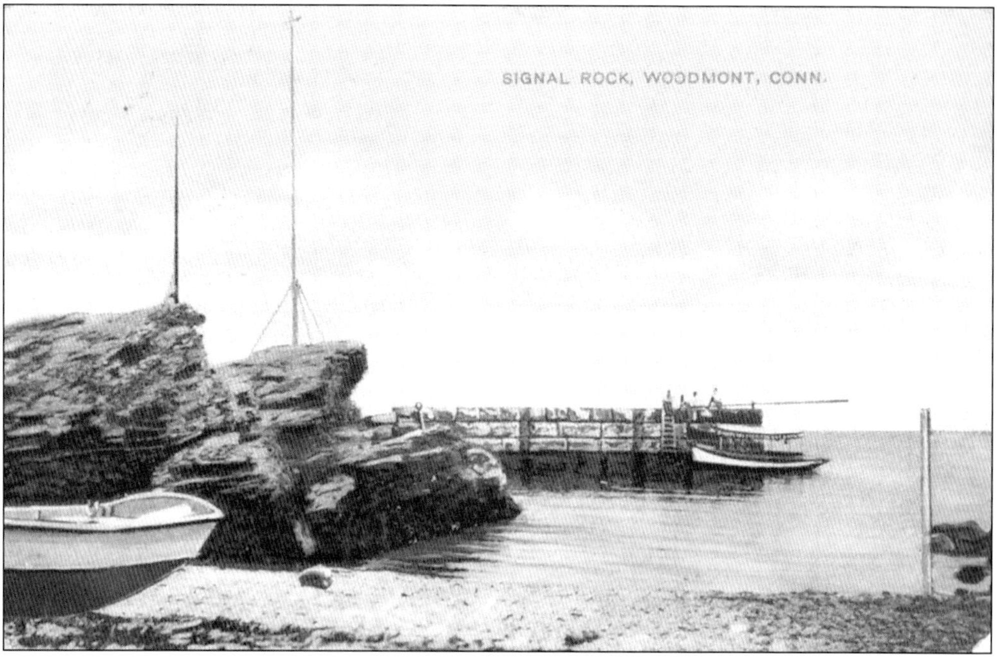

Signal Rock Pleasure Cruise. In the early part of the 20th century, boats from Lighthouse Point in New Haven and Savin Rock in West Haven brought passengers on pleasure cruises, which docked at the granite pier that was connected to Signal Rock until it was destroyed by a hurricane in 1944. This postcard is postmarked 1909.

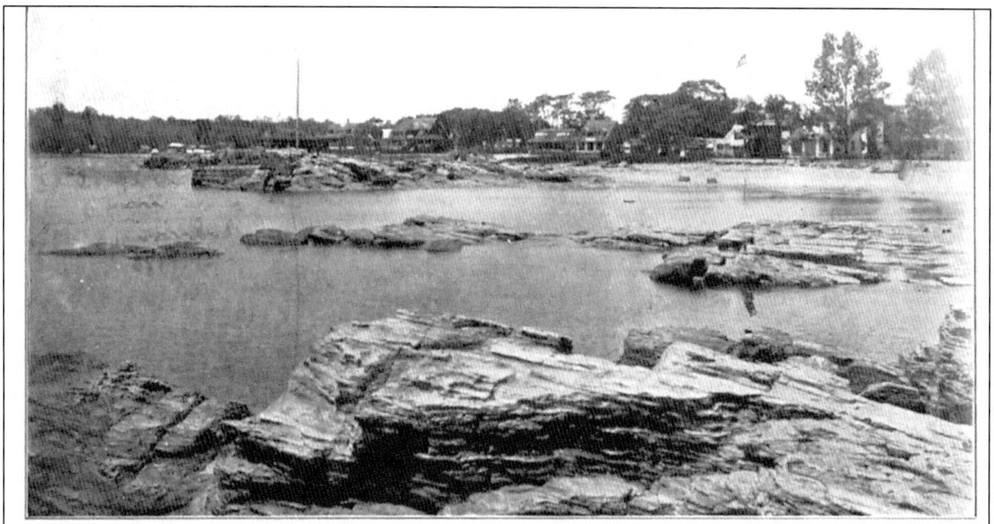

Signal Rock, from the East. Behind and to the left of Signal Rock in this photograph is Great Rock, a rock formation several hundred yards off Anchor Beach, and a haven for many of Woodmont's water fowl, most notably seagulls and cormorants. Many generations of Woodmonters have accepted the dare of swimming to Great Rock at high tide—a far distance for even experienced swimmers. This postcard is postmarked 1907.

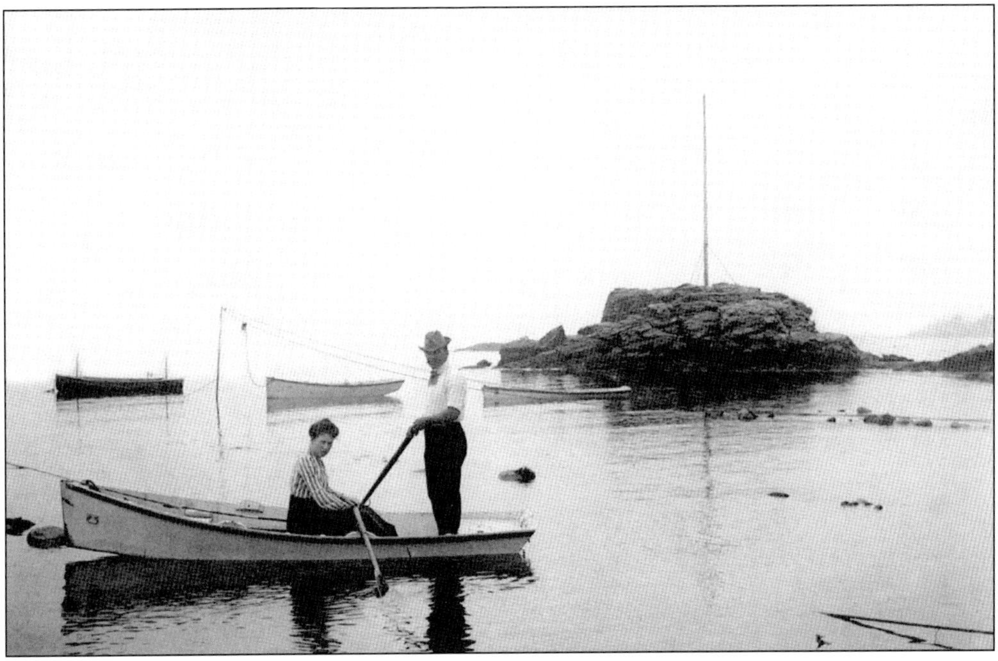

SIGNAL ROCK, *C.* 1900. In its early years, a flag was displayed at Signal Rock for special occasions, but by the 1940s the flagpole had fallen into disrepair. In 1976, the Woodmont Board of Burgesses voted to restore the flagpole for the United States bicentennial celebration, and installed a lighted utility pole on Beach Avenue to allow the flag to be officially flown 24 hours a day.

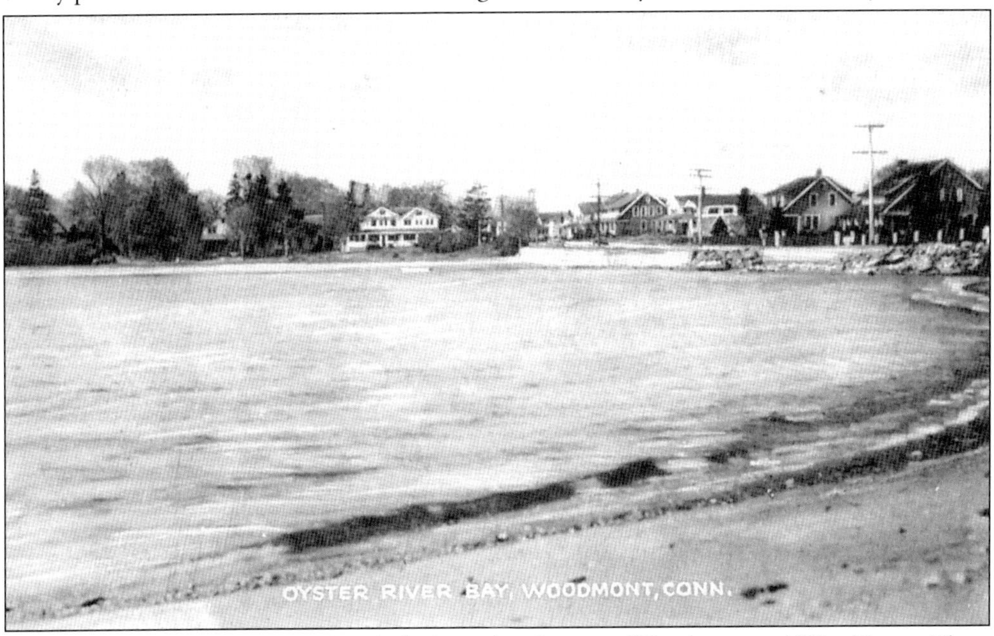

OYSTER RIVER BAY. Oyster River is the boundary between Woodmont and West Haven. There is a bay where the river runs into the sound, which has historically been good for clamming, fishing, bathing, and bird-watching. The white building in the center of the photograph was the Oyster River Inn, built in 1880. The building still exists today as apartments and businesses. This postcard is postmarked 1942.

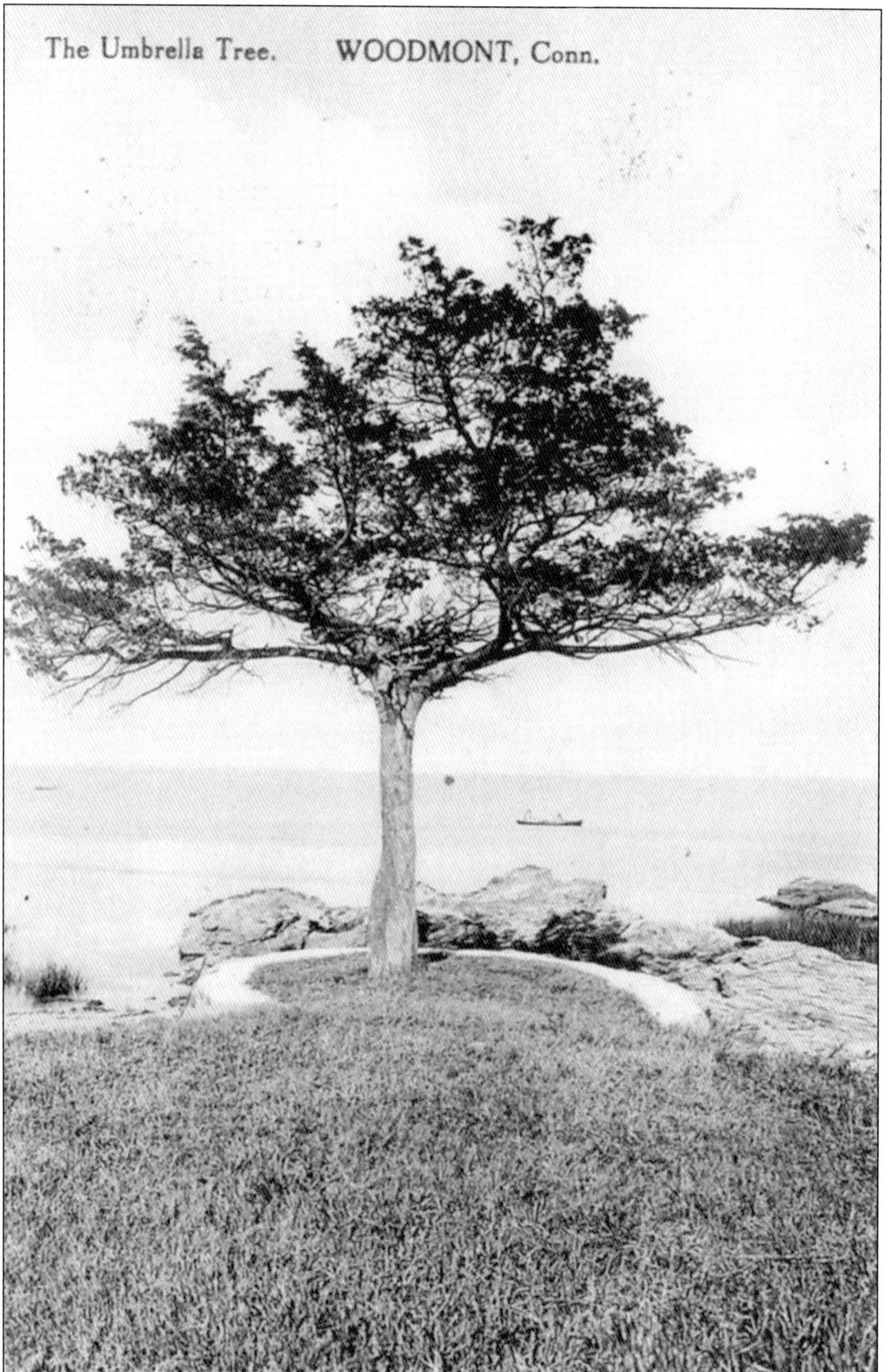

THE UMBRELLA TREE. The Umbrella Tree is a historic landmark on the shore of Woodmont, where Beach Avenue curves north toward Chapel Street. For generations, it has been a favorite spot for marriage proposals—a tradition that continues to this day. This postcard is postmarked 1918.

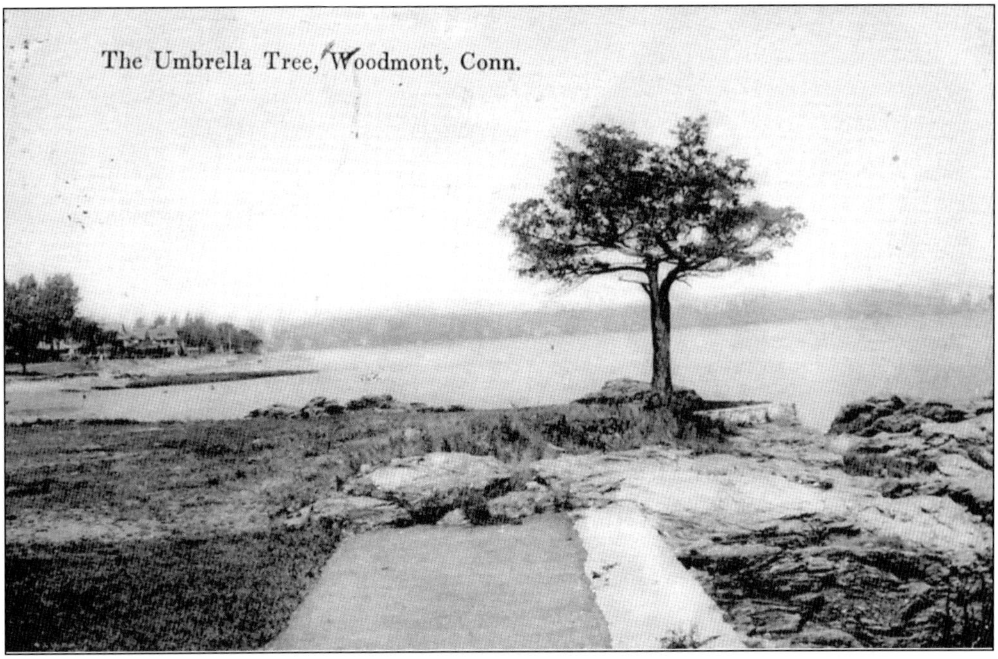

THE UMBRELLA TREE, LOOKING EAST. The message on this postcard, mailed to Nellie Moore in Greenfield, Massachusetts, reads, "Dear Nellie, Pauline and I are here for a rest and change. It is lovely, only Pauline thinks it's pretty quiet not knowing anyone here. This tree on the card, they say here, was brought over from Jerusalem, and is the only one in America. Really, it makes a pretty picture. From Harriet." The Umbrella Tree is a favorite subject for local artists.

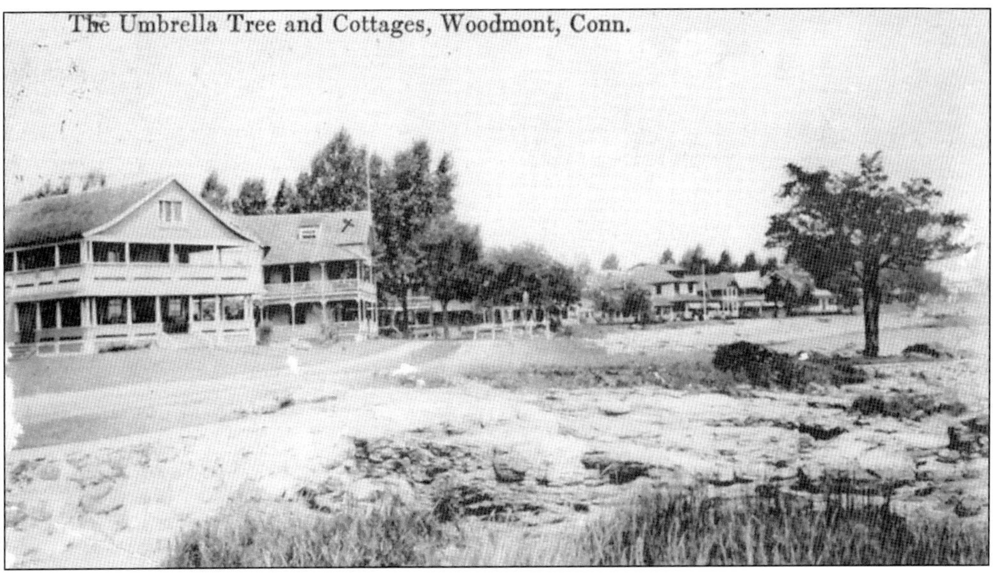

THE UMBRELLA TREE AND COTTAGES. While the Woodmont landmarks never seemed to change, progress was happening all around them. On September 5, 1922, the borough voted "to install electric street lights in the Borough, to begin January 1, 1923 for five years in accordance with a contract submitted by the United Illuminating Co." This postcard is postmarked 1916.

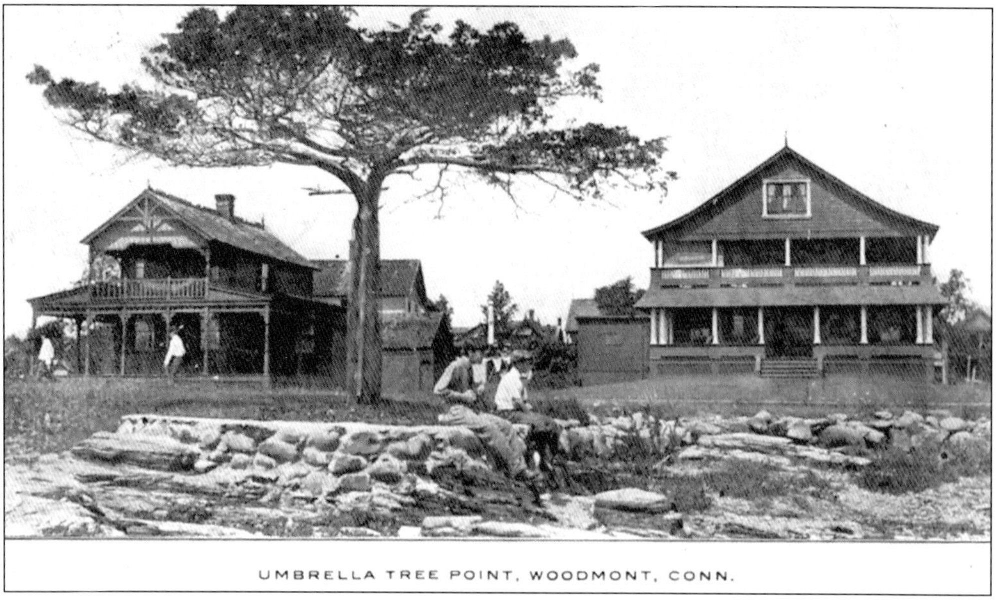

THE UMBRELLA TREE AND COTTAGES. This postcard was mailed to Mrs. J. Burwell in Ansonia, Connecticut, on August 6, 1907. Woodmont was formerly called Burwell's Farm, after the owner, John Burwell, one of Milford's first planters. His grandsons Nathan and Samuel were the first settlers of the area, around 1690.

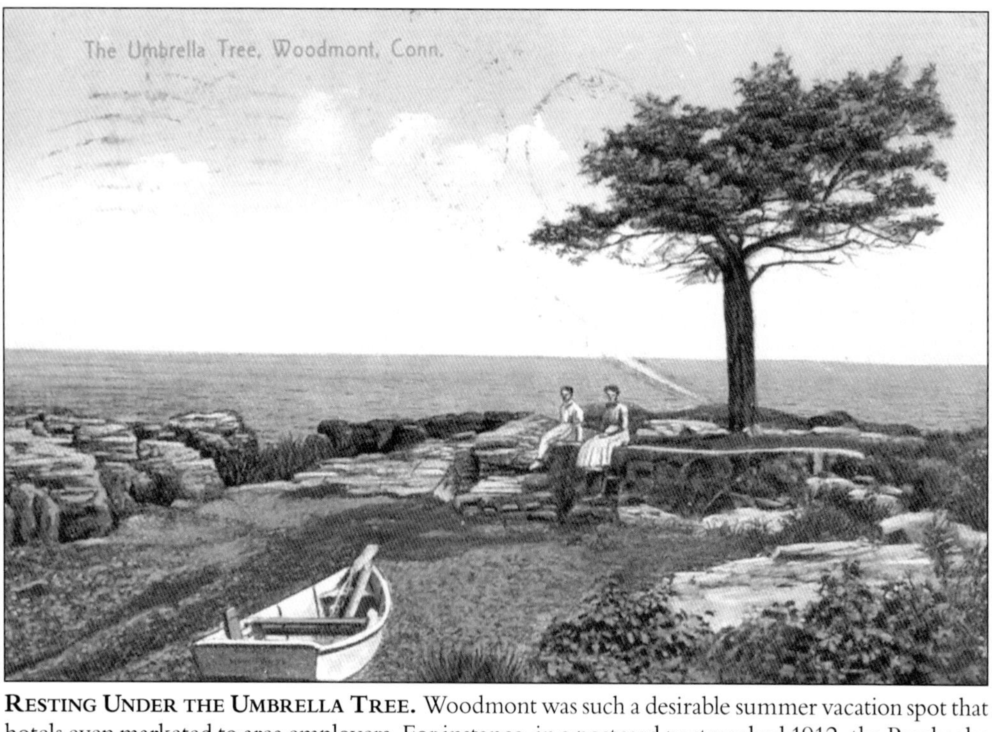

RESTING UNDER THE UMBRELLA TREE. Woodmont was such a desirable summer vacation spot that hotels even marketed to area employers. For instance, in a postcard postmarked 1912, the Pembroke advertised, "Vacation House, Woodmont, Conn., for girl employees of Southern New England Telephone Company. There is no better place on earth to spend your summer vacation."

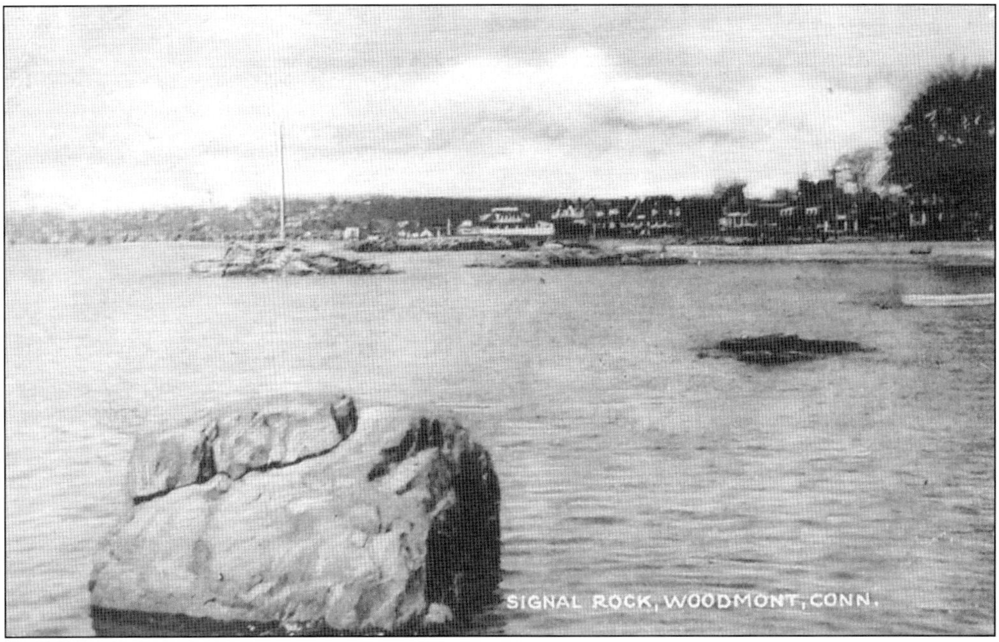

POTATO ROCK. Potato Rock, a famous landmark near Crescent Beach, is not native to the area. Potato Rock is unique in shape and color, unlike the gray shale rock formations in the area. The boulder was likely deposited by glaciers, which created Long Island at the end of the Ice Age. After the beach dredging in the 1950s, Potato Rock was covered by sand so that only its tip was visible; however, erosion has completely unearthed it once again.

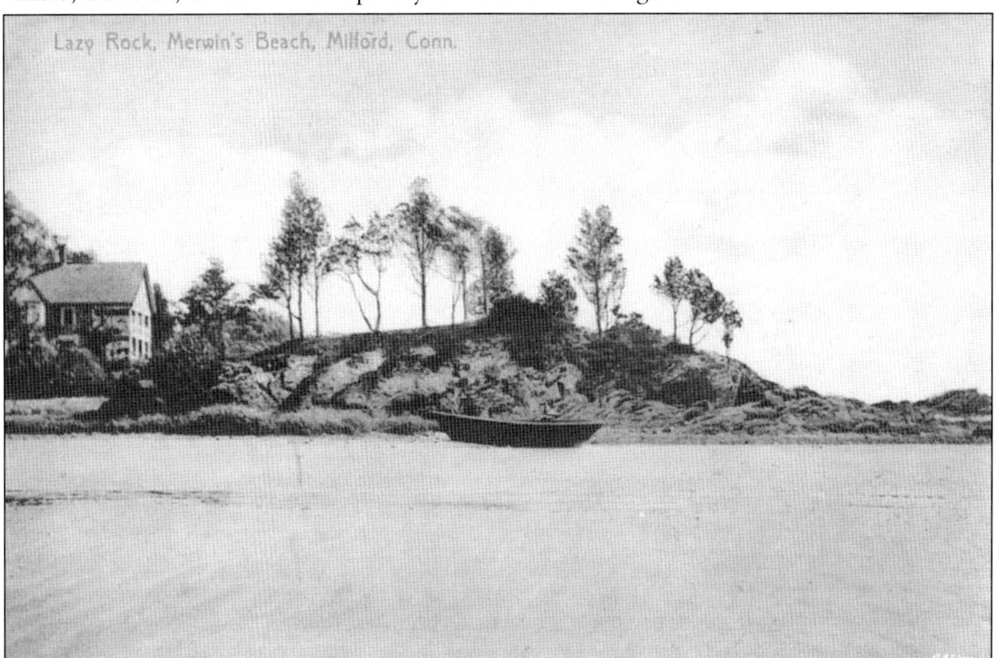

LAZY ROCK, MERWIN'S BEACH. This promontory was just west of Merwin's Point. For many years it was called Lazy Rock. This rocky piece of land was used as part of the property on which the Villa Rosa mansion was later constructed. This postcard is postmarked 1906.

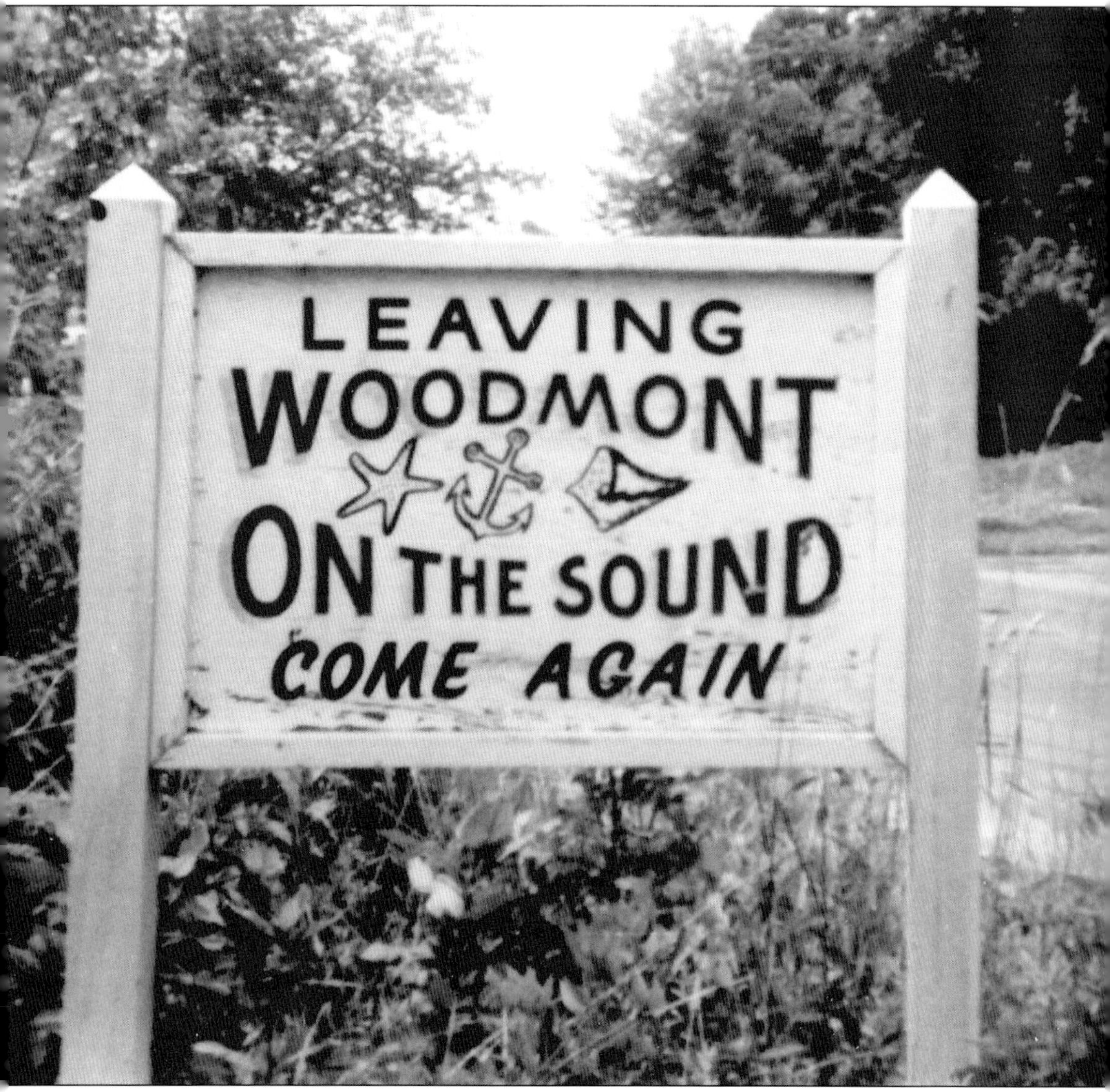

LEAVING WOODMONT ON THE SOUND. Please drive safely after leaving Woodmont, a tiny piece of history, where the shouts of children swimming and the voices of people talking on the front porch still reverberate, where boaters and fishermen share the same sound; where the neighbors not only know each other's names but the names of the neighborhood dogs; where even the rocks and the trees have names; and where the past is cherished.

BIBLIOGRAPHY

Denno, Una; Malone, Letetia; Racz, Harriette; Wolfe, Cynthia, contributing editors. *The History of A New England Hometown, 1639–1989.* Milford, CT: Milford's 350th Commemorative Book, 1989.

Federal Writers' Project of the Work Projects Administration, State of Connecticut. *History of Milford, Connecticut 1839–1939.* The Milford Tercentenary Committee, Bridgeport, CT: Braunworth and Company, 1939.

Saturday Chronicle. New Haven, CT: The Connecticut Press Corporation, 1903–1916.

Smith, DeForest W. *Only in Milford: An Illustrated History.* Milford, CT: George J. Smith and Son Realtors, 1989.

Sykes, Ruth Beach. *Memories of Ruth Frances Beach, Woodmont, Connecticut, United States of America.* Self-published, 1995.